ART

19/4

Mattiwilda Dobbs as the Queen of Shemakhan and
Howell Glynne as Dodon in 'Le Coq d'Or' at Covent Garden.

Action Photograph by Roger Wood

OPERA ANNUAL
1954-1955

EDITED BY

HAROLD ROSENTHAL

WITH AN INTRODUCTION BY

THE EARL OF HAREWOOD

JOHN CALDER (PUBLISHERS) LTD
2 WILTON TERRACE, S.W.1
LONDON
1954

Opera Annual
was first published in 1954 *by*
John Calder (Publishers) Limited
2 Wilton Terrace
*London, S.W.*1
All rights reserved
It was printed in Great Britain by
Richard Madley Ltd.
54 Grafton Way,
*London, W.*1
in 11 *on* 12 *pt. Baskerville*

Foreword

THIS first OPERA ANNUAL is something more than a review of the work of last season's work in the opera-houses of the world. It is an attempt to try to give the reader an overall picture of the post-war opera scene in Europe and America, of the present-day trends in organization and production.

The Introduction by the Earl of Harewood, the essays by Professor Dent, Desmond Shawe-Taylor, Eric White and the directors of the various British operatic organizations, give, I hope, a very good idea of just how post-war Great Britain has come to regard opera as something more than eight weeks of glamorous performances every summer at Covent Garden.

From the review of the past year's events in this country, the reader can judge for himself just how far the various operatic organizations are living up to the aims and ideals they have set themselves, and which are set forth within this volume.

From Germany, Italy and America come reports and essays on the important events of the last few seasons, and accounts of how those countries organize their operatic resources.

I have tried, in assembling the material for this book, to give the reader some idea of contemporary trends in opera production. I hope that the contributions by Dennis Arundell and Hans Busch and the forty-eight pages of photographs will succeed in doing this.

Present-day audiences for opera are not confined to the opera-house; the advent of both television and long-playing gramophone records have put an entirely new complexion on 'opera at home.' The importance of television especially cannot be over-estimated, for not only has it brought opera to a completely new audience, but it has created a new medium for which opera composers, singer and producers may well have to change their whole outlook. Philip Hope-Wallace and Miles Kastendieck have made important contributions to this book on the subject; and Andrew Porter writes about the best of present-day operatic recordings available on long-playing discs.

Between 1939 and 1954 something in the region of 300 new operas have been heard in western Europe and America. Lowenberg's 'Annals of Opera' brought the picture up to 1940. A supplement to Lowenberg would be about the size of this book; but I have attempted to bring Lowenberg's records of premières up to date by listing such details of first performances as there are room for in an appendix.

The operatic obituaries and lists of opera-houses with their singers, conductors and repertories will, I hope, serve a useful purpose as well as being just interesting.

This first OPERA ANNUAL is by its very nature an experiment, if it is a success, then it will be published each year. Then, I hope it will be possible to include many more essays on works of contemporary composers, as well as re-assessments of the great composers of the past, and to increase the scope of our surveys beyond the frontiers of western Europe.   H. D. R.

Contents

CONTENTS (*Continued*)

Introduction

by THE EARL OF HAREWOOD

As I write, we have just finished the tenth full summer of opera in England since the war ended. What began with *Peter Grimes* at Sadler's Wells on June 7th, 1945, has come to a temporary stop with *Don Giovanni* at Glyndebourne on July 24th, 1954—only, of course, to start up again a few weeks later with the Edinburgh Festival, the reopening of Sadler's Wells and the visit of the Vienna Opera in September. During these ten operatic years, London has had ten seasons by Sadler's Wells, eight by Covent Garden, five by the Carl Rosa, six by the English Opera Group, three by Mr. Pomeroy's company at the Cambridge and Stoll Theatres, three by the Intimate Opera; we have had visits by companies from the San Carlo, Naples, the Vienna State Opera, the Opéra-Comique, Paris (*Pelléas* at Covent Garden), la Scala, Milan, the Munich Opera, and the Piccolo Teatro di Roma; we have had a couple of Italian seasons at the Stoll, a couple of seasons in non-operatic theatres with operas by Menotti; occasional productions by the London Opera Club; and a host of amateur or semi-amateur performances. Outside London, several of the above organizations have made extensive tours; the Carl Rosa has been more or less continuously active; Glyndebourne has undertaken six seasons in Sussex and six at the Edinburgh Festival; the Welsh National Opera company has shown signs that it can become the first permanent British company with its base outside London; the Hamburg Opera has visited Edinburgh; there has been opera at seven consecutive Aldeburgh Festivals, at three Festivals at Cheltenham, at two at Bath, at two in Devonshire; and, most notably at Oxford and Cambridge, there has been ceaseless amateur activity.

Can one say that the 'new public for opera,' which was in everybody's mind ten years ago, has truly established itself? We lack, it is true, certain inherited or acquired advantages that are apparent in some other countries. We cannot, for instance, claim in native singers the vocal glamour—it is nothing less—that makes Italian singers rival the film stars in popularity; we do not as audiences possess the inexhaustible appetite of the Germans; nor have we, least of all after the Coronation, that nostalgia for departed Imperial glory which has done so much for so long to fill the Vienna Opera. Still less do we have the invaluable operatic gymnasiums that seem to abound in America, moreover with equipment and funds at their disposal that would turn our opera houses green with envy. All the same, to some extent we clearly have an audience, or the not inconsiderable activity mentioned above would have cost even more than has in fact been the case.

The main trouble is that the operatic habit we have so far formed is too limited in scope, and it has not yet brought with it that natural curiosity which makes people, for example, unable to write off an unfamiliar work without having heard it. The present lack of interest in the unfamiliar can result in the trying position by which an opera like *Elektra*, not heard on the London stage since 1937 and the subject of more " request " letters to Covent Garden, I am told, than any other piece, can be put on in a production that had uniformly excellent press notices and yet failed to draw good houses. The point is not whether *Elektra* is or is not a masterpiece, but that a celebrated work was clearly being condemned unheard by a vast number of opera-goers previously unacquainted with it. The same goes, to an even greater extent perhaps, for Sutermeister's *Romeo and Juliet*, which was mounted at Sadler's Wells in early 1953. In this case, an opera which had had a very considerable success on the Continent was ignored by music-lovers without even the excuse of previous dislike of Sutermeister's musical idiom. As someone wrote recently, it is rather unfair to Covent Garden to complain of standards and then ignore in *Elektra* just the sort of production which, if heard at a Continental Festival, is held up as a model of what Covent Garden ought to do and does not. The same applies to Sadler's Wells and Glyndebourne, criticized for living in the past and then nearly boycotted by the paying public when the former tackles *Romeo and Juliet* and the latter mounts (and excellently, too) *The Rake's Progress*.

Where is the discrepancy ? Is it the depressing one of adequate supply and insufficient demand—but there is no shortage of voices to criticize operatic managements for lack of enterprise; perhaps even *their* owners do not come to hear novelties. Is it lack of confidence in the standards of the organizations concerned—but Glyndebourne fills for *Don Giovanni* and *The Barber*, and Covent Garden for *Aida* and *Carmen*. Or is it a failure of communication between composer and public ? The latter is perhaps the most interesting field for speculation as it is a perennial problem of modern art. Everything unfamiliar is to some extent an acquired taste, but there is a limit to the initial effort people will make; it is one thing to be attracted to what is new and persevere until it changes into the familiar, quite another to be accepted as a novice and expected to go through rites of initiation. Rites (unless they have the luck to be proscribed) are notoriously dull, and it may be that it is dread of being bored by what they fear is in some cases nothing less than initiation that keeps people away from new composers and new music. If that is no more than a problem of Public Relations, there is not so much to worry about; what would be more serious would be if most of the people seeing *Elektra*, *Peter Grimes*, *The Rake's Progress*, *Billy Budd*, *The Consul*, *Gloriana*, *Romeo and Juliet* vowed never to undergo such torture again—in other words, if there was a complete void between artist and public. The responsibility is fairly evenly divided: that nothing worth while comes too easily, is something of which most people are aware; that the paying public must leave the theatre at worst in a state of bewildered enjoyment if what it has unconsciously imbibed is to be properly and painlessly digested, is something which composers and producers sometimes (and mistakenly) ignore.

Perhaps the season of 1954-55 will provide some answers to these questions. Five operas by contemporary British composers will be heard in London (three in world premières) and operatic managements will undoubtedly be studying public reaction with the greatest care. But what will it tell us ?

8

NELL RANKIN and JAMES JOHNSTON. Setting by Wakhevitch

Action photograph by Roger Wood

THE SEASON AT COVENT GARDEN
Two scenes from 'Peter Grimes'

THE SEASON AT COVENT GARDEN

Two scenes from 'Gloriana'

Above:
JOAN CROSS as *Queen Elizabeth*, MONICA SINCLAIR as *Lady Essex*, GERAINT EVANS as *Mountjoy*, JENNIFER VYVYAN as *Penelope Rich*

Below:
JOAN CROSS as *Queen Elizabeth*, PETER PEARS as *Essex*

Action photographs by Roger Wood

THE SEASON AT COVENT GARDEN

King Dodon (HOWELL GLYNNE) and the *Queen of Shemakhan* (MATTIWILDA DOBBS) set out on their wedding procession. Act II of 'Le Coq d'Or'

Action photograph by Roger Wood

13

THE SEASON AT SADLER'S WELLS

Above:

The finale of 'Luisa Miller' (Verdi) with which the season opened

Photograph by Angus McBean

Below:

The finale of 'Don Pasquale' Setting by Osbert Lancaster

Photograph by Denis de Marney

Above left:
PATRICIA HOWARD as *Leila* in 'The Pearl Fishers'

Right:
ROBERT THOMAS as *Nadir*, JOHN HARGREAVES as *Zurga*

Photographs by Denis de Marney

THE SEASON AT SADLER'S WELLS

AMY SHUARD as *Katya* and ROWLAND JONES as *Boris* in the revival of Janacek's 'Katya Kabanova'

Photograph by Angus McBean

Act II of 'Tannhäuser' by the Carl Rosa Company. Setting by Hamish Wilson

A scene from the University College of London Musical Society's production of 'L'Elisir d'Amore'

Photograph by Alan Gabriel

Episode III of Refice's 'Cecilia' by the Dublin Grand Opera Society

Photograph by James O'Callaghan

I. OPERA IN GREAT BRITAIN

National Opera since the War

by EDWARD J. DENT

THE end of the war in 1945 at once brought about a resolute revival of opera in London and indeed all over Great Britain. The Sadler's Wells company returned to their own home after many wanderings and produced *Peter Grimes*, an opera which was immediately taken up all over the Continent with outstanding success. It was a European triumph of English opera which had had no parallel since the days of Balfe and *The Bohemian Girl*. Covent Garden during the war had been converted into a dance hall; Messrs. Boosey and Hawkes courageously took a lease of it for the production of opera and ballet. They formed their own committee of management under the chairmanship of Lord Keynes and thereby secured the friendly co-operation of the Arts Council without the financial support of which neither opera-house could have carried on its work, and opera for the first time in its history, as far as this country is concerned, became a national institution, subsidized by the Government through the Arts Council.

Sadler's Wells, despite all the difficulties under which it had suffered was at any rate a going concern; Covent Garden, as an opera-house, had to be built up from the foundations. The first problem was to find a manager, and on the suggestion of Messrs. Boosey and Hawkes the committee appointed as General Administrator Mr. David Webster of Liverpool, who was hardly known at all in London; in Liverpool he was prominent as a highly successful man of business with a keen interest in music and in the production of amateur opera. It was a wise choice, as subsequent events have amply proved. Those who have studied the history of opera in England since the days of Queen Anne will remember that most operatic managers have been rather dubious characters, to say the least of it, and it was indeed a novelty to have a man at the head of the national opera-house who was not only a most capable business organizer but at the same time a man of scrupulous and unimpeachable integrity. The general management of Covent Garden under the conditions of the present day is an enormously more complicated business than it has ever been before, and we may be indeed thankful to know that it is now in such unfailingly competent hands.

The second problem was to find a chief conductor or musical director. This was a matter of far greater difficulty. The general feeling of the committee was that he ought to be an Englishman. Various names were suggested and various well-known conductors were approached, but all of them were too deeply committed to other engagements. Some, perhaps, might have been willing to accept the position if Covent Garden had been an already flourishing organization, but it was really too much to expect of any ' star ' conductor that he should dedicate himself exclusively to the service of a national opera which was not yet in existence and which might quite possibly have collapsed entirely after a year or two. The right man was again found in Dr. Karl Rankl, a naturalized British subject of Austrian origin with a long experience of operatic conducting in Austria and in Germany.

Mr. Webster saw at once that it would be impossible to start an opera season until a company had been assembled and the nucleus of a repertory formed; it was, however, urgent to get the house opened and to get the public into the habit of frequenting it. The obvious attraction was the Sadler's Wells Ballet, and after some negotiation it was agreed that that body should be transferred complete from Sadler's Wells to Covent Garden. With the history of that Ballet this article is not concerned, but it need hardly be pointed out that the transference of it to a large stage contributed greatly to its own development and also to its international celebrity. The amusing situation arose that Covent Garden had to depend (and still to a large extent depends) on the co-operation of a ballet which still bears the name of a theatre which in the eyes of certain opera-goers was not so much the ' rival ' of Covent Garden as a mere unmentionable fit-up in the slums.

Another problem, and one of the gravest importance, was what were to be the practical relations between Covent Garden and Sadler's Wells. For a hundred years Covent Garden had been the opera-house of the aristocratic and the wealthy; Sadler's Wells (opened in 1931) had been an offshoot of the Royal Victoria Hall (*alias* the Old Vic) founded as a temperance music-hall for the proletariat of Lambeth. Thanks mainly to Lawrance Collingwood, who took over the chief conductorship in 1931, Sadler's Wells had by 1945 become almost the English equivalent of the Paris Opéra-Comique; its repertory had indeed extended far beyond the scope of that famous house, for it had given successful performances of such operas as *Aida*, *Boris Godunov*, *Otello*, *Rosenkavalier* and various other operas which were really much too large and spectacular for its very restricted stage. But it was still limited by its original constitution as a charitable foundation, and although its prices have now risen in conformity with modern conditions, they are still only about half or less of what is demanded at Covent Garden. It is no longer a ' fit-up in the slums,' but it is still a long way off from the theatrical and social centre of London. As to the future, opinions differed; some wanted to ignore Sadler's Wells as far as possible and to return to the old traditions of Covent Garden as an international opera for the rich, with opera sung in foreign languages and mainly by foreign star singers. Others took the view that Covent Garden, being now a state-subsidized institution, should concentrate on opera in English with English singers, and that the two houses should stand more or less in the relation of the two opera-houses of Paris, and further, that they should co-operate intimately in the choice of repertory and as far as practicable in the interchange of singers.

The question settled itself in the course of time, although in practice each house went its own way. It might perhaps be said that the decisive factor was *Peter Grimes*. After the unprecedented success of *Peter Grimes* nobody could say any longer that native English opera was simply negligible; indeed after two years Covent Garden was only too glad to take it up and establish it as a permanent addition to the standard repertory, with every hope of finding new English operas which might be equally successful. As a brave nationalistic gesture, Covent Garden opened its first opera season in 1946 with Purcell's *The Fairy Queen* at the suggestion, needless to say, of Constant Lambert, who made an effective and spectacular arrangement of it in which the ballet played a prominent part; it was in fact a half-way house between the ballet and the opera, which followed immediately with *Carmen* conducted by Dr. Rankl. The solo singing in *The Fairy Queen* was a little disappointing, as very few of the singers seemed to be at ease in the style of Purcell, and it was universally agreed that the main honours went to the chorus which sang magnificently under the training of Mr. Douglas Robinson, who from then until now has continually kept the chorus up to a level which is probably as high as that of any opera-house in the world.

Dr. Rankl's general direction of the opera repertory was very scurvily treated by the critics, both professional and amateur; the general verdict was that he was not sufficiently 'glamorous.' There was no trace of the charlatan about him. Critics, like the general public, tend to judge a conductor by his extravagance of gesture. Some conductors, yes, quite famous ones, have honestly admitted that a dose of charlatanism is a necessity to the concert conductor; it is wasted on the orchestra, and they know it, but it is true that the man who dances an analytical programme is often educating his audience and showing them what to listen for. In the opera-house this 'glamorous' behaviour is utterly out of place; a showy conductor merely distracts attention from the stage. Dr. Rankl was never showy, even in overtures and interludes; what was striking about his performances was the minute care which had been devoted to the preparation of every production. As a typical example I may mention his *Rigoletto*. I have heard many performances of *Rigoletto* in various theatres in England and abroad, and in every one the opening music for military band off stage was revolting in its blatancy and vulgarity. Under Dr. Rankl it sounded for the first time in my experience exactly right, festive and distant, perfectly balanced and joining on with the main orchestra smoothly and imperceptibly. It was such a new experience that I asked Dr. Rankl how he managed it; his answer was simple and practical. The printed full score gives the music of the *banda* in short score on two staves. The publishers send out some thirty separate band parts, and most conductors pick out those for such instruments as they have available, and the players play whatever happens to be in front of them. Dr. Rankl chose the instruments he wanted and himself reorchestrated the *banda* music for that combination so as to achieve exactly the right balance and sonority. With the same skill and judgment he carefully retouched the dynamics of the brass in the scene with Monterone and thereby secured a shattering *crescendo* without ever drowning the singer. Verdi is always a good test of an opera conductor; too many of them, both English and Italian, take the view that since Verdi is always noisy he will be more truly Verdi the noisier they play him. The singers have to bawl their loudest and are drowned all the same. Verdi, Puccini or Wagner, Dr. Rankl never drowned his singers and always showed them every consideration. But Dr. Rankl's main work at Covent Garden was not the performance of the opera but the complete organization and training of the whole company and orchestra, the musical staff included. Dr. Rankl knew, as probably no English opera conductor did or could do, the entire day to day routine in every detail of the work of a first-class large and permanent opera-house giving opera for some nine months of the year or more, like those of Munich or Dresden. Of all this work the general public and the critics naturally saw nothing. To build up an entirely new Covent Garden company and have it in working order within a year was indeed a marvellous achievement for which we can never be sufficiently grateful. But it was not the job for a ' glamorous ' conductor.

Mr. Webster, with his vast experience of ' big business,' saw from the first the essential value of window-dressing and ' making a splash.' If he could not employ star singers of international celebrity he could at least find new scene-designers and producers. As spectacle his first productions were conspicuously extravagant, notably those designed by Oliver Messel. The new management took over a pretty large stock of scenery and costumes, but not much of all this was suitable to the present day, although scenery for *Bohème* and *Tosca* dating back forty or fifty years ago had been extremely well painted and still looked surprisingly effective. Most of the Wagner scenery was usable, but enormously cumbrous and h avy, involving much labour in shifting and quite impracticable for touring. Systematic provincial touring became an important feature of every season, but presented great difficulties, as there were very few provincial theatres (except at Manchester and Liverpool) which were adequately equipped for spectacular productions with large orchestras.

The new producers were almost always criticized with merciless severity. Some had had little or no experience of opera, even when they knew something about music, and the same applied to the designers. A good many mistakes were made at first, mainly owing to a natural temptation to utilize the whole depth of the stage, and it was a long time before the lesson was learned that it is useless to place an important singer a long way back and raised up to a considerable height, however impressive this may be to the eye. Some critics bitterly resented the tendency to keep the stage moving and to multiply dramatic detail for the chorus and subsidiary characters. They demanded an 'experienced Italian producer familiar with the traditions,' in other words a conventional and old-fashioned individual who would range the chorus motionless in a row and bring the principals well down to the footlights. The climax of horror was reached in *Salome* with scenery by Salvador Dali and produced by Peter Brook, who most unjustly was made to bear the blame for the painter's eccentricities. Dali's decor was certainly startling, but it had its justification. *Salome* came out in 1905 at Dresden at a moment when Germany was much occupied with the discussion of sexual abnormalities of every kind. Strauss was himself the very last man to have any inclinations towards such things, but ' perversity ' was in fashion as a subject of general conversation and he approached it from the standpoint of a composer obsessed by technical problems and a virtuoso's ingenuity in solving them. *Salome* was regarded then as the beginning of really 'modern' opera and its music was indeed something that had never been achieved before. It would have been 'perverse' with any sort of scenery or dresses. Now, after half a century, we find it 'dated' and old-fashioned; most of the music shows all too clearly its derivation from the diatonic simplicities of *Das Rheingold*; if it is to recapture its original atmosphere it needs every visual assistance, and Dali's scenery and costumes had undoubtedly the right intention. When the management weakly yielded to the general outcry and re-staged *Salome* in what looked like the ruins of a classical temple, the work seemed to fall hopelessly flat.

During these nine years Sadler's Wells under its new management has pursued a fairly consistent and certainly honourable policy. It is resolutely English; all operas are sung in English and no foreign singers are ever employed. It has no 'stars' and rightly concentrates its efforts on faultless ensemble. Spectacular operas are left entirely to Covent Garden; even *Aida* is seen no more. Sadler's Wells cannot afford expensive productions, but it employs clever designers and producers and by means of intelligence and ingenuity it often achieves quite striking effects. Its public is comparatively unsophisticated and prefers scenery in which it can recognize what it sees; the designers keep reasonably abreast of modern movements in decoration and avoid the conventions which are now quite old-fashioned, but they are determined to have nothing to do with that pretentious parsimony which economic stringencies have imposed upon modern Bayreuth. The repertory has in general been chosen with reference to the size of the house; it is more classical than that of Covent Garden, because the management has discovered that Mozart and other old composers are always popular favourites and that a well-trained ensemble is more attractive than a sprinkling of foreign stars.

The most remarkable characteristic of Sadler's Wells at the present day is its astonishingly high standard of enunciation; there must be few opera-houses in Europe in which words are systematically made to come through with so much clarity and intelligence. This has naturally been a gradual development, initiated by one or two particular producers in operas more or less new to the audience, but by now it seems to have become an ingrained habit and has extended itself to those oldest favourites which used formerly to be thrown on with the minimum of rehearsal. And for this happy habit of clear enunciation we must not forget to thank the established schools of music such as the Royal Academy, the Royal College and the Guildhall School, the opera classes of which have supplied Sadler's Wells with many of its best young singers. In certain quarters it has been continually maintained that London has no real school of opera, and when Covent Garden was reopened there were even suggestions made that Sadler's Wells should be closed altogether as a public theatre and turned into a specialized operatic training-school. The schools named above do not, it was said, teach real 'operatic' singing. They teach their pupils to enunciate English clearly, to sing in time and in tune, to read easily at sight and learn parts intelligently, but they do not encourage them to force their voices in a futile attempt to ' make a big noise like a foreigner.' The admirers of ' operatic ' singing have been corrupted by Italian and German ' traditions ' of the past and still more by the ever-growing habit of listening to gramophone records, and Italian singing, as many Italian musicians are now admitting, is on the road to ruin through the popularity of opera in the open air in such places as the Baths of Caracalla and the Arena at Verona. One of the best of our German guest conductors, and the one from whom our singers learned the most, told them over and over again that they all tried to sing far too loud all the time instead of reserving their extreme efforts for moments of climax. The so-called operatic method leads inevitably to bad enunciation—or none at all—and to the disregard of time and tune.

Covent Garden started out with a definite policy of opera in English, but was soon faced with a shortage of ' dramatic ' sopranos and ' heroic ' tenors; Wales can provide tenors in plenty, and of supremely beautiful quality, but rarely of the *Heldentenor* type. If our leading singers were not to be grossly overworked, it was a necessity to engage guests from abroad. These were often unable—or unwilling—to learn their parts in English, and we were treated to far too many polyglot performances—Aida in Italian, Radames in German and the rest in English; this was deplorable, all the more since a considerable proportion of the imported singers were in any case inadequate and hardly worth their expenses. Our German guests of both sexes were generally on a higher level than the Italians, and when they did sing in English they occasionally set a shining example of determination to know what the words meant as well as to pronounce them correctly.

It was hoped from the beginning that we might have visits from complete foreign ensembles, if possible with their own orchestras as well as their own scenery, but for economic reasons this has proved extremely difficult; and it is on general principle highly undesirable that Covent Garden prices should be doubled for such occasions, even if there are a few people wealthy or foolish enough to pay them. A company of solo singers from Paris gave excellent performances of *Pelléas et Mélisande* in French with our own chorus and orchestra. Vienna sent us some Mozart and Beethoven; *Fidelio* was impressive, for even in Vienna *Fidelio* is taken seriously. The Mozart operas were remarkable chiefly for tiresome affectations of style, both musically and scenically. A company from the Scala (which really has no permanent company as the main German theatres have) brought a fine and full-blooded orchestra and chorus, though some of the principals were rather inadequate. By far the most distinguished foreign company was that of the Munich Opera with three of the later works of Richard Strauss. Unfortunately they came in the summer holidays, and since ' Munich ' apparently does not possess the ' glamour ' attributed to ' Vienna ' and ' Mozart ' they drew poor audiences for their first week, despite the unusual interest of the works themselves and the out-

22

standing all-round excellence of their performance and production. The critics were uncomfortably confronted with operas in which it was indispensable to understand every word ; if the audience failed to do so it was certainly not the fault of the Munich singers.

Covent Garden is beginning to show a dangerous drift away from opera in English to opera in Italian or German (French opera is almost completely ignored, apart from *Carmen*) with mixed casts. There is some excuse for *The Ring* in German, for Wagner's libretto seems not yet to have found its ideal translator. Our critics can sometimes notice if French is sung with a variety of very un-Gallic accents, but if opera is sung in ' Italian ' they are ready to swallow the most horrible pronunciations without a qualm, and Italian enunciation that is both distinct and also distinguished is rare among Italian singers themselves. What is clearly understood by all singers, audiences and critics is that Italian is the ideal language for opera, because it has no consonants and no meaning whatever. No newspaper in the kingdom has a loftier standard of honesty, independent-mindedness and courage than the *Manchester Guardian*, and only the other day (16 July, 1954) one of its musical critics dared to enunciate the appalling heresy that ' there is always much in favour of an opera in a language which the audience understands.' Let us hope that this musical Hussite will not be burned at the stake.

In nine years Covent Garden has actually produced five operas by British composers—*Peter Grimes, Billy Budd, Gloriana, The Olympians* and *Pilgrim's Progress*. There was also a revival of *The Bohemian Girl*, brought up to date by Dennis Arundell, who has done the same for *East Lynne* at Sadler's Wells. At Sadler's Wells *Hugh the Drover* and *The Immortal Hour* have been revived; a more deeply impressive novelty (though first produced many years ago) was *Riders to the Sea*. Native opera is still a grave financial risk, but we are promised more and must be thankful for that much. It can at any rate be said without hesitation that the best all-round performances at Covent Garden have been some of those given in English with almost entirely British casts, such as *Fidelio* (and let us thank Covent Garden for making *Fidelio* at last a popular opera), *Queen of Spades, Lohengrin, Masked Ball, Wozzeck* and *Der Freischütz*—a very mixed bag, but all the better for that. The real test of any opera-house is neither the *prima donna* nor the scenery but the presentation of all the minor characters; if some of our critics are still faithful to the doctrine of Monsieur Valabrègue—*ma femme et cinq poupées*—the management of Covent Garden seems to have abandoned it more or less consistently by now. Sadler's Wells never accepted it for a moment, not even in the days of Miss Baylis. Covent Garden has made mistakes now and then, but on the whole it seems to be on the right road and we may wish it all prosperity.

The Opera Companies of Great Britain

I : COVENT GARDEN

by DAVID WEBSTER

FOR years the Royal Opera House, Covent Garden, led a double life. Three or four months every year it was a theatre, the scene of performances of opera and ballet, for the rest of the year it was a dance hall. For the whole of the last war it was used day in day out for ballroom dancing. In 1944, a group of people determined to restore the theatre to its legitimate life as soon as possible.

These men, brought together at the instance of Boosey and Hawkes, the music publishers, and led by the late Lord Keynes, set themselves a high aim— to develop Covent Garden as a national lyric theatre.

For generations opera in England had led a sporadic existence, almost enough, but not quite, to excuse the American lady thanking me, with tears in her eyes, for bringing ' music back to England after the war ' on the occasion of the visit of the Vienna State Opera in 1947. There was usually an international season of opera once a year at the Royal Opera House. The performances were frequently good, especially on the musical side, but they could not be said to play an important part in the life of the country. The artists were in the main of international fame, trained in the opera-houses of Europe; opportunities for British artists were few and far between. Indeed, so much had opera been looked upon as a foreign affair that it was only after the first world war that a wholly British chorus was employed at Covent Garden.

Founded in 1930, the Sadler's Wells Ballet had achieved great popularity during the war and had, so to speak, come of age in an artistic sense. It was clear that this company could take advantage of the opportunities for development that a permanent home at Covent Garden offered. The Sadler's Wells Company from being popularly acclaimed has, at Covent Garden, become internationally famous. But there was no operatic organization in England of comparable achievement.

It was clear that if opera was to form an integral part of the life of the country, then to found a permanent company rather than to organize a succession of distinguished guest seasons was the course to be followed. What the Trustees decided to do was probably unique in the European history of opera: it was no other than the task of building up from nothing an opera company in one of Europe's chief capitals.

It had been seven years since any British singers had sung under ' Grand ' opera conditions—a large house, a large stage with large musical resources, a numerous chorus and an orchestra of full symphonic strength.

It was decided to form a number of audition panels which, in 1946, travelled

THE 'RING' AT COVENT GARDEN
MAY-JUNE 1954

Above: FERDINAND FRANTZ (*Wotan*), MARGARET HARSHAW (*Brünnhilde*), SET SVANHOLM (*Siegfried*)

Below: HANS BEIRER (*Siegmund*), FREDERICK DALBERG (*Hunding*), SYLVIA FISHER (*Sieglinde*)

Photographs by Derek Allen

C

THE 'RING' AT COVENT GARDEN, MAY-JUNE 1954

Loge (ERICH WITTE) advises *Wotan* (FERDINAND FRANTZ) to bargain with the giants. 'Das Rheingold', scene ii.

Photograph by Wilfred Newton

up and down the country auditioning singers for solo and chorus engagements. The bulk of the Company was formed in this manner. Many of these singers had never appeared in opera before and others were new to the parts they were asked to play; for most of them there had not even been, with the lapse of the war, an opportunity to see established and famous singers in roles they were asked to play. No single person, for example, had played in *Rosenkavalier*, either in the cast or in the orchestra before its production under Karl Rankl in 1947.

Rankl brought to Covent Garden his experience of the routine of established opera-houses, filling exactly the lack of experience which English conductors in this field had been taught to accept. He conducted twenty-two of the thirty operas produced at Covent Garden during his time as Musical Director and did an immense uphill job.

The Covent Garden Opera Company has, in just over seven years, produced thirty-nine different works. Seven of them by living British composers and British librettists. For practical reasons, such as the inability to cast the most of the major parts of works like *The Ring* and *Norma* from native artists, or the desire to have particular singers, some works have been given in their original language. But naturally, the bulk of the repertory has been sung in English, and Covent Garden has been fortunate in having the co-operation of a number of artists of international fame who have sung leading roles in English—artists like Flagstad, Goltz, Mödl, Schwarzkopf, Seefried, Welitsch, Patzak, Hotter, Rothmüller, Silveri and Uhde.

In any case every opera company requires guests; no national opera company exists on the work of its own nationals, and it was clear from the beginning that apart from the desire of the public to hear great singers, there are parts in the repertory for which there are or have been no British singers available.

Besides the artists mentioned above, other memorable guests have included Callas, de los Angeles, Harshaw, Schlüter, Simionato, Stignani, Varnay, Christoff, Rossi-Lemeni, Schoeffler and Weber. While the company has also enjoyed the co-operation of Barbirolli, Beecham, Britten, Capuana, Dobrowen, Gui, Kempe, Kleiber, Krauss and other great conductors. It surely is a testimony to the standard of the Company that Covent Garden has been able to attract the co-operation of these distinguished conductors and singers.

The public, too, have responded to the general policy of Covent Garden during the past eight years. Indeed, since the war, the doors of the opera-house have been open to the public for eleven months in the year, a unique record in the theatre's history. Since the war the average paying audience at Covent Garden has been 86 per cent. of capacity. Opera in its first year averaged 68.5 per cent. and has been as high as 88.2 per cent.

It is no accident that the general standard of the English works performed at Covent Garden has been high. None of the great opera companies of the world is good in all sections of the operatic repertory, Vienna excels in Mozart, Munich in Strauss, the Scala in Verdi. Covent Garden averages a production of a new work by a British composer each season. This is a deliberate policy on the part of Covent Garden's direction. Not only are the works of contemporary British composers worthy of the investment of time and money these new productions represent, but it is through performances of native works that British singers will achieve style and high standard.

The best assurance of the development of English Opera is in the continuity of the work of Covent Garden, Sadler's Wells and Carl Rosa. The Ballet Company has been able to attract many of its most distinguished members from Australia, New Zealand and South Africa. British singers have always included among them a distinguished contingent from Australia. The present Covent Garden Opera Company is no exception to this custom, but a more direct and formal liaison not only with Australia, but other parts of the Commonwealth, especially with Canada ought to be productive.

Potential singers in most countries of Europe grow up with the opportunities from their earliest days of hearing the great parts of the operatic repertory performed more or less adequately, just as the potential actor in England grows up not only with the great parts of Shakespeare in his blood, but able to see in the course of early life many performances of Hamlet. Such has not been the opportunity of the young British singer in the past. Indeed, circumstances have been such that the young singer has looked to the concert platform rather than to the operatic stage for a career.

In a country which maintains several opera-houses, the opportunity exists for experience which is denied to the vocal aspirants in our own country. Nor does the young opera company enjoy the same advantages as the young ballet company; works are not specially written and composed for them, they must tackle from the beginning the great works of the repertory. The Trustees were clear that an extended period of training was impossible for the new opera singers, they must learn by performance. The problem has been to secure a good standard of performance while the singers have, professionally speaking, been growing up. This work is still going on and the ranks of British singers are not only gradually filling but Covent Garden artists are beginning to be in demand abroad.

It has often been assumed that an opera-school must precede an opera company; this may be a logical order of development but, in practical economics, it is necessary to create employment before individuals can be persuaded to study for that employment.

The opera-school is post-graduate in nature. The capacity to sing develops comparatively late in life. Ideally training for opera follows the training of the College or School of Music.

While, therefore, the Directors of Covent Garden have offered small part contracts to enable potential singers to pursue their studies or to determine whether they have sufficient talent to make an operatic career, and in some cases have subsidized members of the company to study abroad for periods, they have not taken active steps to promote a school.

It may be that when it is demonstrated that there exists the possibility of operatic careers in this country this somewhat viscious circle may be broken. In the meantime, the physical and to some considerable extent the financial means of developing an active school of opera which exists at the Royal College of Music, might become more useful through active co-operation with the existing opera companies.

II : SADLER'S WELLS

by NORMAN TUCKER

WHO among those present will forget that evening in 1945 when Sadler's Wells re-opened with *Peter Grimes?* Before a capacity audience an accomplished Company performed a work which seemed to herald the new birth of the native English repertory for which all hoped. And the foreign repertory drew full houses. And there was no competition. And there was money in reserve earned largely in the war years by prudent management of both opera and ballet companies. How does Sadler's Wells stand now, nearly ten years later?

The Company has almost completely changed. Several valuable singers difficult to replace have left for Covent Garden or the concert platform, and their successors have been found after long and patient hours of auditioning. As with those before them it has often been a case of sink or swim : but they mostly swam and now there is a cadre of youngish singers of great talent and growing experience. In consequence of this the newcomers can be eased more gently into the arduous life of an operatic artist. Apart from the permanent company most of the best English singers with talents for opera have appeared at the theatre as guests, at sometime or other.

The look of our composers' list has improved from the British point of view by the mounting of short works such as *The Shepherds of the Delectable Mountains* of Vaughan Williams, and *Lady Rohesia*, a new opera by Antony Hopkins, which did not take as much time or money as a full-length work. Efforts have been made to get the only obvious conductor of *The Village Romeo and Juliet* to direct the work at Sadler's Wells. It was financial difficulties alone that prevented the première of *Billy Budd* being given by Sadler's Wells at the Edinburgh Festival. The nearest to repertory pieces has been *Hugh the Drover*, the same composer's *Riders to the Sea* preceding it. Boughton's *The Immortal Hour*, was brought into the repertory in 1953, and the 1954-5 season opened with the première of Lennox Berkeley's *Nelson*. A new opera based on Somerset Maugham's ' The Moon and Sixpence ' has also been commissioned from the young English composer, John Gardner.

What of the foreign repertory ? On the debit side, there have been too many performances of the Italian and French war-horses of the 19th century which have been the staple fare of opera-houses everywhere for the past 40 years, and too few performances of all that is more interesting to the experienced opera-goer. On the credit side, the war-time management of Sadler's Wells has the distinction of actually adding one to the popular repertory—*The Bartered Bride*. There has been a gratifying number of evenings devoted to four of the five great Mozart operas, works for which the house is ideally suited in size and resources. There have been four English premières, *School for Fathers*, by Wolf-Ferrari, a brilliant production which gave great musical and theatrical pleasure, but which never drew the public ; Verdi's *Simon Boccanegra* which drew capacity audiences for at least one season, Janacek's *Katya Kabanova*, a work of extraordinary originality and beauty which is slowly attracting the attention it deserves from the public, and Sutermeister's *Romeo and Juliet*. Four operas were given their first Sadler's Wells performance, *Schwanda the Bagpiper* by Weinberger, which still has good money in it, Massenet's *Werther*, which may never achieve wide popularity but which attracted far better audiences than was expected from its previous record in this country, *Luisa Miller* and *Don Pasquale*. Finally, there are half a dozen works from the astonishing list of operas given at Sadler's Wells before the war, *Falstaff* and *Don Carlo* of Verdi, *Il Tabarro* and *Gianni Schicchi* from the *Trittico* and, reflecting the pre-war interest in Russian opera for which Lawrance Collingwood was mainly responsible, *Snow Maiden* and *Onegin*. The hard fact is that you can give 25 performances of *Carmen* in a season and your theatre will be 90 per cent. full. Give 4 performances of *Falstaff*, which takes a disproportionate amount of rehearsal time, and you will be lucky if your theatre is more than half full. In other words, out of London's population of 8,000,000 some 40,000 in a season are anxious to hear *Carmen* and only 3,400 can be persuaded to hear *Falstaff*. Even 40,000 does not seem very many. Here is the toughest problem of British opera—how to induce the ordinary music lover to go to hear works which he would certainly enjoy if he would only make the venture.

Competition. Before the war and just after it Sadler's Wells was the only permanent opera company in London, and the only one in the kingdom with a home to call its own. It had first call on the English singers who wished to devote themselves to opera and it made good use of its advantage. Then the scene changed. The great adventure of Covent Garden as a full-time national opera began, and almost at the same time the New London Company at the Cambridge Theatre embarked upon a run of *La Bohème* of a length which threatened to exhaust public interest in the work for some time to come. On a long-term view this was all to the good as it meant that the audience for opera was being widened.

It was clear that, given a national plan for opera, the heaviest works such as *Die Walküre* and *Aida* ought never again to be given at Sadler's Wells. Nor even should near popular works of a large-scale character such as *Samson and Delilah* be given if Covent Garden planned to present them. Conversely, Sadler's Wells is just the place for the smaller-scale works such as Mozart and Rossini. There is, however, a common ground consisting in the main of the French and Italian operas mentioned earlier. It is often asked why Covent Garden puts on *The Marriage of Figaro* and Sadler's Wells *Il Trovatore*. It may be that in the future the repertory will be still more clearly divided between the two houses according to suitability, but there will probably always be a public for the ' common ' operas if they are produced at Sadler's Wells with the best British singers and at Covent Garden with a star element. Furthermore, given the comparatively slender repertory at both house at the present time and the urgent need to create stable and indeed increased audiences, neither house can afford to disregard works which are well established in the public favour. Such a situation could not arise in a continental capital. In England, however, it has arisen and we can do little more at present than avoid a direct clash of performances and stagger the production of ' common ' operas as far as possible. There is one operatic genre that hitherto has found its way very little into the repertory of permanent opera-houses, in England—the operetta. Following on the great popularity of *Die Fledermaus*, Sadler's Wells plan to extend their repertory by the occasional inclusion of the best works in this form.

And what of the financial situation now ? Despite a high level of box-office receipts, increases in admission prices, and steep rises in Arts Council grants, the accumulated reserves have all gone. In other words, the costs of running opera and ballet at Sadler's Wells have risen out of proportion to the income. The reserves were not such an enormous sum after all, but they were badly missed when they had gone. Some of the money spent in the past could no doubt have been put to better use. On the other hand, the position of the company might be easier in some respects to-day if we had spent a little more freely in certain directions such as the engagement of young singers. The bulk of the money went to meet the rising costs that have faced every organization since the war. Salaries have tended upwards and the day has gone when artists could be expected to take a kind of charitable or missionary view of their work at Sadler's Wells.

The standard of production has risen and with it, the cost. Few people realise that, apart from scenery and properties, 120 costumes may well be required in a new production at Sadler's Wells and we can get some idea of what this item means in a production budget if we compare the cost of our own personal clothing now and at the end of the war. There is another source of economic difficulty—the fact that the Theatre has to support both an opera and a ballet company. It is an artistic fact that ballet can do without opera but opera cannot do without ballet.

Almost all French and Slav operas contain dancing as a matter of course calling for dancers of experience and quality. Hence the need for an opera ballet, but good dancers of the quality required cannot be expected to content themselves with this work. Hence again the growth before the war of the Sadler's Wells Ballet now based on Covent Garden, and the exactly parallel growth after the war of the Sadler's Wells Theatre Ballet Company. We need this Company for our ballet operas and yet we find it hard to meet the salary bill when both companies are in the theatre together.

The future? That is very largely a matter of time and money. It will take time to achieve what we want and it will certainly cost money. The aim? To continue the development of a British style and tradition of opera and maintain Sadler's Wells as a people's opera house in the best sense of the word.

III : THE CARL ROSA OPERA COMPANY
by ANNETTE PHILLIPS

TOWARDS the end of the War conditions for touring opera were abnormally prosperous, since people everywhere had money to spend on entertainment. For a time the Carl Rosa Company was able to tour all the year round; night after night you could not, as my husband used to say, get a mouse in, and the non-profit distributing Company that was then operating Carl Rosa tours was able within three or four years to renovate scenery and costumes for several operas and to put some £20,000 in the bank. This money enabled the Company to continue during succeeding years when ever-increasing costs were gradually making it impossible to pay our way in any but the largest theatres. The opera companies competing with us, both for public patronage and for artists' services, were now subsidized, and in 1952 there came a break of fifteen months in our activities, until last September when we also were given a grant from the Arts Council that enabled us to take the road again.

Since the days of Carl Rosa himself it has been the business of this Company to give the public in provincial towns regular seasons of opera in English at ordinary theatre prices. The mainstay of the repertory has always been the few popular masterpieces that the public everywhere continues to demand, but through good times and bad the Carl Rosa Company has constantly introduced one or two novelties or interesting revivals into its seasons, so that the total number of operas performed since 1875 is something like one hundred and fifty, of which more than forty, not counting British works, were given their first performance in English. This part of the Company's work has been rendered most difficult by the high production costs of the present day, especially since war damage to the stores resulted in the loss of much of our stock scenery and costumes; however, in 1949 we gave the first professional performance in England of Smetana's *The Kiss*, in 1950 we revived Cherubini's *The Water Carrier* to celebrate our Jubilee, and in 1951, with the assistance of the Arts Council's special grant for the Festival of Britain, we produced a new English Opera, *John Socman*. Carl Rosa expressed his own faith in British opera by performing and even commissioning operas from British composers whenever he could. Bearing in mind the invariably discouraging box-office response the Company's subsequent record in the production of native works is not a bad one. During the past thirty years we have given two operas by de Lara (*The Three Musketeers* and *Messalina*), Colin Campbell's *Thaïs and Talmaae*, Reginald Somerville's *David Garrick* and, most important, Holbrooke's *Bronwen*, and when I had the opportunity to select a British composer for the Festival of 1951, I chose George Lloyd, a young man who had shown in two previous operas a quite exceptional talent for the stage. I am extremely sorry that for financial reasons we cannot keep *John Socman* in the repertory, because it is an enjoyable work and the audiences, though small, were most enthusiastic.

In certain quarters our respect for the traditional manner of performing the old operas has been condemned as 'old-fashioned' or 'too robust,' but I think we may claim some understanding of the public that has for so many years supported us, and strange though it may seem, they often prefer their favourite operas given as we play them to much more ambitious productions. The public in the provinces cares most for *singing* in opera, and it is that element that suffers when the traditional style of performance is departed from. I consider that the modern producer who tries to make something new and different out of the work of such masters of the opera-stage as Verdi, Wagner and Puccini is wasting his time. One must always move with the times, but not so as to change the spirit and feeling of a masterpiece.

The Carl Rosa Company from its earliest days cultivated a team spirit, an *ensemble*, that does not go with a too frequent engagement of guest artists, and I consider this to be one of the most valuable features of our work and one that counts most in keeping faith with our public. Young artists fresh from College and Academy learn, what cannot be taught, by working with older artists of perhaps thirty years' service with the Company, who themselves learnt in the same way from artists of the past. There is an abundance of talent amongst the younger generation of singers to-day that promises well for the future of opera.

With no home of its own, the Carl Rosa Company is dependent upon the larger provincial towns to keep it working a sufficient number of weeks in the year to hold the artists whom I find and train. At one time Carl Rosa owned the Court Theatre in Liverpool, and made his twelve-week seasons there the base for all his activities. My foremost aim is to find such a home in the provinces where we could stay long enough to rehearse new productions and to train artists to carry on the Carl Rosa tradition. A Company that has survived all its rivals for seventy-nine years can only have done so through its ability to serve the public. Critics, who dismiss us as 'provincial,' may not appreciate that we are proud to be so, nor that the public in the provinces, less sophisticated perhaps, but more solid than London, has played its part in the past history of opera and may well influence the future. I am thankful that, so far, the Arts Council have accepted us for what we are, and I hope that those whose control of State subsidies gives them so powerful an influence on music to-day will never, in their desire to give the public what they consider it should have, deprive it of something it likes, and is willing, within its means, to support.

IV : GLYNDEBOURNE

by DESMOND SHAWE-TAYLOR

WITHOUT being a Marxist, one can discern an analogy between the economics of the last 150 years and the styles of theatrical and operatic presentation which have been in vogue during the same period. The nineteenth century was the heyday of unbridled competition, of riches unabashed, of free trade and free enterprise ; in the theatre, it was the age of the star, the *prima donna assoluta*, the individual performer of genius to whom everyone else more or less willingly deferred. Now, in our age of planned economy and state control, the theatrical centre of gravity has also shifted : stars are regarded with suspicion and virtue is held to reside almost exclusively in ensemble and production. In some quarters things have moved so fast and so far that the producer has become more autocratic than any prima donna ; we have changed Queen Log for King Stork, a situation all too familiar in the political sphere.

In the dramatic criticism of the nineteenth century, we find no mention of a producer, and we can read dozens of nineteenth century operatic notices without encountering the name of the conductor. In those days one went to hear Patti in *La Sonnambula*, and one could be reasonably confident that the arias would be sung, not only with beautiful tone and technique, but in a beautiful style. The ' supporting company ' might be good too; very often it was, for the all-star cast is not a modern invention. A good theatre was furthermore expected to provide a ' superior band ' and ' splendid stage decorations.' But these were the trimmings, not the essential feature of the evening's entertainment.

It was Wagner, more than any other man, who dethroned the individual star in favour of the *Gesamtkunstwerk*, the ' complete work of art ' as imagined by its creators, with a more equal balance between the component parts: voice and orchestra, drama and music, eye and ear. The impact of Bayreuth was tremendous, but there was a time-lag in the diffusion of its principles ; the first notable victory was the Mahler epoch at the Vienna Hofoper (1897-1907). By the 1920's all the principal opera-houses in Germany were deeply concerned about production and unified ' style '; the change came more gradually in Italy, with its powerful *bel canto* traditions; and more slowly still in France, where the opera always seems like a branch of the Civil Service. Meanwhile, England was hardly in a position to indulge in innovations. The International Seasons at Covent Garden were committed to the older conception of opera; and it was not until the first Glyndebourne Festival of 1934 that we enjoyed, under ideal conditions, our first real taste of the *Gesamtkunstwerk*.

The experiment, over which many people had shaken their heads, was from the outset successful. John Christie had shown unerring judgment in placing the whole enterprise under the joint control of two men of genius (Fritz Busch and Carl Ebert) whose gifts were perfectly matched; and in handing over the practical side to a third (Rudolf Bing) whose enthusiasm and knowledge of opera were far greater than those of the average impresario. Bing's departure for the Metropolitan in 1950 was followed, a year later, by the untimely death of Fritz Busch; these were heavy losses for Glyndebourne, but in Moran Caplat and Vittorio Gui, respectively, worthy successors have been found. Glyndebourne audiences can still enjoy operatic performances of superlative quality. This quality is due, not only to the skill and taste of conductor and producer, but to the unique conditions of rehearsal. The long, undistracted summer days in a country house beneath the Sussex Downs are something new for the international artists. They respond with enthusiasm, and become infected with the idealism which inspired the creators of the Festival.

In the opening Glyndebourne seasons, it was above all the execution of the ensembles in *Figaro* and *Così*, and their exact realization in terms of stage action, which came as a revelation: nothing quite like that had been known in England before. Confirmed opera-haters conceded that the performances were almost as enjoyable as listening to a string quartet ; confirmed opera-lovers discovered a fresh delight in familiar music. Even those who had heard these operas conducted by Richard Strauss in the exquisite Residenztheater in Munich, or by Bruno Walter in the Landestheater in Salzburg, found at Glyndebourne one enchanting new experience: that of hearing them sung to the original Italian texts. Mozart's Italian operas suffer terribly in German translation—rather more so than in English. Of course the Germans themselves, who are in this matter as smugly nationalistic as many people would like the English to become, see nothing wrong with their German texts ; they accept them as inevitable, and probably many of them believe them to be the original texts set by Mozart. But a German singer who has sung much at Glyndebourne confessed to me that, since coming to know the three Da Ponte operas by heart in the original, he could no longer bear the German texts. Nor am I surprised when I compare the insinuating grace of the Count's *Crudel, perchè finora farmi languir così* with *So lang' hab' ich geschmachtet*, or Don Giovanni's *Deh vieni alla finestra* with *Horch auf dem Klang der Zither*.

The casts at Glyndebourne have always been international, with British and foreign singers side by side. In the circumstances, the authenticity of the Italian

37

accents has varied widely, and I remember Ernest Newman's remark, *à propos* of one of the earlier performances, that 'all schools of pronunciation were represented, including the preparatory.' But no one has seriously questioned the wisdom of using the original texts, and many listeners will have noticed how much more vivid and stylish has been the work of English singers at Glyndebourne than elsewhere. I believe this to be due, not only to inspiring artistic direction and to the stimulus of working with artists of the calibre of Stabile and Baccaloni, but to the satisfaction of singing in the language to which the music of the opera rightly belongs. Of all the Mozart operas, none gains more than *Così fan tutte* from its original Italian dress. I have seen elsewhere finer individual performances; for instance, I can recall two Despinas whose equal has not yet been seen at Glyndebourne. One of these was Lotte Schöne at Salzburg in 1927; another was Elisabeth Schumann about the same date at Munich (when Mme Schumann sniffed the cup of chocolate at her first entry, I remember how Richard Strauss, accompanying the recitative, used to play a crystalline upward flourish in illustration of her gesture). Nowhere, however, has *Così fan tutte* come so entirely and unequivocally into its own as at Glyndebourne; it is the Glyndebourne opera *par excellence*.

And yet even *Così* awaits one more collaborator to complete the ideal performance: a scenic designer with a sense of style and a feeling for voluptuous Neapolitan beauty. Décor has in the past been the weak spot at Glyndebourne; but the post-war employment of Oliver Messel, John Piper and Osbert Lancaster is an augury of better things. Before the war, with one notable exception, Glyndebourne obstinately pinned its faith on the tasteless fantasies of Hamish Wilson; but, little as I cared for his notion of *Così*, it was better, I think, than the current sets by Rolf Gérard: modish shop-windows framed in black. The Neapolitan sensuousness of *Così* ought surely to make an irresistible appeal to answering qualities in the designer; and I think regretfully of the ravishing sets and costumes we might have had from a pleasure-loving artist such as Christian Bérard. When *Così* is redesigned (and may it be soon), I beg the artist to read first an exquisite page of Taine, in which the atmosphere and ambience of this most perfect and sensuous of operas is wonderfully evoked: he will find it quoted at length in the fifth volume of St. Foix's study of Mozart.

There was one great exception to the prevailing mediocrity of décor, namely the *Macbeth* of 1938-39, in which Caspar Neher's magnificent Berlin designs were adapted for use on the smaller Glyndebourne stage. But this *Macbeth* was altogether exceptional, in some ways the most remarkable of all Glyndebourne's achievements. With Mozart, it was a case of realizing to the full an ideal beauty universally acknowledged; with *Macbeth*, of rehabilitating a work of genius, often of crude genius, not very successful in Verdi's lifetime, and since then largely neglected. Never was unity of music and drama more splendidly achieved than in the *Macbeth* of 1939, when the astonishing Margherita Grandi (herself more or less a Glyndebourne discovery) took over the part of Lady Macbeth. Though it took the public some time to realize it, the Glyndebourne *Macbeth* revealed this opera as a master-piece of early Verdi.

Now, with the help of Vittorio Gui, perhaps the greatest contemporary advocate and exponent of Rossini's music, it looks as though Glyndebourne intends to bring into its repertory as many as possible of the lighter works of this neglected master. Since 1952 we have had *La Cenerentola*, *Il Barbiere di Siviglia* and *Le Comte Ory*; perhaps before long *L'Italiana in Algeri* and *La Gazza Ladra* may also be heard.

In the post-war Glyndebourne seasons we have made the acquaintance of a new generation of singers, of whom Sena Jurinac and Richard Lewis deserve special mention; the former's Fiordiligi, Donna Elvira and Composer (in *Ariadne auf Naxos*) and the latter's Bacchus and Tom Rakewell are interpretations that will not soon be forgotten.

The brilliant artistic success of Glyndebourne had for long seemed to rest on somewhat precarious material foundations. So far as possible, our apprehensions have now been dispelled. The recent establishment of Glyndebourne as a charitable trust and the success of the Glyndebourne Festival Society enable the future to be faced with some measure of confidence.

V : THE ENGLISH OPERA GROUP

by BASIL DOUGLAS

THIS is a short account of the origins, purposes and achievements of the English Opera Group. At the end of the recent war Britain's need for opera was new, widespread and more serious than ever before, but there was extraordinarily little to satisfy it. With one or two exceptions, our theatres were inadequate (and still are) for large orchestras and choruses, and the costs of producing and running opera were already beyond all relation to possible ticket-sales (they still are and increase rapidly every year). Moreover, there had never been a tradition of opera in Britain, as there was, for example, in Italy, France or Germany. The works had mainly been foreign and the translations more or less unsatisfactory. Our artists and technicians, therefore, had had little chance of developing an English style of performance.

The obvious way out of this difficulty, by means of government subsidy, could not be realized at once. Was there another way ? The group of artists which included the composer Benjamin Britten, the painter John Piper, the author Ronald Duncan, the producer Eric Crozier, and the singers Joan Cross and Peter Pears, thought that there was. Soon after the first performance of *Peter Grimes* at Sadlers' Wells in 1945, which had been rehearsed with enormous difficulty and at huge cost

39

on tour, Britten had the idea of writing an opera with no chorus at all, a cast of only eight and an orchestra of twelve. Eric Crozier suggested the theme of *Le Viol de Lucrèce* as dramatized by André Obey. Ronald Duncan agreed to provide the libretto, and John Piper the designs for scenery and costumes. The result was *The Rape of Lucretia*, and John Christie offered to present it at Glyndebourne.

That was in 1946, and in the following year the English Opera Group was officially constituted. New operas followed—*Albert Herring* in 1947, *The Beggar's Opera* in 1948, *Let's Make an Opera!* in 1949. There were tours and London seasons, and invitations to Switzerland, Belgium, Germany and Scandinavia; it was the first British opera company to be invited abroad.

It is remarkable how successful the Group's continental visits have been and how quickly the operas that were written for the Group have found their way into the repertories of foreign opera houses. It has been much harder to secure recognition at home. It was in fact quickly realised that with the solitary exception of *Let's make an Opera!*, the Group's performances could not be a commercial proposition, in the ordinary sense of the term, for some years to come, and that although its expenses were tiny when compared with those of 'grand' opera, they were still too high to make it possible to operate without subsidy. Additional funds had to be sought, by giving concerts in London and the provinces and by founding the English Opera Group Association with the object of raising money for new productions; this Association now has more than five hundred members who pay a guinea a year by way of subscription, and their indefatigable efforts in this and other directions provide essential assistance. The Group enjoys no other private subsidy, and without the annual grant of the Arts Council, its activities in this country must quickly cease, and indeed they are strictly limited by the amount of assistance the Council can give. The problem of reconciling artistic policy with available cash is always acute.

In its Artistic Directors the Group has been lucky. They have always been clear in their own minds that the importance of the Group's work transcends the importance of their own work as individual artists, and it is not merely for his music, for example, that the Group owes so much to Britten. Not only does his wide knowledge and experience cover every aspect of the operatic scene, but also his consistent aim has always been to persuade other composers to write for the Group; and when one considers its short life and the lack of funds for commissioning young composers, one must admit that he has been remarkably successful. Arthur Oldham and John Addison have both made new musical versions of ballad operas and original works have been contributed by Brian Easdale and Lennox Berkeley. Moreover, these works have actually been performed, a significant fact which should be an encouragement to others. Librettists also, and producers, designers, and of course singers, are having the opportunity of gaining valuable experience with the Group. By stimulating the Aldeburgh and Devon Festivals, the Group has helped to bring the arts to parts of the country where there was previously very little;

40

and by founding the Opera School in 1948, it provided an incentive to the study of the *performance* of opera as distinct from merely singing it (the School is now flourishing and independent).

In comparison with Covent Garden, Sadler's Wells and the Carl Rosa, the extent of the Group's work is inevitably modest, but its directors like to think that it is having a disproportionate effect on the future of opera in England and on the development of a national style of performance. The year 1954 marks the beginning of a new phase in its story. The struggle for existence continues, but whereas hitherto it has been a fight for recognition, from now on it will be a fight for consolidation—for new achievements, but on a recognized pattern.

VI: THE WELSH NATIONAL OPERA

by W. H. SMITH

THE Welsh National Opera Company was formed to fill a long-felt need in Welsh musical and cultural life. In a country which had earned so much well-deserved fame for its choral singings, the almost complete neglect of Grand Opera had become a serious omission, and the formation of this company was an attempt to fill that gap.

The first full productions by the company were launched in April 1946, and aroused considerable interest throughout the whole of South Wales, with the result that numerous requests for auditions began to come in from people anxious to be actively associated with the company.

In May 1948, it was decided to place the Company on a permanent basis, and so the Welsh National Opera Company Limited was established and registered under the Companies' Act, as a non-profit making Company for the promotion and presentation of Grand Opera in Wales and elsewhere, and to contribute to the musical cultural and educational life of the community. Indeed, the success of the company has attracted notice outside Wales, and singers trained by the Welsh National Opera have been invited to appear as guest artists elsewhere.

Soon it was decided to extend the sphere of activities of the company, and a training centre was established in Swansea, which was able to draw on the talent in which West Wales abounds. This met with an immediate and enthusiastic response. The Chorus now draws its members from valleys of South Wales as well as from Swansea and the West. The regular attendances of practically one hundred per cent. at the many rehearsals in various centres, is a measure of the enthusiasm of the singers. It is now planned to establish training centres in Mid and North Wales, and additional strength is confidently expected when this takes place.

The company has a repertory of thirteen operas, including *Nabucco* (Verdi) and *Menna*, the new Welsh Opera by Arwell Hughes, with libretto by Wyn Griffith.

At the National Eisteddfod in Llanrwst in 1951, the company gave a Concert version of *Cavalleria Rusticana* in Welsh, and in Aberystwyth, the following year, a similar performance of *Carmen*. For the first time in the history of the Eisteddfod, an opera was given on the stage in August 1954, when the company performed *Menna*, in Welsh, at Ystradgynlais.

As for the future, we want to play operas which make a substantial call on our Chorus, and we have planned a production of Verdi's *Vespri Siciliani* for the November season (1954) at Cardiff. We have recently revived *The Bartered Bride*, and it is well within the bounds of possibility that we shall do a Russian opera early in 1955. We also have in mind the Johann Strauss operas, and are considering a revival of his *Gypsy Baron*.

VII: INTIMATE OPERA

by ANTONY HOPKINS

SINCE I became the musical director of the Intimate Opera Company some eighteen months ago, I have gradually brought about a considerable change in its programme building policy. For over twenty years the company has been primarily associated in the public's mind with operas of the eighteenth and early nineteenth centuries. Admirable though these might be in themselves, the repertory is not limitless; and there is no doubt that such music demands the finesse and delicacy of accompaniment that can only be given by a group of professional string players. As the majority of our engagements come from music clubs who cannot possibly afford the additional outlay that such an accompaniment would demand, a musical compromise has to be accepted, and the operas are consistently accompanied by piano alone. The unsatisfactory nature of this compromise is only too obvious, and the solution we have arrived at is, I think, very much more satisfying from an artistic point of view.

Briefly, we are attempting to create virtually a new art form—contemporary opera designed to be accompanied by the piano alone. It is only when the piano is attempting to reproduce the sounds of an orchestra that its limitations are particularly noticeable. If the accompaniment is specifically designed by the composer to be played by piano only, there is every chance of achieving a satisfactory, if somewhat unorthodox, result. The inevitable outcome of such a policy is, of course, a gradual transfer to a completely modern repertory, all of which is tailor-made to our own particular requirements. It gives me the greatest personal satisfaction to say that this policy is already bearing considerable fruit. By the winter of 1954, we will have in production four operas specially written for us, *The Dumb Wife* by Joseph Horovitz, *Apollo and Persephone* by Gerald Cockshott, my own *Three's Company*, and a new opera called *Second Chance* by Freda Swain. The première of this was planned to take place at the Bryanston Summer School of Music, at Dartington Hall, on 21 August 1954, but unfortunately lack of rehearsal time owing to summer holidays caused its postponement. In addition, we hope very much to have works from John Addison and Malcolm Arnold before long.

Of the four operas mentioned above, only the Cockshott is not entirely satisfactory with piano. It was conceived and written by the composer before the new policy was completely envisaged, and it would undoubtedly benefit from having the string accompaniment which he had hoped for. This is not to say that it hasn't had a great success with audiences already, but only to bewail the fact that financial considerations do not allow us to do it full justice.

We do not claim to be making an overwhelmingly significant contribution to modern culture, but in our small way, we are doing something that is not only worthwhile, but is, so far as I know, unique. Present-day economic conditions demand a highly practical approach; that our efforts to meet those conditions wihout artistic compromise are being appreciated is, I believe, shown very clearly by the remarkably promising season which is opening up before us.

Review of the Year

FOR many opera-goers the 1953-4 season began with the Richard Strauss festival given by the Munich State Opera at Covent Garden. This short season introduced Strauss's last two works, *Capriccio* and *Die Liebe der Danae* to this country, and gave us another opportunity of hearing *Arabella* (last given here in 1934). This last work, which had failed in London some twenty years ago because many people had thought that it would be a second *Rosenkavalier*, now came into its own. Not the least reason for its success was the dazzling performance in the title role by Lisa della Casa.

The Munich company, with Rudolf Hartmann as its Intendant and Rudolf Kempe as its chief conductor, showed itself to be one of Europe's finest operatic ensembles, though it is only fair to say that London saw them exhibiting their choicest and most special wares. Routine repertory performances in their home town, as the editor can testify, are not always of the same high standard.

The other great event of the year at Covent Garden was the new production of *The Ring*. A mammoth undertaking for any repertory theatre. Covent Garden, unlike most European opera-houses produced its new *Ring* in one season, the operas following one on the other within the short period of a month. As usual Covent Garden was criticized for its choice of designer, conductor, artists, lighting, *et al*.

Of course there were weaknesses and mistakes, of course, some of the parts could have been better sung; but the fact remains that the whole work was approached in the right spirit. *The Ring* is now to become an annual event, which means that improvements will be carried out and mistakes rectified. By 1958, we will probably have the Covent Garden *Ring* in an edition that will satisfy both the opera-house authorities and their audiences.

Leslie Hurry's sets were an attempt to compromise between the old realistic scenery and post-war Bayreuth. Falling between the two, Hurry failed in the romantic scenes such as Act 1 of *Walküre*, Act 2 of *Siegfried*, and Act 3, scene 1 of *Götterdämmerung*, all of which were lacking in poetry, but was eminently successful in all of *Rheingold* (except for the Walhalla projection), and the mountain top scenes in all the other operas. Hartmann's production was mainly 'traditional,' and notable for its effective groupings. The conducting of Fritz Stiedry was a great disappointment, lacking poetry and grandeur.

Of the new singers, Margaret Harshaw (Brünnhilde) displayed a beautiful voice, but little sense of grandeur. Ferdinand Frantz (Wotan) was out of voice, and though one never doubted for a moment his fine musicianship and great musical intelligence, he never thrilled his listeners. Eric Witte (Loge), Maria von Ilosvay (Fricka and Waltraute) and Hermann Uhde (Gunther) were all first-rate artists whose re-appearances will be eagerly awaited.

THREE SCENES FROM 'DIE WALKÜRE'

Top right:

    The Valkyries' Rock

Top left:

Siegmund (HANS BEIRER) and *Sieglinde* (SYLVIA FISHER)

Right:

Wotan (FERDINAND FRANTZ) and *Brünnhilde* (MARGARET HARSHAW)

Photographs by Wilfred Newton

THE 'RING' AT COVENT GARDEN, MAY-JUNE 1954

TWO SCENES FROM 'SIEGFRIED'

Left:

Siegfried (Set Svanholm) forges the sword.

Below:

Siegfried and *Mime* (Paul Kuen) in the Forest.

Photographs by Wilfred Newton

THE 'RING' AT COVENT GARDEN, MAY-JUNE 1954

THE 'RING' AT COVENT GARDEN, MAY-JUNE 1954
'Götterdämmerung', Act II.   *Hagen* (DESZO ERNSTER) and *Alberich* (OTAKAR KRAUS).

Photograph by Wilfred Newton

47

THE 'RING' AT COVENT GARDEN, MAY-JUNE 1954

Three scenes from 'Götterdämmerung'.   The three Norns; *Siegfried's* oath; *Brünnhilde, Gunther* and *Hagen* in a scer
from Act II

Photographs by Wilfred Newto

48

Of the ' old hands ' Svanholm has never sung so well in London as he did on this occasion, he was in great form, and is undoubtedly the best Siegfried of the day, as Sylvia Fisher is the best of Sieglindes and Otakar Kraus the finest Alberich.

H. D. R.

After *The Ring*, the big new production of the season was Rimsky-Korsakov's *The Golden Cockerel*. A Diaghilev glamour still tends to hang over things Russian, and it was presumably with some idea of exoticism in mind that Covent Garden, usually staunch adherents of opera in the vernacular, chose to bill the piece as *Le Coq d'Or*. Edward Agate's English translation was used, and glamour there was: not in the garish settings of Loudon Sainthill, nor in the rather matter-of-fact conducting of Igor Markevitch, making his Covent Garden début—but in Mattiwilda Dobbs's Queen of Shemakhan. Apart from a Glyndebourne Zerbinetta, this was her first major operatic appearance in England. Rimsky's vocal writing implies a more full-blooded, more voluptuous personality than that created by Miss Dobbs's gamine charm (in the summer reprises of the opera she realized more fully the sinister side of the Queen's character); but all that sweet, pretty tone, agility and delicate phrasing could provide were there to charm us; Miss Dobbs won the hearts of her public. Hugues Cuénod, another Covent Garden débutant, scored a success as the Astrologer.

Other characters were cast from the resident company. Howell Glynne played Dodon as an operatic Baron Hard-up—a rounded study, successful within those limits, and Frederick Dalberg was an assured and convincing Polkan. But Robert Helpmann, producing, imposed on the whole a jittery, fluttery, unmusical style of gesture and movement. The success with the public was immediate; the opera was chosen for a command performance before the King and Queen of Sweden; but the artistic level was uneven.

Unanimous, however, was the acclaim for the revival of Benjamin Britten's *Peter Grimes*, with Peter Pears repeating his magnificent study of the title-role, and Sylvia Fisher as a touching Ellen Orford. The opera was newly produced by John Cranko; apart from some over-stylized crowd movement, and the rather crude symbolism of having the mad Peter struggle through nets, his work was successful. The over-elaborate settings of Tanya Moiswiewitsch were retained, with some modifications, especially in the hut scene.

Reginald Goodall, whose triumphs generally seem to be reserved for the company's tours, gave an alert, flexible, impressive reading of the score. Minor characters, too many to name, were almost without exception excellent. The Covent Garden chorus (who had to rush about waving their hands in *The Golden Cockerel*) now could show their true ability; they looked, acted and sang extremely well. In later performances Edgar Evans took over the role of Peter.

Two repertory pieces at Covent Garden, *Rigoletto* and *Traviata*, form a striking contrast. No one takes responsibility in the programme for the décors and produc-

49

E

tion of the former; those of the latter are by the late Sophie Fedorovitch and Tyrone Guthrie respectively. *Rigoletto* is entirely successful on both counts; and *Traviata* equally unsuccessful. The *Rigoletto* sets are, in fact, the pre-war ones, worked over by James Bailey, one of the best of our operatic designers. The present state of the production is due to the resident producer, Christopher West, and ranks with his *Bohème* (also uncredited in the programme) as being little less than first-rate. There were two *Rigoletto* casts during the season, but common to both was the Gilda of Mattiwilda Dobbs. She was entrancing. We have had equally exact, perhaps more exact Gildas since the war, but none who has shown so caressing a touch with the phrases, so ambitious a determination that the full beauty of the part should be revealed. The role suited her much better than the Queen of Shemakhan. The first Duke was Oreste Kirkop, a Maltese tenor developed by the Carl Rosa and Sadler's Wells, making three Covent Garden appearances before being claimed by Hollywood. With an easy presence, a ringing voice, and the rare ability to forge the words of the translation into musical phrases, he was notably successful; more so than Nicolai Gedda, who seemed rather insipid at his Covent Garden début. There was no swagger, either vocal or physical, in his Duke; but neat, musical singing told in his favour. Marko Rothmüller's Rigoletto is an assumption of Shakespearean stature, magnificently carried through in each gesture and inflexion. Jess Walters, in the same part, was impressive, but he did not carry the big guns, the dramatic and vocal reserves for the climaxes, which made Rothmüller's impersonation unforgettable. John Pritchard conducted, and brought something of Fritz Busch's intensity to his realization of the score. His tendency to push the singers, however, had not entirely disappeared.

In looking for a Violetta, Covent Garden turned their eyes—as so often they do when needing Italian heroines who can sing in English—towards Germany, and imported from Frankfurt the Swiss soprano, Colette Lorand. This proved an unhappy piece of casting. Art production and Art décor told further against the performance; all muslin and twirls, and lights going up and down during the parties to underline the emotional situation. On the credit side we must set warm, Italianate singing from Jess Walters as Germont *père*, and good singing in three small parts: Flora (Barbara Howitt), Annina (Leah Roberts) and the Doctor (Inia te Wiata). Clever casting of minor roles has been one of the notable features of the 1953-4 season. Mr. Pritchard gave a brittle account of the score.

Covent Garden has three Richard Strauss operas in the repertory: *Rosenkavalier*, *Salome* and *Elektra*. All three, in the season just ended, were conducted by Rudolf Kempe, who brought to the scores much vitality, if not the finesse to which Erich Kleiber has accustomed us. Kempe made his début with the resident company with *Salome*. This revival brought back Ljuba Welitsch in the title-role; opinions of her varied, and were largely dependant on where one sat. Had Richard Strauss been placed in the back-stalls, he would have had no cause to shout: " Louder, louder, I can still hear the singers," for Mme. Welitsch's voice was like a small-scale model of its former self. Even in this reduced state it still held its characteristic quality, while her portrayal of the character was a marvel of artistry and stage-wisdom. Rothmüller's Jokanaan was noble and moving. The set is a clever concoction by Clement Glock which embodies parts of the scrapped Dali décor for this opera and elements from Arthur Bliss's ill-fated *Olympians*. Mr. West's production can be faulted in details, but his general conception is sound.

Elektra, too, brought a famous interpreter of the title-role who is now past her vocal prime: Erna Schlüter. That she lacked reserves of power, particularly in the great evocation of Agamemnon, none would seek to deny. Equally indisputable was the affecting sweetness of tone in the recognition scene. But the over-riding consideration in this performance was that word and tone, movement and bearing, were fused in an impersonation on the grand tragic scale. Leonie Rysanek brought radiant tones to Chrysothemis; Edith Coates was too energetic a Klytemnestra, Otakar Kraus an adequate Orest. The whole performance, lucidly produced by Rudolf Hartmann in a towering and well-proportioned set by Isabel Lambert, remains one of Covent Garden's best offerings.

Andrew Porter.

Of the producer staging *Der Freischütz* in the mid-twentieth century the chief requirement is that he should enable the audience to achieve the suspension of disbelief. Scarcely any other opera of comparable musical value and dramatic force (and I have not forgotten the *Ring*) is so hard to mount persuasively. Nearly anything that goes out of focus is good for a laugh, and a laugh in the wrong place can dispel the illusion of a whole scene.

On the surface, the main problem of *Freischütz* would seem to be to find a proper way of handling its supernatural elements—not merely the rites and materializations of the Wolf's Glen Scene, but the entire paraphernalia of omens, dreams, and superstitious apprehensions, and above all else the uncomfortably naturalistic personal appearances of the diabolic Zamiel.

But there are other, and subtler, problems, for *Der Freischütz* was conceived in a mixture of styles. It is concerned with the presentation of the idea of Evil *vs.* Good in naively black-and-white terms prefiguring those of *Tannhäuser*. It exploits bits of the Faust story in the contractual relationship between Zamiel (and, almost, Max) and the Devil. Snippets of Bohemian folk-lore are sandwiched in among musical structures derived from *Fidelio* and the Singspiel tradition.

I can see only one way of dealing satisfactorily with this musical and theatrical Mulligan stew: Treat the opera, as nearly as possible, as Weber expected it to be treated in 1821. Only in this way can the dangers of false emphasis implicit in a 'modern' viewpoint be avoided.

In his first full-scale production at Covent Garden, Christopher West, the resident producer, followed this line. As a result the performance was right in intention and vigorous in effect, even if there were, inevitably, occasional minor errors in judgment. The Wolf's Glen scene, through the frank use of all the stage machinery Mr. West could lay his hands on, reactivated much of the chilling horror the spectacle must have projected to a less sophisticated audience 133 years ago. The glowering vultures on wires, the horridly life-like wild boar, the phosphorescent skeleton of a horse upon which Zamiel appeared—these were all part of an authentic and appropriately traditional mode of presentation. If the phantoms on the back-cloth were shades who had too obviously been trained in the Sadler's Wells Ballet School; if the astral Agathe had only a fraction of the displacement of the corporeal Sylvia Fisher; and if the backstage public-address system obtruded a specifically twentieth-century noise, these were only passing defects. More important, perhaps, was Mr. West's failure to realize the importance of defining geographically the difference between the actions taking place within the magic circle and the horrors outside it. Roger Furse's stage designs and costumes, attractively old-fashioned, made a valid contribution throughout the opera to the attempt to make both the natural and the supernatural aspects believable.

For this opera Edward Downes was advanced to conductorial status. Not only did he know the score completely—its tempi, textures, and transitions, and the orchestra's varying functions of dramatic commentary, lyric exposition, and accompaniment—but he held everything together on the stage and in the pit with admirable clarity and cleanliness.

On the stage Otakar Kraus's Caspar was the dominant figure. He was not afraid to use the broadest resources of melodramatic delivery, and gave renewed proof of the scope of his attainments as a singing actor. Adele Leigh was delightful to watch as Aennchen, and delightful to hear when she did not cloud and uglify her tone with bad vowels. The two lovers, however, were disappointing. Miss Fisher is not by nature an Agathe. Dramatically she failed to make any real contact with her audience, and her singing was rocky and short of breath. James Johnston's Max had little or no punch, and his particular brand of flowing tone turned many of the consonants to mush and obliterated many of the requisite accents. To the speaking role of Zamiel, David Franklin did not bring the impact the character requires.

Edward J. Dent's English translation (not brand-new, since it was used in an Edinburgh performance in 1950) sometimes finds words and vowel sounds that retain most of the values of the German original. But there are trying moments, especially in Aennchen's songs and in the spoken dialogue between Aennchen and Agathe, some of which had to be revised. On the whole the translation is neither better nor worse than an 1895 one by J. C. Macy which I have in my possession.

Once upon a time opera-houses thought it necessary to have a Carmen in order to give *Carmen*. But that halcyon era is moving farther and farther into the past, as year after year goes by without the emergence of a single singer able to do justice to the part. I have not run across a first-class Carmen since I last heard Lily Djanel in the role, nine years ago; perhaps she still sings it in Brussels, which is a lucky city if she does. Solange Michel understands the role, and is quite adequate to the family-style *Carmen* performances they give at the Opéra-Comique, but she is hardly a personality of international scale. At the Metropolitan, Risë Stevens makes quite an effect, but she sees her task from a Hollywood viewpoint.

So it is not surprising that Covent Garden could not come up with a satisfying Carmen, since there is apparently none to be had. I do think, however, that it would be possible to find someone better than the Alabama mezzo-soprano Nell Rankin, whose sole virtues are good looks, good grooming, and a placidly even scale. She left the opera with a great big void right in the middle. and indirectly helped Frances Yeend to score a success with her expert, sympathetic, vigorously sung (almost too vigorously) Micaela. And her passivity made the final scene lopsided, when James Johnston suddenly came to life and sang and acted with fire and passion.

Whenever a good Carmen does come along, Covent Garden will now be equipped with a background worthy of her talents. For the new settings by Georges Wakhevitch are a magnificent exercise in stage-Spanish, evocative of the real thing, yet splashingly handsome, rich in vivid-hued detail, well conceived in form, and useful to the action. Some people were shocked by the shrine with a sculptured Crucifixion right next to the bull-ring, but I found it wholly consonant with the spirit of Latin Catholicism.

Anthony Asquith was borrowed from the films to stage his first opera. In the opening act he showed his skill by the naturalness and appositeness of the action he devised, and by his ability to keep it always related to both Wakhevitch and Bizet. But he was evidently unaccustomed to Covent Garden's rehearsal pace. He simply did not finish his job. From act to act the registration became a constantly greater shambles, until in the end it was impossible even to guess what he had hoped his production might look like. This was a great shame, for in all probability the management will now merely try to pick up the pieces, and we shall not see a consistently developed performance for years.

I wish I could share the enthusiasm some people expressed for John Pritchard's conducting. I found it thin, rigid, often at tempi which either did not work or were theatrically inexpressive, and generally devoid of the richness and savour of one of the greatest and most individual orchestral scores in all opera.

Cecil Smith.

This revival of *Lohengrin* is easy to write about, for there is almost nothing to say about it, beyond praising the darkly powerful Telramund of Hermann Uhde, who was not prevented by the English language from repeating the forceful impression he had given at Bayreuth a few months earlier. Scenery, costumes and *mise-en-scène* all came from the warehouse; they were neither good nor bad, but merely character-

53

less. John Pritchard's conducting of the score had little breadth or depth, though I thought he showed somewhat less than his customary callousness to the needs and intentions of the singers. But then, the singers, apart from Mr. Uhde, did little more than go through the requisite motions. Sylvia Fisher was in reasonably happy voice as Elsa, but she brought to the music none of the special conviction that elevates her Leonore and her Marschallin to an international level of excellence. Nell Rankin, as Ortrud, sang as she always does—with a suave vocal method of which she may well be proud, but without the innate sense of drama which alone could make her even scale and modest volume seem colourless. Set Svanholm's voice has always been too dry to give Lohengrin's presence the gleaming radiance it needs, and on this occasion it sounded rough and often went off pitch. Frederick Dalberg made the King as droning a bore as he really is in Wagner's score; one wondered, without knowing the answer, how such rare basses as Alexander Kipnis and Ludwig Weber ever learned to make Wagnerian barking-bass declamations interesting, and even attractive. Even the chorus let the opera down, for it had been given too little time, or perhaps merely too little inspiration, to get into the spirit of the work. The Wolfgang Wagner production at Bayreuth, with its stunning clarification of the two-sided character (opera vs. music drama) of this transitional work, was wholly wasted upon Covent Garden. It will be best, surely, to let *Lohengrin* go back to the warehouse and remain there until the management is ready to insure it an honourable restoration.

Cecil Smith.

The Sadler's Wells season saw the addition of three works to the repertory, *Luisa Miller*, *Don Pasquale* and *The Pearl Fishers*, and revivals of *Hansel and Gretel*, *The Snow Maiden* and *Katya Kabanova*.

Luisa Miller was the third 'unfamiliar' Verdi work to be given at Sadler's Wells since the war (*Simon Boccanegra* and *Don Carlo* were the other two). Unfortunately it did not receive the kind of performance or production which was a credit to Sadler's Wells or one which served faithfully the composer.

The new English translation was trite to a degree, and James Robertson's conducting of the piece was loud, vulgar and unsympathetic. The settings were of a utility nature and the cast, which included Victoria Elliott, Jean Watson, Oreste Kirkop, John Hargreaves, David Ward and Harold Blackburn ranged from the incompetent to the adequate.

Don Pasquale, with settings by Osbert Lancaster and in Professor Dent's translation, was produced by Basil Coleman in an arty-crafty manner. There was no Italian spirit evident, and British opera singers' views of 'buffo' style are often embarrassing.

Of the cast, only Dennis Dowling, as Malatesta, got within hailing distance of the right style, but neither he nor his colleagues were helped by the conductor, James Robertson, whose reading of the score was quite lacking in charm.

The Pearl Fishers was by far and away the best of the new productions at Sadler's Wells. Basil Coleman, in his third opera of the season, eschewed the fussy and the clever and allowed his chorus to stand still and sing. He made great effect with the magnificent crowd scenes.

Vilem Tausky, who had conducted an admirable *Hansel and Gretel* at Christmas time, treated the score and singers with respect. John Piper's designs, while not pleasing those who like geographical verisimilitude in the opera-house, were excellent.

Patricia Howard sang a beautiful Leila, Robert Thomas, once he had got over the hazards of *Je crois entendre encore* was a fine Nadir and John Hargreaves and David Ward were in good form as Zurga and Nourabad.

H. D. R.

The Snow Maiden does not belong at Sadler's Wells, or, for that matter, on any small stage anywhere. It was intended for treatment as spectacular as that awarded *Le Coq d'Or* at Covent Garden.

It is not captious to demand the elaborate visual effects the libretto specifies. For the opera is about the scenery; it is a legend of the vernal equinox, not a love story about the unrequited affection of Misgir for the Snow Maiden. By pretending that the human element is the main concern of the opera rather than the mythical element, Sadler's Wells turns the work upside down, and distorts it beyond recognition. The attenuated and repetitious Rimsky-Korsakov score will not support a producer who emphasizes the human aspects and disregards the spectacular ones. When I saw the opera in Chicago with the magnificent scenery and costumes of Nicholas Roerich, dances choreographed in *bona fide* Russian style by Adolph Bolm, a Misgir (Georges Baklanoff) who looked and behaved like a moody Russian, a Snegourotchka (Edith Mason) whose voice has a spangled fairy glitter, and a chorus who did not disport themselves like holiday-makers at a Butlin camp, I thought that *The Snow Maiden* compared favourably with *Le Coq d'Or*. At Sadler's Wells it was milk and water, a fit companion to *The Immortal Hour* in the department of dreariness.

Elsie Morison, to be sure, sang very prettily, for the music fitted her voice and did not tempt her to force it into the ugly fortissimos she sometimes uses in the larger reaches of Covent Garden. But she left the character a nobody among nobodies. In the entire cast I thought only Gwent Lewis's peasant, Bobyl, gave some inkling of the texture the acting ought to have. The Tumblers' Dance conferred no distinction upon Ninette de Valois, who choreographed it, nor did the pacing or sound of the score confer any upon James Robertson, who conducted. In fact, we can truly say that we have scarcely seen or heard *The Snow Maiden* at all. The management was incautious to revive this production at a time when Covent Garden was displaying its brilliant *Coq d'Or*, which does—whatever you may say against this or that facet of the performance—represent the work for what it is.

55

When Janacek's *Katya Kabanova* was first staged in England at Sadler's Wells in April, 1951, it aroused virtually no enthusiasm except among a small band of consecrated Janacek-lovers. When it was revived in June, 1954, in token of the centenary of the composer's birth, it was widely hailed as a considerable masterpiece. The production was the same (by Dennis Arundell, with scenery by John Glass and L. W. Anson and costumes by Anthony Boyes). All but three of the ten members of the cast were the same; only one of the newcomers (Edith Coates, as Marfa Kabanova) sang a role of more than secondary importance.

It was the conductor, Rafael Kubelik, who wrought the alchemy. At the 1951 première the conductor had been Charles Mackerras, a bright but inexperienced musician to whom the Janacek music remained a considerable mystery. *Katya Kabanova* is no piece for a tyro, or even a *Wunderkind* ; looking back on it from our present improved point of vantage we can see what an episodic and erratic affair Mr. Mackerras made of the opera. Mr. Kubelik, on the other hand, pulled Janacek's short-breathed phrase patterns and dactylic declamation-rhythms into a sweeping continuity. His drive and his ardour were unflagging, and he gave the music a theatrical vigour that made the audience's hair stand on end. Mr. Kubelik's interpretation of the work was one of the peak achievements of Sadler's Wells history, and its effect upon instrumentalists and vocalists alike was electric.

Amy Shuard's performance as the self-punishing heroine was altogether remarkable, and more than justified the patience of those who have waited confidently to see the young soprano grow into a mature artist. In the centre of Dennis Arundell's wonderfully evocative Tchekhovian production, she held firmly to the line of the character, portraying a bottled-up, frustrated neurotic with a conviction I have seldom seen equalled on the musical stage. Her opulent singing had subtle and apposite colorations that matched and reflected her acting. This was a new and impressive Amy Shuard, a singing actress of present distinction and high future potentialities.

Edith Coates's mean, snarling impersonation of the icy mother-in-law was a portrait of no less imaginative power; the reality she gave to the character greatly clarified the reasons for both the unhappiness of Katya and the milksoppishness of the son-and-husband Tichon (John Kentish). Among the other admirable individual contributions were Marion Studholme's vivacious, but not empty, foster-sister Barbara and Robert Thomas's beguiling singing of Vanya's music. And all the principals and the chorus were brought together by Mr. Arundell in a production so perfect that it would be a pleasure to detail all the excellences—if only this book were twice as long.

Cecil Smith.

Glyndebourne this summer added two more Rossini operas to its repertory, the immortal *Il Barbiere di Siviglia* in Sussex, and *Le Comte Ory* at Edinburgh. Strawinsky's *The Rake's Progress* conducted by Paul Sacher, was given a performance superior in most respects to that of 1953 Edinburgh Festival; *Alceste*, under Gui, with the title role inadequately realized by Magda Laszlò, was repeated, as was Strauss's *Ariadne auf Naxos* with the incomparable Sena Jurinac once again as the Composer.

Oxford saw the first performance in Great Britain of Marschner's *Hans Heiling*—a dull dreary piece and I doubt whether it will be heard again.

The Carl Rosa revived *Tannhäuser*, the first performance of the work in this country since 1939, and continued to take opera to the provinces. An Italian company, with Virginea Zeani, Kyra Vayne and Gianni Raimondi as its chief attractions brought a breath of Italy to this country.

The season, as a whole, was not such a vintage one as 1952-3, but for a country which has only recently turned to opera, it was a highly interesting one.

H. D. R.

Television Opera in Great Britain

by PHILIP HOPE-WALLACE

T HE problem of televised opera looms large, far larger than a 12 × 9 home viewing screen. And the first root of the problem seems to me a social one. To pretend that there is not always a social problem in opera is a mistake: from its very origins, opera has properly been so considered. Consider televised opera in that light (which is to say with the parlour lamps duly dimmed) and you must admit some formidable implications. Opera as an art form spread downwards from the nobility. Television as a medium and as an art even more so, has come from the people up. Opera, we like to think in a book such as this, has a great following in Great Britain and indeed the most pessimistic must see that there is a new and growing public for opera, fostered by the gramophone and by radio. But it would be idiotic to imagine that nearly everyone ' likes ' opera, and with a monopoly of television as yet and a single wavelength one must accept the fact that into many of the homes which a television performance of even the most popular opera penetrates there is likely to be a large measure of resistance to start with. The hard core of opera lovers is I believe a quite small but intensely enthusiastic body which knows exactly what it wants and will reject any way of promoting opera which seems to them to belie or traduce the fundamental spirit of operatic excitement and interest. So the B.B.C. will get surprisingly little help from them: especially as in trying to please a large popular audience, the corporation is unlikely to commend itself to purists and connoisseurs by serving up the operas which enthusiasts are clamouring to see. In the nature of the case, the choice will tend to fall on the tried and sometimes rather tired successes; these, as adapted, will probably annoy their most persistent ad- mirers. Of the risk of putting *on* operas in such a way that the uninitiated are put *off* opera in particular and general for ever, there is no need to speak, so obvious is it.

To the average Briton as to the average news editor a visual event is of incal- culably greater importance than an audible one. Eyes are ten times better trained than ears. An appalling bit of singing, for instance, a cracked high B makes no stir at all: but let a tenor split his breeches, as did Robert Thomas at Sadler's Wells when reaching for Carmen's carnation, and the news is on the front page of every paper in the world. What sounds musically absurd and jejune goes uncondemned; but an extravagantly plain soprano, or falling scenery, as viewed in the family circle, away from the heat and communal excitement of the footlights, will be ferociously derided. If the B.B.C. has sometimes pulled it off, as I think we may say they have, it has been in the teeth or rather the highly critical eyes of a vast and by no means sympathetic audience.

This question of better trained eyes—everyone can spot a hunchback but how few people can spot the equivalent deformation in a voice!—bedevils all our opera production, not only in television. And eyes trained to the fast, restless, urgent visual language of the cinema (the ' flicks,—well named) find the television screen slow in the first place—even in fairly rapid drama. How much more so then in televised opera. I speak here of opera designed for the opera house originally: the handful of operas or melodramas aimed primarily at the television screen would hardly compose a repertory worth the name. The nature of opera in the opera house makes for the static stage picture. From a dramaturgical aspect nearly all opera is a series of crises, prepared for to some extent but above all expatiated upon in music. Note your reactions in the opera house and you will find (as also in much poetic drama, Shakespeare included) that your attention is seldom that of eye and ear at equal pressure *simultaneously*. You look and then, so to speak, ' turn off your eyes ' and listen, with your visual sense in abeyance. Now, with overtrained eyes, undertrained ears ' glued ' to the screen, this mode of attention is not at all easily acquired, especially after perhaps two hours of old news reels or a lamentable session with puppets where if you stopped watching the whole entertainment ceased to exist.

Ideally, one ought to see on the screen the crucial action: after which, e.g. during the aria or duet of consternation, the screen would fall into a merciful twilight. But of course as in the cinema, a nearly blank television means that the entertainment *qua* television simply *non est*.

So what happens ? Ah, dear reader, too well you know what happens. Either we remain gazing with a scrutiny no human should have to bear while in full song at the face, wig, stomach and clutching hands of Signor X; or possibly worse the camera eye carries us vaguely, resentfully and impatiently on a tour of the 'scenery', dwelling on a crucifix here, a glittering candle or a spray of flowers there. Sometimes, and possibly worst of all, it will wander, as it did during Queen Gertrude's speech in the Olivier *Hamlet* film, on a descriptive lecture, so that we actually *see* what is being sung about—*la mia vecchia madre* or worse, *la mia cuffietta rosa* !

Ingenuity of the kind exercised by a Christian Simpson or a George Foa, true artists fully cognisant of the terrible difficulty, will do much. I recall an admirable series of shots of Rome at dawn accompanying the introduction to *Tosca*, Act III. But the basic trouble, what one may call the eyes v. ears war, is always lurking.

Musically, there ought to be less to worry us: I mean, music is reproduced by a TV set getting a good signal with more fidelity much than the average radio set. In theory, and in future perhaps, one ought to be able to enjoy a TV *Tristan* quite as well as a live broadcast from Bayreuth, illustrated, for as much time as you will, by ' views '. Why then does everyone who likes opera feel obscurely that even the best television performance lacks, to use a slang shorthand, ' binge,' i.e. that wonderful fusion of various exciting elements which everyone recognizes in the opera house ?

The trouble again is largely practical. Until recently, and for all I know even today, singers and orchestra had to inhabit separate studios ! In order that the camera eye may approach them and move freely in front of them the singers must be out on the floor (as in a cinema studio). In theory the orchestra might, I suppose,

59

the Workers' Music Association commissioned and produced Inglis Gundry's *The Partisans*. Five years later the Universities of Oxford and Cambridge produced two new operas as part of their celebrations during the Festival of Britain. None of the operas Egon Wellesz wrote before his naturalization has been played here as yet; and to the Oxford University Opera Club fell the honour of producing *Incognita*, the first of his operas to be written to an English libretto. Elizabeth Mackenzie had based the book on Congreve's novel of the same title; but in performance Wellesz's musical setting did not seem to overcome the confusion engendered by the criss-cross intrigues in this comedy of errors. Peter Tranchell's first opera, *The Mayor of Casterbridge*, was produced at the Arts Theatre, Cambridge. The composer had made his own adaptation of Hardy's novel, which, if anything, erred on the side of over-simplification. In 1952 the students at the Royal College of Music tried out *All at Sea*, new ballad opera written by Geoffrey Shaw to a libretto by Margaret Delamere and Sebastian Shaw in the same sort of convention as the Playfair adaptations of 18th-century light operas at the Lyric Theatre, Hammersmith, in the 1920's.

Purcell's *Dido and Aeneas*, having been originally written for the young ladies at Josias Priest's School at Chelsea, remains one of the most suitable English operas for amateur production; and indeed its present vogue dates from its revival in 1895 at the Royal College of Music under Stanford. Recent productions include those by the City Opera Club (1947) and the Royal Academy of Music (1952). Purcell's semi-operas are more difficult to produce—they call for a rather extravagant deployment of actors, singers, dancers, instrumentalists and designers—but these are the sort of problems universities delight to overcome. Fired by Edward J. Dent's enthusiasm, Cambridge led the way with its revival of *The Fairy Queen* in 1920; and there have been recent Cambridge productions of *Dioclesian* (1947) and *King Arthur* (1949). The Bristol Opera School produced *The Fairy Queen* in 1951.

Although there is an immense amount of 18th-century operatic material waiting to be used, it is difficult for amateurs to tackle it. Original scores of the ballad operas, pasticcio operas and comic operas of the period can hardly be said to exist. Each musical generation has to make its own realization of the work in question, and such adaptations call for a consummate degree of musicianship. *The Beggar's Opera* is the best known of the ballad operas, and the musical material of the Austin, Dent and Britten versions is readily available. The Dent version was given by the Oxford University Opera Club (1948) and the Austin version by the Guildhall School of Music (1951). Considerable initiative was shown by the Leighton Park School, Reading, which prepared *The Quaker's Opera* for performance in 1950 and *The Duenna* in 1954, and by Jesus College, Cambridge, which produced *The Tragedy of Tragedies* with Arne's music in 1952. Arne's musical entertainment, *Thomas and Sally*, was given by the Liverpool Opera Company in 1952, and Dibdins' *The Padlock* by the Maddermarket Theatre, Norwich, in 1949.

62

The English romantic operas of the mid-19th century are at the moment an almost entirely neglected field. Apart from productions of *The Bohemian Girl* by the Barfield Grand Opera Company (1950) and *Maritana* by the Barfield Company (1946), the Devon Amateur Opera Company (1950), the Glasgow Grand Opera Society (1952) and the Hebburn Music and Amateur Operatic Society (1954), the other operas of Balfe and Wallace have been neglected, and also the whole output of Barnett, Benedict, Loder and Macfarren. It is not as if the romantic conventions of the early part of the 19th century were uncongenial to present-day audiences, for considerable success has been scored by the City Opera Club with Weber's *Der Freischütz* (1952) and by the Oxford University Opera Club with Marschner's *Hans Heiling* (1953). It is true, of course, that some of Balfe's works call for a display of vocal pyrotechnics that makes them difficult to cast; but, instead of *The Maid of Artois* or *The Rose of Castile*, societies might be well advised to consider a lighter work like *The Castle of Aymon* that had a considerable vogue in Germany in its day.

Interest continues to be shown in the operatic works of the English musical renaissance at the turn of the century. Stanford has been well served with productions of *Much Ado About Nothing* (Oxford University Opera Club, 1949), *Shamus O'Brien* (Sutton Coldfield Operatic Society, 1950) and *The Travelling Companion* (Swindon Musical Society, 1951). Dame Ethel Smyth's *Fête Galante* and *The Boatswain's Mate* were given in a dual bill by the Wilderness Opera Group (1949); and the Opera School produced the latter opera at Dartington Hall in 1954. The Falmouth Opera Singers produced *The Immortal Hour* in honour of Boughton's 70th birthday (1951); and his *Bethlehem*, which seems almost ideally suited to amateur requirements, was given by the Wilderness Group in 1945 and 1948. Students of the Royal Colleges have been active with works by Holst and Arthur Benjamin: *Savitri* was produced at the College in 1950 and the Academy in 1952, and the College gave *The Devil Take Her* in 1950 and *Prima Donna* in 1954. Delius seems to have been neglected; but Vaughan Williams has had a handsome deal, as can be seen from the following list which covers all the operas he has written:—

Hugh the Drover	Swindon Musical Society	1948
	Liverpool Opera Company	1952
	Bristol Opera School	1953
	Isle of Wight Grand Opera Society	1953
The Shepherds of the Delectable Mountains	Wilderness Opera Group	1949
	Falmouth Opera Singers	1950
Sir John in Love	Wilderness Opera Group	1946
The Poisoned Kiss	Royal Academy of Music	1947
Riders to the Sea	Royal College of Music	1950
	Wolverhampton Technical College	1950
The Pilgrim's Progress	Cambridge University Musical Society	1954

Of Britten's operas, mention should be made of the R.A.M. production of *Albert Herring* in 1950.

A number of important foreign operas have been introduced to this country for the first time by students and amateurs. In 1949, about three and a half centuries after its original production in Rome, Cavalieri's musical morality, *Rappresentazione di Anima e di Corpo*, was produced in Cambridge by the Girton College Musical Society. (Girton also revived Monteverdi's *Orfeo* the following year.) Maisie and Evelyn Radford translated Gluck's *Cythère Assiégée* as *Love's Citadel Besieged*, and it was given by the Falmouth Opera Singers in 1950. The honour of a Mozart première fell to the City Opera Club when they produced *Zaide* in 1953. The Oxford production of Marschner's *Hans Heiling* has already been referred to above. Two of Dvorak's operas should be mentioned here—*The Jacobin* (W.M.A., 1947) and *Rusalka* (John Lewis Partnership Music Society, 1950)—and also Granados's *Goyescas* (R.C.M., 1951 and Swindon M.S., 1952).

The names of Gluck and Mozart are bound to appear frequently in any account like this. There are nearly as many amateur performances of *Orpheus* to chronicle as of *Dido and Aeneas*; and *The Marriage of Figaro*, *Don Giovanni*, *Così fan tutte* and *The Magic Flute* are staple fare for operatic students. But other works by these composers have not been neglected. The Falmouth Opera Singers have played *Armide* (1947), *Alcestis* (1949), *La Clemenza di Tito* (1951) and *Il Seraglio* (1952); the City Opera Club has produced ten of Mozart's operas, including *The Impresario* (1947), *Il Seraglio* (1948), *La Clemenza di Tito* (1949), *Bastien and Bastienne* (1950), *Idomeneo* (1951) and *Zaide* (1953) already mentioned above; and the Oxford University Opera Club has given *Idomeneo* (1947) and *Iphigenia in Tauris* (1949).

In considering 19th-century operas, apart from two national groups that deserve separate consideration (the Italian and the Russian), there are two strikingly ambitious productions to chronicle—Berlioz's *The Trojans*, which was done by the Midland Music Makers in 1948 and by the Oxford University Opera Club in 1950; and Meyerbeer's *Les Huguenots* (Midland M.M., 1951). Lighter works include Flotow's *Martha* (Leicester O.C., 1947; Barfield G.O.C., 1948; Palmer's Green and Southgate G.O.S., 1950; Sheffield Singers G.O.S., 1953), Mendelssohn's *Son and Stranger* (Wolverhampton Technical College, 1951), Bizet's *The Pearl Fishers* (Glasgow G.O.C., 1950) and *The Fair Maid of Perth* (Sutton Coldfield O.S., 1951), Gounod's *Romeo and Juliet* (Barfield G.O.C., 1949), Lalo's *Le Roi d'Ys* (Glasgow G.O.C., 1953), and Massenet's *Werther* (Opera school, 1951) and *Cinderella* (Swindon M.S., 1954). Smetana's *The Bartered Bride* has been particularly popular during this period (Leicester O.C., 1946; R.A.M., 1949; Guildhall S.M., 1949; Bourneville Musical Society, 1950; Cambs. Opera Group, 1951 and 1953; West Riding Opera Circle, 1954).

The Falmouth Opera Singers, always in the van of progress, revived Spontini's *La Vestale* in 1954 in a translation specially made by the Misses Radford. This followed their 1953 production of Rossini's *Moses in Egypt*. Two Italian operas of this period that must have been exceptionally difficult to cast were Rossini's *William Tell* (Midland M.M., 1949) and Bellini's *I Puritani* (Cadoxton Amateur Operatic

ᴇORGE LONDON in *Scarpia's* death scene. Act II of 'Tosca'

Photograph by Erich Lessing

THE SEASON IN
VIENNA

Three scenes from
Einems 'Der Prozess'

Top left:
MAX LORENZ as *Josef K.*, LASZ
SZEMERE as the *Painter*

Top right:
LISA DELLA CASA as the *Nurse*, M
LORENZ as *Josef K.*

Bottom left:
The execution of Josef K.

Photographs by Erich Lessi

Three scenes from Lortzing's 'Zar und Zimmermann', with EMMY LOOSE, PETER KLEIN, ALFRED POELL

Photographs by Erich Lessing

Above: Monteverdi's 'Orfeo' in Hindemith's realization at the Vienna Festival

Below: Felsenstein's production of 'Die Zauberflöte' at the Komische Oper, Berlin

Photograph by David Herr

Photograph by Jurjen Si

68

Society, 1954). But interest in Italian opera of the 19th century has been mainly directed to Verdi, as the following table shows:—

Nabucco	Clydach and District Operatic Society	1952
	Glasgow Grand Opera Society	1952
I Lombardi alla Prima Crociata	Midland Music Makers	1953
Ernani	Sheffield Singers Grand Operatic Society	1952
Il Trovatore	Barfield Grand Opera Company	1953
	Palmer's Green and Southgate Grand Opera Society	1951
La Traviata	Isle of Wight Grand Opera Society	1953
The Sicilian Vespers	City Opera Club	1954
A Masked Ball	Glasgow Grand Opera Society	1949
Otello	Leicester Opera Club	1951
Falstaff	Guildhall School of Music	1952
	Royal Academy of Music	1954

New translations were made for some of these productions; and it seems likely that *I Lombardi* and *The Sicilian Vespers* had never before been performed in this country in English. It is significant that since the above performances of *Nabucco* and *The Sicilian Vespers*, both operas have been taken into the repertory of the Welsh National Opera Company with outstanding success. Of later Italian operas, mention should be made of Boito's *Mefistofele* (Glasgow G.O.S., 1951), Ponchielli's *La Gioconda* (Palmer's Green and Southgate G.O.S., 1951), Mascagni's *L'Amico Fritz* (Philopera Circle, 1954,) and also the one-act operas of Puccini's *Trittico* which are frequently given by the students of the Royal Colleges.

For initiative in the presentation of Russian operas, one has to look primarily to the Swindon Musical Society, and the Midland Music Makers. Both Societies produced Borodin's *Prince Igor* in 1946 and Rimsky-Korsakov's *The Snow Maiden* (Midland M.M., 1946; Swindon M.S., 1953). Other operas by Rimsky-Korsakov performed by the Swindon M.S. were *Mlada* (1947) and *Sadko* (1949). Mussorgsky's *Boris Godunov* was produced by the Midland M.M. in 1952.

It is worth notice that practically no operas by living foreign composers come into this record. The only exceptions appear to be Menotti's *The Telephone* (Opera School, 1953 and 1954) and Sutermeister's *Die Schwarze Spinne* (John Lewis Partnership M.S., 1954).

A survey like this is bound to be selective, partial and incomplete; but at least it shows that there is a deep and widespread enthusiasm for opera throughout this country. Although opera comes to life only at the moment of performance, the prime purpose of these productions is not to entertain the audience—it is, rather, to train the students to become professionals in their own right and to give amateurs the sort of experience that will help them to comprehend something of the mystery of this particular art, which shapes drama according to the exigencies of musical form, subjects music to the task of accompanying words and action, and at times transcends the limitations of each of these individual elements.

II. OPERA IN EUROPE

The Turn of the Wheel

SOME THOUGHTS ON THE STAGING OF OPERA SINCE THE WAR

by DENNIS ARUNDELL

OPERA production in England since the war has quite naturally followed the usual tendency after a period of drabness and economic restriction in everyday life to introduce as much colour and visual stimulus on to the stage as possible. When opera was first introduced to this country in 1656 it was after an uneasy twenty years, of which about ten had been spent under the eye of a pleasure-disapproving authority: so when the theatres began to open unsurreptitiously, it was natural that the theatre public, tired of the buff-coats of the Parliamentary Army, flocked to see the magnificent novelty of spectacular scenes and machines, which were imported to bring new life to the new theatre, having been borrowed from the recent Italian invention, opera, of which they were the chief attraction.

So too after the 1914 war of khaki and mud the theatre aimed at colour and life in the setting of scenes, but instead of overflowing with expensive naturalistic touches such as real water and real rabbits, there was often—especially in Germany—an attempt to achieve visual glamour by playing with interesting lighting and shadows in conjunction with either simply angled sets or serviceable shapes of solid structures and skeleton silhouettes.

After the last war with its khaki, denim, dirty grey-blue and the blackout, except for some exceptional productions, scenery—especially in any form of repertory theatre—tended to consist of as few built-up backgrounds as possible owing to the shortage of reasonably-priced seasoned wood, though different practicable levels of solidly built platforms were used to allow for variety of grouping in front, perhaps, of a plain sky; this comparatively simplified scenery was also naturally made interesting by the use of lighting effects—and, many would say, of darkening effects, though why dark scenes should not be dark many people who never saw a limelight follow a stage-star cannot understand.

At the same time ballet with its escapism from the ordinary life of rationing achieved an ever increasing popularity—just as it did in seventeenth century London—and as the average ballet, where space is the first essential, only needs a painted backcloth as scenery, this encouraged non-theatrical artists to design lovely pictorial backgrounds. With this infusion of new blood perspective painting—another seventeenth century craze—returned, one of the most remarkable achievements being Cecil Beaton's designs for Sir Laurence Olivier's *School for Scandal*, in which perspective backcloths appeared as solidly real as did the wall-paintings both inside and outside Mr. Povy's house that Pepys so much admired.

In the search for further economy the film-method of projecting scenes by light on to a background has now been tried both abroad, as in Rossellini's production of Honegger's *Jeanne d'Arc au Bûcher* at the San Carlo, and here with Hurry's designs for this year's *Ring* at Covent Garden; incidentally this was unsuccessfully tried out in the eighteenth century in London, but no doubt the artists at that time, without the example of the films, only botched up those ' Italian Shades, a larger Kind of magick Lanthorn, an Expedient so low that it would disgrase a Puppet-Show.' The method failed at Covent Garden before the war, though it succeeded at times under Strohbach at Cologne in the 1920's.

The danger of non-theatrical artists designing more than ballet is that often they have neither the time nor the opportunity to study the problems of the stage, which are so different from anything they have dealt with before and which can really only be learned in some hard school such as a weekly repertory theatre: the result is that their beautiful flat design usually has to be translated by others into practical construction that takes into account such things as line of sight, masking, manoeuvrability, storage and so on. Many sincere art-lovers think that the active interest such artists have begun to show in the theatre is so welcome that they should not be expected to have to deal with practical problems: but practical problems of theatrecraft are of the first importance in stage-design, as Sir Hugh Casson so admirably admitted in print after designing his first theatre-settings for Gluck's *Alceste* at Glyndebourne last summer.

At the Opéra-Comique two years ago Paris saw a production of *Louise* with scenery after maquettes by Utrillo: of course the backcloth of Paris was, in the best sense, as pretty as the prettiest picture, full of the nostalgic magic of the mysteriously alive city at night, but as realized by the practical theatre-man the lovely background was framed—and inevitably framed—by two flat sides, as it were, a picture frame extended in depth: this uninteresting framing—the inevitable result of realizing for the stage a picture that is complete in itself—certainly allowed for a full view of the whole beauty of the design, but it made the singers intrusive, especially as the only place for a tree was right in front of the very door out of which Louise appeared to the crowd (had the artist not been Utrillo, the prima donna might justifiably have demanded the tree's removal): and that design could not have been " realized " at all except in such a non-theatrical fashion, simply because it was a non-theatrical design. Such framed pictures have often been seen in London recently.

At the same time the Paris Opéra gave *Salome* with a minimum of solid levels against a changing sky with effective lighting that was quite nullified at the first performance by the distracting fidgeting of the undisciplined supers: shortly afterwards the complicatedly stupendous production of Rameau's *Les Indes Galantes* with its choking eruption and staggeringly sumptuous dresses completely swamped whatever merit there might have been in this not very good example of a Rameau opera, as ' realized ' by the same musician who has ' improved ' and added to Weber's no less spectacular *Oberon* recently.

71

Italy of course has always loved scenic spectacle coupled with fine solo singing, sometimes even at the expense of the opera: in a production of *Forza del Destino* at the San Carlo, Naples, last spring there was an extraordinarily inept mixture of scenic styles—after an enormous realistic waterfall had done its best to distract from Tebaldi's lovely singing of the prayer there came a pantomimically naturalistic forest-cloth that might have looked well at a distance suitably lit, but which looked overwhelmingly music-hall so far in front of the stage that Alvaro caught his sword in the wings at his entrance, while the next two scenes were a shoddy vamped-up unfurnished room of vast size for the wounded scene and a completely empty stylized slope up to the sky for Preziosilla's scene with the huge crowd—a complete jumble.

Far better from the production point of view was *Forza* as done last year (1953) at Innsbruck: this was entirely staged with a view to economy but with the addition of that great essential of the theatre—sincere imagination: the method might not work with many operas, but for this opera it was successful—it was all staged inside heavy black curtains with a minimum of scenic suggestion and only the necessary acting areas lit. Most moving was the sight of the black-robed monks in the initiation scene standing motionless in a semicircle facing upstage with tall lighted candles in their hands beneath a thirty-foot crucifix with the huge naturalistic figure of the Christ leaning forward from the darkness: here the impressive simplicity of the settings made the good singers, Sperlich and Lechleitner seem even better, while at Naples Tebaldi could almost have lost her personality in front of the glitteringly trickling waterfall unless one shut one's eyes and only listened to the fine and moving singing.

How difficult it is to achieve the right balance between sight, sound and sense, those three partners that are so often encouraged by their prejudiced followers to fall out—especially abroad! It is surely about time this was said, for here we are always under a delusion that the Continent performs opera better than elsewhere. Occasionally no doubt a special effort is made for a famous Festival, and Stockholm, Zurich and Vienna at least may usually maintain a generally high standard, but routine performances in Italy and France—even at opera-houses of repute—are in most ways far inferior to the normal performances at Covent Garden or Sadler's Wells. At neither of these opera-houses would scenery as old and obviously torn and patched as the Opéra-Comique *Mireille* settings be allowed, nor would such slovenly, haphazard casualness among the performers be tolerated.

Better voices may be more often found on the Continent than here—after all it is a larger place, but this is not invariably the case and Continental singers are not always wise in singing the varied parts they do: however, they do have the one supreme advantage over our singers—they have for many years been able to learn their craft in an opera-house with its practical tradition, as some young singers are now able to do in our opera-companies. But though individual singers may pack a house, as they have always done, the number who can do that is limited, and there is no harm in developing the other ingredients of opera which, if rightly used, may improve a good performance or disguise an adequate one, but which, if not considered, may well stultify a brilliant performance. As Sir Thomas Beecham once said, there is no point in getting the music of an opera right if the stage-production is wrong.

This is what, I am sure, all opera-producers in London today have in mind, though their methods vary: above all, they are beginning to agree in looking at opera and in encouraging conductors and other musicians to look at opera as a theatrical art, as Sir Thomas has always done. This can be seen from the number of purely dramatic producers and choreographers who have recently staged operas: those in the audience who are not solely interested in music and vocalisation are always ready to be excited by a theatrical device or to criticise it when it obtrudes distractingly on the emotion of the work—and this section of the audience that appreciates sense as well as sound and sight is increasing and will soon fill the opera-houses regularly, if their predelictions are taken into account as much as are those of the enthusiasts for the two arts of music and design (design, which Ben Jonson said was the invariable excuse of the artist who disregarded the requirements of the drama and of the theatre). But when working on opera designers of ballet backcloths should study stage-craft, and theatre producers should have knowledge of music and be led by it.

Several have already set the example, and perhaps one day we shall see the grandeur of Messel, the detail of Beaton, the drama of Hurry, the modesty of Mosceiwitch, the texture of Piper and the special qualities of other artists merged together by the drive of Guthrie, the movement of Helpmann, the sincerity of Devine, the adaptability of Coleman and whatever else of value other producers can give, so that worthwhile examples of the true operatic combination of the sound of fine singing and playing, the sight of fine scenes and costumes and the sense of fine emotions and dramatic contrasts can be enjoyed and remembered by opera-lovers of all kinds, whether expert or ignorant, but all enthusiastic.

Trends in Post-war Germany

by HANS BUSCH

THE opportunity to study post-war production of opera in Europe has been offered to me by the generous award of a Ford Foundation Fellowship recommended by Indiana University, U.S.A., on whose faculty I am. Travelling some 14,000 miles by car through Germany, Austria, Italy and Switzerland I have so far visited 43 theatres and opera houses in 22 cities. This unique and most inspiring experience and personal contacts with a great number of artists, directors, producers, designers and managers have brought about a wealth of information and answered many questions I had asked for some time.

To form a fair and objective opinion of present trends, standards and accomplishments on the European opera stage, I am visiting as many of the major opera houses and smaller theatres, radio and television studios as is possible within a given, comparatively short period of time. After some twenty years of absence from Germany and Austria where the teamwork of opera production had been developed more widely and effectively than anywhere else, my main interest is naturally focused on these particular countries. I am trying to learn to what extent the disaster of the Hitler régime, the war and subsequent reconstruction have affected the arts and the artist, mainly as far as the theatre in general and opera in particular are concerned. A fairly complete description and discussion of the many contrasting answers I have found to this single question would fill a book. However, here they are in a nutshell, as well as I am able to present them before the end of this trip, while still absorbing new impressions every day.

The spiritual and physical rebirth of the German theatre since 1945 reflects the so called " German Miracle " of survival and reconstruction achieved with astounding faith and energy and the aid of the Marshall Plan. In the ruins of 1945 there was and there still is today a widespread and genuine need for " Kultur " and artistic expression which in most instances is still promoted and subsidized, as it was in the days of royalty and the Weimar Republic, but no more propagated by the state. Apart from its purpose of entertainment, the theatre is still considered a " moralische Anstalt," a moral institution without which the Germans refuse to live. Today many of them, readjusted to a normal way of life, speak of the events the first performances after the war used to be for artist and audience alike. From their enthusiastic, almost nostalgic descriptions of the incredibly improvised performances in the ruins of 1945 one may gather that the theatre had never and nowhere been in greater, even more desperate demand. Without a stage, scenery and costumes or the money and material to make them, words and music became of greater importance than ever before. So did their interpreters returning from the battlefields, bombed out and starving, but longing to sing and play no matter what salary they received.

74

Very little seems to be left of that spirit today. Some of the severe simplicity caused by the lack of buildings and of other necessities which had proved to be no longer necessary at the end of the war, is still reflected in some very stylized costumes and scenic design. As in the case of the post-war Bayreuth Festival, the usually convincing simplicity of such productions today is motivated by artistic rather than economic considerations. Most of the important theatres and opera houses in Western Germany have been repaired or rebuilt with enormous sums allotted by the cities and/or the government. No time has been lost in this process, but a good deal of money has been wasted on ugly and impractical constructions. Most German cities have missed their great chance to rebuild their theatres as efficiently and beautifully as many of their industries and private homes.

On the other hand, many of the ardent, idealistic performers of 1945 today have become economically secure employees of government subsidized theatres— employees to whom music and theatre often mean a routine job rather than an art; more or less talented people some of whom are more interested in their privileges than in their duties, and more concerned with their personal comfort than their service to the company. This is one of the major disadvantages of the protection offered by government subsidized theatres. In America, unions like A.G.M.A. and EQUITY, are not powerful enough to protect those of their members who are not constantly at their best from receiving that two weeks' notice terminating their contract. No German Intendant can dismiss any of his artists, chorus, orchestra and staff, many of whom enjoy the security of lifelong contracts and subsequent pensions, so fast if at all, unless the member becomes guilty of some criminal offence. The majority of German theatrical artists, musicians and staff are too efficient and too proud of their profession to take undue advantage of the privileges they deserve and enjoy; but the few who do are sometimes liable to affect the morale and efficiency of many a subsidized company. Few German theatrical artists and staff protected by the rights of government employees realize how fortunate they are compared to most of their colleagues often fighting for their lives under the commercial, competitive systems of free enterprise elsewhere. One of the greatest benefits offered to them by the government subsidized system lies in the fact that instead of having to worry about their next job like so many of their British and American colleagues, they can settle down and concentrate on their artistic work and development. Both systems have their advantages and disadvantages which are quite interesting to compare. The benefits and drawbacks of the government subsidized system explain many of the extraordinary accomplishments as well as some of the worst mediocrity I have observed on the German stage of today.

Mediocre performances of opera I have attended in German cities, large and small, are mainly caused by inadequate musicianship and vocal talent still prevailing in many German theatres and opera houses, despite the fact that Western Germany of today, as far as the employment of foreign artists is concerned, is the most generous and liberal country I have known. This open-minded, hospitable attitude toward the foreign artist and foreigners in general is a natural reaction to the walls of the fortress by which the Germans were separated from the rest of the world under the Nazi régime. Their interest in world affairs, in music, art and literature of other countries, and their desire to absorb foreign influences in every field of culture and civilization account for much of Western Germany's spiritual and economic rebirth. The general cordiality extended to the visitor from abroad seems to derive from some sincere regret of Germany's guilt in the past, perhaps also from the fear of the East. Whatever the motives of this most pleasant and intelligent attitude may be, may it last and benefit mankind and the arts in general and opera in particular !

This impressive worldliness, which is by no means limited to the large cities, lives side by side with the utmost provincialism. On the surface it is amusing and even touching to watch the German provincial theatregoer sit through the dullest and most inadequate performances of plays and operas which are a community project, and in taxes cost him far more than the price of his seat. The stubborn routine by which such performances are presented and accepted besides other excellent ones in the German province, can only be explained by the naive pride the German bourgeois takes in his local " Stadttheater." Once he has paid for his subscription he goes to his theatre week after week for ten or eleven months year after year; and often his reaction may not differ from that of the last King of Saxony, who when urged by his adjutant to leave his box after having fallen asleep observed: " My grandfather could stand it, my father could stand it, and I am going to stand it, too!" In Germany the arts and the theatre are a tradition which is taken for granted; to have been to a certain performance is sometimes a matter of the " educated " citizen's or the pseudo-intellectual's social pride rather than of genuine need and enlightenment. Wherever this situation predominates, an opera performance, too, ceases to be the exciting event which it *always* is for performers and audience alike in the remotest Italian province, good or bad, but *never* indifferent. One cannot help wondering why mediocre companies in the German province offering an overwhelming choice of operas, plays and concerts throughout the year can be accepted and supported by the citizens, when sometimes only a few miles away in often more than one theatre excellent performances can be heard and seen. The only explanation of this phenomenon seems to be the somewhat mediaeval way of life in the German small city or town. The desire of its citizens to have their own theatre on the one hand causes much waste of public funds; on the other, it must be admitted that it furnishes the young artist with a training and a springboard, and in some instances even leads to some remarkable artistic results in the provinces.

Opera, if properly produced, as is generally known, is a costly affair. By the very nature of its complicated and expensive organism it is bound to lose money and cannot live without some kind of private or public support. Today it flourishes in Germany, Austria and Italy more than anywhere else in the world, because of the generous subsidies it receives from the governments of those countries. Since

Richard Wagner's reforms, opera in Germany and Austria has always been regarded and treated as music-drama and a " Gesamtkunstwerk," an integration of the arts of music, drama, dance, architecture and painting. In Germany today the emphasis is laid on the theatrical rather than the musical aspect of the production. Although I happen to be a producer and as deeply impressed as I am with a number of German opera productions, I must reluctantly confess that a comparatively insignificant opera performance in Florence—the first I attended in Italy since years— provided the greatest thrill of my entire voyage through the lands of opera. This impression was consolidated by other performances in Italy, for I cannot help feeling that in opera the music is even more important than the word and all that goes with it. Naturally, the ideal performance is born from the completely successful marriage of music and drama; but how seldom does such a marriage occur. At times it did occur in Vienna, Dresden, Munich, Berlin and Bayreuth before and in between the two world wars, and in Glyndebourne, too, when a great conductor and producer joined in close and harmonious collaboration. With very few exceptions, in Germany and Austria the era of the great opera conductor seems to be past. Producers and designers of exceptional talent bring new life to opera from dramatic and visual angles; but in most instances opera's musical and vocal elements are being treated as if they were of secondary importance. Rare performances, in which music and drama are presented with the same talent and care, such as Strawinsky's *Oedipus Rex*, *Mavra* and *Renard* under Georg Solti and Günter Rennert in Frankfurt only make one realize that something is wrong with opera when an interesting or brilliant *mise-en-scène* overshadows the musical values of the work. While a few powerful producers have come into being, the small number of successors to the generation of great opera conductors in Germany and Austria is not the only reason for the importance attributed to the theatrical function of opera. World War II and its consequences have sadly curtailed the quality and quantity of German and Austrian opera singers. The very few outstanding ones are so much in demand that they seldom concentrate their efforts on a single opera house or on a particular role. A good deal and sometimes even more than half their time is spent in guest appearances at other opera houses in Germany, Austria and abroad. Naturally, such lucrative overactivity of the individual artist prevents the continuous cohesive teamwork required to achieve top rate productions, particularly from a musical point of view. The same restlessness has befallen the few outstanding conductors, producers and designers. Their eagerness to compensate for years lost through the Nazi régime and the war has prompted the remark that German and Austrian theatres and opera houses no longer depend on production and rehearsal schedules, but on the arrival and departure of aeroplanes and trains. For many an artist even Bayreuth has become just another stopping place between Barcelona and Salzburg. The Vienna State Opera, still playing at the Theater an der Wien while its former building is being restored, appears to be more critically affected by this situation than any other company. In spite of some allegiance to Vienna for artistic, prestige and sentimental reasons Austrian and German artists there are attracted by better economic conditions abroad, particularly in Germany and Italy. Karl Böhm, the new head of the Vienna State Opera, must be a man of the highest integrity and strength to tie himself and his ensemble to Vienna, if that city's reputation of one of the great centres of opera in the world is to survive. The fantastic sums spent for the reconstruction of the Opera House am Kärntner Tor, which is being furnished with the most modern stage and technical equipment in the history of opera, could otherwise not be explained and accounted for. How the transition from the Theater an der Wien and the Volksoper is going to work out, and what role those two theatres will play thereafter, is anyone's guess.

Two features in the field of German opera production and scenic design have struck me as being most effective when properly applied: the perspective slope on which an entire stylized, remarkably simple and convincing production of *Don Carlo* was staged by Kurt Ehrhardt and the designer Rudolf Schulz; and the sloped round plate on which *Fidelio*, another stylized production of similar simplicity and strength was produced by Reinhard Lehmann and the designer Rolf Christiansen in the small city of Freiburg. Both devices, of ancient origin, also appear in the much debated productions of the Wagner brothers in Bayreuth. These slopes create a feeling of unexpected depth and dimensions and often provide for more dynamic acting than a flat or only slightly rising stage. Lighting, in which the Germans are masters, replaces much scenic detail and with the aid of projections, at times practically entire sets. A production of *Così fan tutte* staged by Wiesbaden's newly appointed Intendant Friedrich Schramm with the designer Ruodi Barth was another highlight of my opera impressions on the Continent as far as *mise-en-scène* and design are concerned. Singing actors in colourful costumes moved with grace and intelligence within a black and white set inspired by Paul Klee's designs. Overcoming some initial surprise I soon felt that Mozart and Paul Klee made a team which appeared more convincing than many a rococo set I had associated with *Così fan tutte* before this fascinating experience. A production of similar taste and charm, though on an entirely different level and for reasons which I cannot explain frowned upon by the Viennese, was that of the old French operetta *Giroflé-Giroflá* directed by Hans Jaray and designed by Erni Kniepert and Walter Hoesslin.

Whatever his criticisms, the visitor from abroad cannot stop marvelling at the enormous activity of European opera today. In view of the fact that production costs are considerably higher than in the days of the Weimar Republic and that all these stages depend on government subsidies higher than ever, considering that Germany has lost the most terrible war in history and that her talent is limited, some of the best informed observers in Western Germany conclude that the present opera boom has reached saturation point. Whatever artistic, economic and political concern one might have in this situation, the opera lover leaves the Continent enriched and rejuvenated and with a feeling of gratitude for the inspiration he has received.

Opera in Western Germany

By STEWART MANVILLE

IN Western Germany at the present time there are approximately fifty-six theatres which regularly give opera, of these eight are Staatsoper organizations, Braunschweig, Hamburg, Karlsruhe, Kassel, Munich, Oldenburg, Stuttgart and Wiesbaden. I think also it is permissible to include in this list a ninth, the Berlin Städtiche Oper, which is in the Western Sector of Berlin. The remainder of the theatres are supported by their respective cities as Städtische Bühnen with the exception of the few Landestheaters, which are supported by their respective provinces (Coburg, Darmstadt, Detmold and Hanover).

Each opera ensemble is, without exception, part of a larger organization which also sponsors a drama ensemble, an operetta ensemble, and in the case of Düsseldorf, Munich, Stuttgart and one or two other cities, a ballet ensemble of independent rank. Many of the theatres housing these companies were of course either damaged or totally destroyed by bombing during the war; and although many have been rebuilt, a number of opera companies still perform in make-shift houses. The Darmstadt ensemble, for example, plays in the Orangerie of the local palace, the Kassel company in a remodelled ballroom, and the Munich State Opera in the Festival Theatre, the Prinzregenten.

In the majority of the opera companies, the works announced for performance during the 1953-4 season were nearly all *new* productions. Each theatre on an average has mounted eight or nine new works during the current year, the most successful of which are performed again a second season, and sometimes a third; but the major portion of the season's performances are new. This is quite in contrast to the repertory system that is in operation in Vienna, Berlin, Cologne, Munich, Stuttgart, and most other European countries.

Another feature of operatic organization in most of the smaller German towns is the large number of performances given of a single opera in a short period of time. In Nürnberg, for example, the new production of *Figaro* received between twenty-five and thirty performances during October and November (1953), including those given at Fürth and in the outlying cities of Bayreuth, Erlangen and Arnsbach. When Nürnberg produces *Figaro* again, in perhaps five or six seasons' time, it will again receive an entirely new production. This is in direct contrast to the Metropolitan, New York for example, where the 1940 production of *Figaro* is still being given, and which receives perhaps four performances each season for something like a generation regardless of the constantly changing ideas of production and improved methods of stage lighting, scenic design and other techniques. Once the season's list of productions is announced there are few deviations from it, though the outstanding success of one work can crowd another from the season's schedule.

An examination of the season's repertories in the sixty odd German theatres provides several interesting factors. Without exception there is one Mozart opera in every repertory; indeed such is this composer's popularity that *Titus* has been given at Stuttgart, *La finta Giardiniera* at Karlsruhe and Mannheim, and *Idomeneo* at Bremen. Ticket sales for performances of Mozart throughout Germany surpass even those for Lortzing's works. Nearly every theatre, too, includes at least one work by this composer in their repertory. Lortzing attracts quite a different audience to the opera house, and it is often by attending performances of this composer that the operetta-minded individual is won over to opera. At Stuttgart where *Zar und Zimmermann* is a popular repertory work, Orff's *Trionfi* was sold out for nearly forty performances.

Contemporary operas are everywhere in evidence in Germany. Twelve companies produced works by Orff last season: *Die Kluge*, *Der Mond* and *Carmina Burana* are the favourites, and they have been performed frequently enough during recent years to be counted as almost ' standard ' repertory works ! Britten was represented by new productions of *Albert Herring* at Krefeld, *The Rape of Lucretia* at Wiesbaden, Stuttgart and Hamburg, *Let's Make an Opera* at Hanover. *Wozzeck* has been produced at Heidelberg, Hamburg and Gelsinkirchen. Although relatively little French opera is produced in Germany, Milhaud is represented by *Les Malheurs d'Orphée* at Freiburg, *Orestie* at Darmstadt, *Maximilian* at Oldenburg and three short works at Mannheim. The new version of Hindemith's *Cardillac* is being given in Detmold, Frankfurt and Nürnberg. New works like Einem's *Der Prozess* which had its première at the 1953 Salzburg Festival has been given in Berlin, Hamburg, Mannheim, Wuppertal and, outside Germany in Vienna, and Berne. When *The Rake's Progress* was new in the 1951-1952 season it was performed on no less than twenty German stages, and the public bought tickets.

Why does a German public purchase tickets for *The Rake*, and why does the public of the Metropolitan Opera, New York, stay away from the same opera or from *Peter Grimes* ? Surely because German companies perform contemporary works each season, and their public thereby become familiar with them, understand them and accept them. In a theatre like the Metropolitan which gives the standard repertory year after year, and then suddenly springs *Grimes* or *The Rake* on its public, it finds that public totally unprepared for contemporary opera.

New productions of Wagner outdistance those of Strauss by nearly two to one—there have been approximately sixty-three new productions of Wagnerian works and thirty-six of Strauss. *Arabella* and *Ariadne* received eight and six new productions respectively, *Die schweigsame Frau* two, *Die Frau ohne Schatten* two, *Rosenkavalier* eight, *Daphne* one, *Elektra* four and *Salome* five.

Another interesting fact that can be deduced from the season's repertories is the popularity in Germany of such operas as Cimarosa's *Secret Marriage*, and Adam's *Postillon von Longumeau*, and interest in such works as Humperdinck's *Königskinder* and Nessler's *Trompeter von Sackingen*. Handel and Gluck too have been surprisingly well represented; with the latter's *Orpheus* at Hamburg, Karlsruhe and Oberhausen,

Armide at Bielefeld, *Iphigénie en Aulide* at Oldenburg and the former's *Julius Caesar* at Freiburg, *Saul* at Mannheim and *Deidamia* at Hamburg.

On further examining the season's repertories in Germany, one is struck by the large number of theatres all performing the same work. This may be explained in three ways. First, a publisher may print a new edition of a score which has previously been available in limited quantities; *Arabella*, for example, was newly edited a year ago, and now nearly every opera *ensemble* in Germany will have performed *Arabella* within the next two or three years. Secondly, when one company has an unusual success with an opera, others will immediately rush to perform it the next season; this was again true with *Arabella*. Thirdly, small houses cannot afford a double cast, and are therefore likely to perform operas which their neighbouring cities also perform currently or have performed the previous season, in order to obtain singers who know the roles when they are needed in an emergency.

Summing up, one is forced to the conclusion that the ' production ' system is preferable to the ' repertory ' system, for over a period of a few years the public is able to become acquainted with many more operas. In a repertory theatre like the Metropolitan, there are perhaps thirty operas in mountable condition. These same operas will be performed over a period of say twenty years, in rotation, with a novelty here or there and an occasional revival, making the total of operas available to a New York opera-goer in that period something in the region of forty. In a German provincial theatre, say Nürnberg, a minimum of ten new operas will be produced each season. Thus, theoretically, one should be able to see two hundred different operas there over a similar period of time. Indeed, between 1920 and 1952 nearly all the one hundred and seventy operas listed in Reclam's *Opera Guide*, have been performed at Nürnberg, which has a population of some 390,000. New York has a population of eight million. Is there a lesson to be learned from this ? This writer thinks that there is.

The Vienna Opera Festival, 1954
by JOSEPH WECHSBERG

'FESTIVAL' is becoming a much misused word.   A festival should be made up of festive performances, carried in a festive spirit.   It is not sufficient to lure visitors by promises of great things to come and then offer them sub-standard repertory.   Perhaps we in Vienna were spoiled by the *Festwochen* in 1952 and 1953, when the Staatsoper im Theater an der Wien gave a brilliant galaxy of fine opera performances during the annual June Festival.   This year, the *Festwochen* opened and closed with spectacular events; in between were stretches of arid mediocrity. There seemed to be a general lack of organization.   It is bad luck when a number of first-rate singers are suddenly getting indisposed; it is poor management when a 'Festival' is organized without adequate replacements.   On two successive evenings the performances had to be changed at the last minute.   On other nights, there was appalling improvisation.   The old era Hilbert is finished and the new era Böhm (who takes over as director in September) had not yet started.   During the interregnum no one seemed to care what happened.   The present director, Franz Salmhofer, was overheard saying that 'improvisation is everything.' Visitors from abroad, who had travelled to Vienna expecting to hear great things, sat in dismay, bored by voiceless singing, superannuated acting, sloppy orchestra playing and a virtual lack of musical direction.   No opera-house is better than its conductors and some of the State Opera's present conductors just do not belong there.

There were two outstanding performances in twenty-two days.   Both were conducted by Dr. Karl Böhm.   This is no accident.   Things being what they are now in Vienna only the future director, who can hire and fire, seems able to extract that extra effort from the performers which makes the difference between a mediocre performance and a great one.

The two outstanding performances were *Meistersinger* and *Elektra*.   Paul Schoeffler sang a Hans Sachs of great poetic beauty, with the necessary humorous and robust undertones.   Rarely have veteran *Meistersinger* fans, to whom I belong, heard the tragic of the ageing man (*Mein Kind, von Tristan und Isolde kenn ich ein traurig Lied*) with such eloquent understanding.   The *Fliedermonolog* and the scene with Eva (Irmgard Seefried) were magnificent, and so was the entire *Schusterstube*. The quintet reminded me of the great days of Lotte Lehmann, Leo Slezak and Emil Schipper.   Kunz was *the* Beckmesser (he refrained from exaggeration) and Murray Dickie and Rosette Anday were their reliable selves.   The Mastersingers could be heard, the *Prügelszene* was a cabinet piece of exactness, and the *Festwiese* was impressive.   What an evening that was !

Elektra is the single greatest performance in Vienna, and the one during the Festival was even more gripping and moving than usualy.   Böhm kept the large orchestra down to chamber-musical lucidity and there were minutes of unbroken lyrical beauty, such as Elektra's meeting with Orest and the final duet of the two sisters. In the title part Christel Goltz made it clear once again that she is the finest Elektra of our day; one would wish though she would not sing this taxing part so much, for there were signs of fatigue, particularly her around B and B flat; her C's are magnificent. The rest of the cast, Elisabeth Hoengen as Klytemnestra, Hilde Zadek as Chrysothemis, Schoeffler as Orest and Max Lorenz as Aegisth, were equally spectacular. The orchestra, under Böhm, was marvellous.

There were also a few good evenings. A *Don Giovanni* with George London, vocally and in appearance superb, though in his characterization sometimes conventional, and with a trio of beautiful women, Zadek as Donna Anna, Lisa della Casa as Elvira, Hilde Gueden as Zerlina. Ludwig Weber as the Commandator sang the cemetery scene with impressive resonance. There was also an exciting *Tristan* with the great Martha Mödl and Max Lorenz. Both performances (as well as a fine *Ariadne*) were conducted by Rudolf Moralt, the State Opera's always-reliable maestro, a fine technician and a man of sound musical intelligence. There are rumours that he may not stay on in Vienna. It is to be hoped that Böhm will not repeat the mistake of some of his predecessors who surrounded themselves with a string of second-rate conductors so they would shine themselves. This may be quite effective for the *Herr Direktor* who conducts all outstanding performances, but it is not the right way to keep a high-class establishment.

In *Ariadne*, Seefried demonstrated again that her Komponist is perhaps the finest of her parts, and the long legato phrases are so-to-speak tailor-made for Zadek's beautiful, warm voice. Richard Strauss's ninetieth birthday was celebrated with a good performance of *Daphne* (with Maria Reining). As Boris Godunov, George London, singing beautifully, was surrounded by a hopeless cast and hardly helped by a sloppy orchestra.

By way of contributing to the new Handel Renaissance, the State Opera produced *Julius Caesar*. No expense was saved. Impressive baroque scenery and costumes were designed by Caspar Neher. A selected orchestra (two first desk concertmasters, Boskowsky and Sedlak) was under Böhm. And there was a first-class cast (Shoeffler, Seefried, Hoengen, Dermota, Frick). The performance was very good, in spite of several indispositions. It was repeated just once, and it will not be given again before next year. A very fine contribution to *kultura* but one wonders whether the work couldn't have been given as oratorio in the concert hall—last year, *Die Frau ohne Schatten* was performed there—while the money could have been spent to bolster the repertory, say, to buy new sets for the such much-performed productions as *Carmen*, or *Hoffman's Erzählungen*, which need badly a new make-up. Very little Mozart was given this year. The State Opera travels with its de-luxe *Così fan tutte*, but at home they never play it. And Alban Berg's *Wozzek*, an opera in the repertory, was not performed during the Festival which was said to be devoted partly to Berg.

83

Opera in Post-War Italy

A Critical Perspective of Rediscoveries and First Performances

by CYNTHIA JOLLY

NOVELTY in Italy is the spice of life, a psychological necessity. And, fortunately, operatic life still profits from it, presenting an impartial and international galaxy of musical activity calculated to turn the head of a foreign guest. Nor can its richness and adventurousness be understood without reference to the background, where individual enterprise and State help flourish side by side. The first refreshing phenomenon is the way contemporary composers are hunted down for performance. The Scala handles this side with great seriousness, commissions generously and ensures careful performance. The concert-careers of composers are watched by the Artistic Directors of the various theatres and festivals, and everyone may get heard. So far, so good. But there are disadvantages inherent in the system, which a Commission, now sitting, is striving against countless odds to improve.

The risky age of the unscrupulous impresario gave way to State protection and subsidy in the twenties. Very sensibly, the higher taxes of football and cinemas go to meet the needs of their less popular brothers (theatre and opera), which are thus artificially fostered. The autonomous and highly competitive opera-houses receive block subsidies according to their size, personnel, etc., and the Government then washes its hands and expects no financial return. The native operas are chosen quite casually for a variety of reasons, too often non-artistic; living contact with public opinion is limited to the dramatic reception often afforded new works, which by an uneconomical practice receive a maximum of three to four performances. Official honour and the public desire for novelty being alike satisfied, the work, however important and however stimulating its performance, returns to its shelf. This helps to explain why Italy seldom gives its best composers the rating they are given abroad, and why so many have sought a truer assessment outside. How very few of the contemporary works discussed below have been afforded a second hearing ! Yet there are many which would merit it. *Wozzeck* (performed at Rome in 1942 and post-war at Naples and the Scala) is the only shining exception. Even the older masterpieces which come to light enter the repertory slowly—Rossini's *Turco in Italia* and Cherubini's *Medea* are recent examples.

In the presentation of old works State patronage performs an undisputed and invaluable function with vital repercussions in the whole musical world. Furthermore, in recent years it has come to encourage the formation of ' Piccoli Teatri ' attached to the big centres, which perform the small-scale works, once somewhat scorned, and left to the pioneer work of the Accademia Chigiana and a few enterprising Conservatoires.

THE SEASON IN GERMANY

Above:
A scene from the new production of Weber's 'Euryanthe'

Below:
A scene from Britten's 'The Rape of Lucretia', both at Stuttgart

Photograph by Weizzacher

Above left:
C. Köhnly's set for 'Euryanthe'

Above right:
A scene from Lualdi's 'Il Diavolo nel Campanile'.   Setting
by Dino Buzzati

**THE FLORENCE
FESTIVAL 1954**

LUCILLE UDOVICK (*Agnese*) and ENZO MASCHERINI (*The Duke of Borgogna*)
in Spontini's 'Agnese di Hohenstaufen'

Photographs by Levi

A word about performance conditions. As opera companies and tours do not exist, conductors and singers are open to bidding and go the rounds on contract. Rehearsal is therefore scanty and the producer often unable to build an ensemble. The festivals are more successful in this because they come at a less crowded time of year, and existing for the tourist public are anxious for favourable publicity. Generally speaking, the Florence Maggio concerns itself with older works and Venice with untried contemporary ones, but they are apt to interchange functions. Of the four big theatres (Milan, Rome, Florence, Naples) the San Carlo at Naples has a natural zest for modernity. But the Scala and Rome tend to include a good proportion (about 20 per cent.) of non-repertory works, which they balance out against stock repertory. This means that post-war activity has been so fervid that a brief survey cannot hope to do it justice, simply indicating main lines with a hint of the reactions of press and public.

First of all, the ' riprese ' or ' exhumations ' as they are graphically called. The most striking single initiative was the musical profile of Rossini offered by the Maggio Musicale in 1952. Apart from two known operas in the French style, they staged two comic operas (*Pietra del Paragone* and *Scala di Seta*) and two *opere serie* (*Tancredi* and *Armida*). The way to this revaluation had been opened up in Rome in 1950 by a courageous *ad hoc* society, the Amfiparnaso, who had put the *Turco in Italia* and Maria Callas together in an enchanting production, to discover a major comic opera and a magnificent Rossini interpreter. (Previtali, Guerrieri, Maccari: Callas, Stabile, Bruscantini.) *Armida*, however, received a mixed press without substantially altering musical opinion of Rossini: the libretto and an over-elaborate vocal line disturbed contemporary critics, even though Callas probably equalled La Colbran. Savinio's opulent and un-Rossinian sets came in for much comment. (Serafin, Savinio : Callas, Albanese, Filippeschi, Ziliani.) In general, there emerged, as d'Amico pointed out, the fact that a Rossini opera in performance never sounds dull because of the architectural skill hidden behind the succession of so-called complete numbers. This was equally true of *Tancredi* where production was less successful. (Serafin, Frigerio, Cagli : Stich-Randall, Albanese, Simionato, Petri.) The comic operas were all performed with immense brio and were extremely successful, notably the *Pietra del Paragone*, found to have the invention and impetuousness which in *Conte Ory* (unearthed by Zandonai before the war) have given way to formal perfection and balance. (PP. Serafin, Bragaglia, Vagnetti ; Simionato, Corsi, Petri, Luise.) *La Scala di Seta* (Tieri, Chiari sets) inaugurated the Florentine Piccolo Teatro, sung by members of the Opera School attached to the Comunale.

Cherubini and Spontini are two other Italian composers who have been entirely reconsidered as a result of recent performance (which over and over again proves to differ from a score-reading opinion). Both of them are now gaining from what for so long has been their disadvantage: their historical position at the vital transition period between the eighteenth and nineteenth centuries, and their geographical position as expatriots. Cherubini's *Medea*, rich in anticipations, might in fact have been a modern opera, so great was the *éclat* aroused, and so deep, one might say, the correspondence with the modern spirit, so patently missing in the 1909 centenary production. Its very granite strength and unity of purpose proved a stumbling-block for some critics, who found a stiffness in melodic invention. Some, like Abbiati, objected to a discrepancy between the 'mannered' spectacular side and the unrelenting dramatic development. But to all it meant an 'authentic revelation,' enhanced by production in the grand manner, in which Callas made operatic history. It was a pity that the sets and costumes were in questionable relationship to the spirit of the work. (Gui, Barsacq, Coutaud : Callas, Barbieri, Guichandut, Petri.)

Spontini has had his most triumphant revindication this year at the Maggio with a production, not uncriticized, of his Berlin opera *Agnese di Hohenstaufen*. (Gui, Lualdi Carboni: Udovick, Dow, Corelli.) The operas of his Paris period had already seen performance, *Olimpia*, with its rhetoric and long formal ballets, at the 1950 Maggio, the significant *Fernando Cortez* at Naples in 1951 in an apparently magnificent production. (Santini, Cristini : Tebaldi, Penno, Tajo.) *Agnese* represents the fusion of all his cosmopolitan qualities, his *ne plus ultra* and his own favourite. In spite of the obscurity of the libretto plot (translated into Italian *prose*!) and copious cuts, the structural unity of the work and its rich symphonic and polyphonic texture have met universal admiration from the major critics. 'We find ourselves faced with living people,' added Pannain: characters who lead straight to Verdi and to Wagner. The careful preparation of the performing edition was universally praised.

Less conspicuously successful but not unimportant events were Haydn's *Orfeo e Euridice* (Kleiber, Salvini : Christoff, Callas, Tygesen) and Schumann's *Genoveva* (Cluytens, Grundgens, Böhm : Cunitz, Mödl, Gester, Hofermayer) ; both at the 1951 Maggio. They were not considered to be more than sidelines of their illustrious authors, and to lack dramatic impact. *Orfeo e Euridice* was given its very first performance, being commissioned for the King's Theatre, London, which was then closed under a prohibition of George III.

Monteverdi's *Orfeo* had an important revival in a much-discussed but seemingly effective transcription by Vito Frazzi. Cavalli's *Didone*, the 'courtyard' opera of the 1952 Maggio, was a revival after three centuries, and musically highly praised in Nielsen's transcription. Like the imported French production of *Les Indes Galantes* (Boboli Gardens, 1953) the music really required a theatre, and in Cavalli's case some hint of the fantastic stage-machines dear to the Venetians. (Giulini, Gründgens: Petrella, Radev, Tajo.) Gluck's *Ifigenia in Aulide*, however, which was revived in 1950, survived the rigours of the open-air, and with Graf's lakeside production of Weber's *Oberon* (Maggio 1951) took the palm for spectacular open-air production.

94

An unexpected and 'intoxicating' experience—according to the critic of *Il Mondo*—was the production of Handel's *Giulio Cesare* in the ruins of the Teatro Grande of Pompei in July 1952. Unperformed since an Opera Festival at Göttingen in 1922, the opera made an indelible impression in spite of a mangled nineteenth-century transcription which caused some critics in all seriousness to exclaim ' C'e già Verdi ! ' (Albert, Graf: Tebaldi, Siepi, Nicolai, Sinimberghi.)

The fiftieth anniversary of Verdi's death (1951) saw three Verdi revivals, one of them the discovery of the 'gigantic stature' of *Macbeth* (Gui, Gründegens, Böhm: Varnay, Penno, Tajo: a superb performance). *Aroldo* proved to have a genuine dramatic force, and its fourth Act interested critics, who found in it anticipations of later Verdi. (Serafin, Graf, Vagnetti: Penno, Stella, Protti.) Even *Oberto* had a successful revival at the Scala, 111 years after the first performance ! (Capuana, Ratto sets: Caniglia, Stignani, Poggi.)

The revival of interest in nineteenth-century Russian opera in Italy is a widespread phenomenon. Besides the better-known works, *Pique-Dame* (Florence 1953) enjoyed immense critical esteem; *Prince Igor* and *Kitesch* were welcomed at the Scala; Rimsky-Korsakov's *Snow-Maiden* was heard at Rome (1954) and *Kascey the Immortal* at Naples (1950). His short opera *Mozart and Salieri* which followed *Boulevard Solitude* at Naples (1954) found less critical approval. In April 1954, the Piccolo Teatro of Florence staged Dargomizhsky's *Stone-Guest* for two evenings, before an enthusiastic public of some 300 (a striking example of the waste of talent involved in the arch-individualistic system). Never before performed out of Russia, this boldly experimental opera was claimed by d'Amico as the authentic musical ancestor of Mussorgsky's most important works, possessing a host of stylistic finds which all serve to reinforce the drama. Not even Rimsky-Korsakov's alteration of its harmonies seems to have prevented its impact.

In this field of smaller operas, one of the earliest post-war revivals was that of *Dido and Aeneas* at the Quirino, Rome, in 1947: a fine fusion of elements was not found again when the opera was repeated at the Rome Opera House in 1948. The initiative of Count Chigi was responsible for Mortari's transcription and the Siena production of Galuppi's *L'Amante di Tutti* in 1948. (Gavazzeni; Perea-Labia, Gardino.) Like this composer's *Diavolessa* which Venice performed in 1952, the music and treatment both anticipate Mozart and show the art of the concerted ensemble already highly developed. (Giulini, Pavolini, Luzzatti: Rizzieri, Noni, Cadoni, Bruscantini.) Cimarosa's *Tre Amanti* and smaller Neapolitan intermezzi marked the re-opening of the Teatro dei Rinnovati in Siena (1950). Another brilliant piece of reconstruction was afforded by Boccherini's 'zarzuela', *Clementina* (Venice 1951). The libretto was never found and so speaking characters and dialogue were added without damaging the spirit of farcical caricature. (Dobrowen, Guerrieri, Guttuso: Rizzieri, Simionato, Sciutti, Bruscantini.)

At the Pergola in Florence in 1949, Emidio Tieri conducted a revival of three works which have since been played everywhere: Cimarosa's *Maestro di Capella*,

Pergolesi's *Contadina Astuta* and Cherubini's *Osteria portoghese*. At the Angelicum, Milan, in 1952, the latter was played with the medieval *Jeu de Robin et Marion* of Adam de la Halle in a free orchestral adaptation by Mompellio. And last, but not least, the *Amfiparnaso* society of 1950 built its contemporary repertory round an incomparable production of the Vecchi *commedia harmonica*, which Mario Soldati solved by putting the chorus in the orchestral pit and dividing the stagework between actors and dancers.

Judgments on contemporary operas suffer from lack of disinterestedness among the majority of critics and a lack of preparation in the public, who tend to listen to each ' *novita* ' as an isolated phenomenon. (There are hardly any critical biographies available in Italy, and even if available, are read only by specialists.) Any analysis perforce needs this proviso. While foreign operas suffer from incredible, often unsingable translations and ' rhythmic adaptations.' At least three, recently performed, Liebermann's *Leonora* 40-45 (Scala 1954), *Boulevard Solitude* (Henze) and Einem's *Prozess* (Naples 1954) have owed some of their harsh reception to this sad fact. For the *prime mondiale* it is another story: *The Rake's Progress*, for example, had the Scala chorus dutifully singing in phonetic English and the critics commenting that the less Anglo-American was the soloist, the clearer the diction !

The performance-right tussle between the Scala and the Biennale which by a happy compromise gave Strawinsky's first English opera to Venice with Scala orchestral and choral resources is by now familiar history. Strawinsky was presumably the last to object, since he knew the Fenice to be the ideal setting. ' The Scala performance has given oxygen to the dying Venice Festival ' commented one critic cruelly. The production aroused few adverse comments among the Italian press who were perhaps too nonplussed by the music to pay attention, though Mila wishes that Hogarth could have been more in evidence. They managed all the same to document the highest price paid for a seat (L. 100,000 or £60 !) and to count the curtain-calls ! With very few exceptions they found it exasperating, enigmatic, or simply as Mila puts it, ' a harmonious capitulation of old worlds.' ' It has drawn an enormous question-mark on the blackboard of contemporary music,' commented Abbiati, who waxed eloquent. A general irritation that Strawinsky should deliberately stride backwards over a century and a half of musical development found vent in *La Stampa*'s critic, who insisted that it was a thorough-going music-drama all the same, in an illogical and bizarre mixture of styles. One of its champions, on the other hand, took up another extreme position, asserting that it was the only real twentieth-century opera, *Wozzeck* being the last extreme of romantic melodrama. *Il Mondo*, with more detachment, found it the most complete and amusing of his pastiches, a ' paper model held together with pins on the old marionette of *Petrushka*.' Several critics welcomed the real expressiveness which entered through the character of Anne to be fully developed in the third act. The cemetery scene and the auction sale came in for general admiration, the latter considered a modern equivalent of the inn-scene of *Boris*. (Strawinsky/Leitner, Ebert, Ratto: Schwarzkopf, Rounseville, Tourel, Kraus.)

The first Western performance at the 1953 Maggio of another Russian work, Prokofiev's *War and Peace*, caused a war of rival versions which has meant that the expurgated version approved by Prokofiev before his death has not yet been heard. The shortened Rodzinski version brought from the States was certainly acceptable to the public, as Gavazzeni points out in the *Rassegna Musicale*, although in common with many others he found its language had become mere rhetorical mannerism, which generally leaves audiences cold. He also comments very pertinently that nobody can write a people's opera by act of will, be it *Boris* or *Cavalleria*. Most of the critics, complaining of poverty of imagination, found the relationship with Tolstoy non-existent (his name was, in fact, missed off the programme) but were willing to allow that the score showed the occasional " mark of the lion." Vigolo of *Il Mondo* took up an intermediate position between the general disapproval and the advocacy of d'Amico, considering that perhaps contemporary music may arrive at new development by passing through a phase of relative banality. D'Amico went further and found a deliberate renunciation of complex sonorities to attain a genuine singing opera. The performance, in general, was conducted on a very realistic plain and was convincing as spectacle. (Rodzinski, Pavlova, Sciltian: and over thirty singers—Carteri, Barbieri, Tajo, Corelli).

Prokofiev's *Gambler*, performed at Naples in 1953 in an exemplary performance (Scherchen, Frigerio, Cristini: Barbato, Gardino, Pirazzini, Tajo) found a much warmer welcome in spite of a failure in the last act, which besides being unfaithful to Dostoievsky left things in the air. The melodic spontaneity and successful transmission of the comic spirit was by some interpreted as brilliant superficiality.

Shostakovitch's *Lady Macbeth of Mtsensk* (Venice 1947) had a poor reception, partly due to his conspicuous comic talent, which, leaning towards parody, touched on sacrosanct matters. Mila commented on the lack of stylistic unity and objected to the blatant tragic effects. (Sanzogno, Millosz, Guttuso: Fortunati, Cassinelli, Voyer.) Turning to home waters, Britten reaped a positive success with *Peter Grimes* at the Scala in 1947: *Lucretia*, performed at Rome in 1949 (Santini; Lattuada, Clerici: Gardino, Manurita) was appreciated musically, though the theatre was considered over-large for it with the effect of distorting many dramatic effects. A small-size, well-written American work, Foss's *Jumping Frog*, had the advantage of staging in the Fenice (Venice 1953) and showed up as it should with a fresh, invigorating performance by young co-nationals (Sanzogno: Harrower, Wittstein: Luciano, Tozzi, Brown).

In spite of a Premio Italia and other signs of official favour, the unfortunate Henze fell foul of press and public alike with his *Boulevard Solitude*, produced at Naples in March 1954 and at Rome in April, made all the more famous by Strawinsky's sartorial adventure and the grotesque clamour of the Romans. The more responsible critics admitted him to be a well-equipped musician, but to be working in an expressionistic cul-de-sac. Like Menotti, Henze does his own producing, insisting on including dancers whose enigmatic symbolism infuriated many. (Naples. Perlea, Russo: Stix, Munteanu, Borriello.)

One of its parent works, Berg's *Lulu*, had its first Italian performance at Venice in 1949 in an interesting production. (Sanzogno, Strehler: Stix, Rehfuss.) In spite of its inferior dramatic quality, Mila found the use of twelve-note technique more successful than in *Wozzeck*, producing a compactness of language so prodigious that it was sometimes paralyzing.

The Hindemith stage works of this period have encountered critical comprehension and acceptance in Italy: first with *Cardillac* (Venice 1948; Sanzogno, Fritz-Schuh, Neher: Torres, Christoff) and then with *Mathis der Maler* (the Stuttgart Opera under Leitner at Rome 1951 in a stupendous production). The witty comic satire *Neues vom Tage* was recently presented at Naples in its revised edition (Hindemith, Brissoni, Cristini: Fortunati, Valdengo) and met favourable assessment which was not, alas, afforded a similar opera of the same period—Schönberg's *Von heute auf morgen* (Naples 1953. Scherchen, Reich, Otto: Krämmer, Stix).

Milhaud, too, has found scope in Italy, culminating in the 'colossale'— the production of *Christophe Colombe* at Rome in 1954, which pleased the press more for its music than for its success as a dramatic representation, to present which, however, the Rome Opera spared no pains. (Santini, Graf, Colasanti: Guelfi, Pirazzini—a cast of thirty-seven singers.) The exquisite *Malheurs d'Orphée* has had a quantity of radio performances since its successful production at Venice in 1948: but *La Sagesse*, given its first stage setting at Rome in 1950, failed dismally with many puns upon its name. *Bolivar* came to the San Carlo with the Paris Opéra and the beautiful Léger sets, which exercised a strong visual appeal in spite of reservations about Milhaud's talent as an opera composer and comments on his 'facile eloquence.'

The diffusion of Honegger's *Jeanne d' Arc au Bûcher* (Rome 1949) is as much due to the fame of Bergman's interpretation in the Rossellini production (Naples 1953 and Scala 1954) as to a strong appreciation of what is considered a very hybrid work. It forms one of the few instances of a repeat of a modern opera. Strauss's *Danae* received a *succes d'estime* at the Scala in 1952.

Last of the important foreign composers, Orff gained an easy public success with *Die Kluge* (Rome 1951) and the opulent production of the *Trionfi* at the Scala (1953), of which the *Catulli Carmina* was a first performance for Italy and the third part, the *Trionfi d'Afrodite* was a *prima assoluta*. He was criticized for trying to repeat an earlier successful formula and considered a decadent in many quarters. (Karajan, Fenneker sets: Schwarzkopf, Gedda.)

When we come to the scene of contemporary Italian opera, the plot thickens even more, because scores of conflicting interests come into play. It would not be blessed Italy if it were otherwise. Added to this, there is a basic division of opinion as to what constitutes a successful opera. For the fact remains that the best musicians in Italy today have not necessarily written the best operas. This is not a new general phenomenon but it is new for Italy. Menotti (who is still an Italian national) has split the ranks of the critics in twain (but the larger half is in opposition). The public, meanwhile, has joyfully flocked to one opera after another (*Telephone*, Venice 1948, *Medium*, Genoa 1951, *Consul*, Scala 1951, *Amahl*, Florence 1953). The problem is the same as elsewhere, only the expression is more violent (the sober pages of the *Rassegna Musicale* record that critics organized whistling squadrons at the *prima* of the *Consul*. (Sanzogno, Wakhevitch: Petrella, Powers, Gardino, Guelfi.) One critic put it nicely when he said that the opera problem was like a large car, broken-down, with experienced mechanics standing helplessly by: along comes a youngster who with a touch makes it go. Menotti seems to have the same genius with his conductors and performers, too. It is years since Stokowski conducted an opera as he did the ' sugar-water ' *Amahl*. (Stokowski, Menotti, Coltellacci, Balanchine: Cordova, Simionato.)

Much influenced by Menotti's methods, Peragallo, however, met a dramatic fate at the hands of the Scala public in March 1954, with a one-act opera *Gita in Campagna*, which had much to recommend it, but suffered from a libretto taken over too directly from a realist post-war tale of Moravia: its title, *Andare verso il popolo* has acquired an ironic connotation, because Peragallo's was a genuine attempt to bridge the gulf. His older dramatic madrigal, *La Collina* (Scala, May 1951) showed a promise which many critics find Peragallo to be fulfilling in his recent works. As to the performance of *Gita in Campagna*, one trustworthy critic considered Guttuso's sets the best ever at the Scala. Though a jeep appeared with impunity on the Fenice stage for Martinu's *Comedy on the Bridge* (Venice 1951) Topolino was not tolerated for Peragallo by the subscription ticket holders of the Scala ! (Sanzogno, Colosimo, Guttuso: Ribetti, Bertocci, Cadoni.)

Two other young composers have met success with comic operas which pivot round a clever stage-contrivance. Such was Tosatti's *Partita a Pugni* (Venice 1953) which, with no small virtuosity, reproduced in veristic terms a live Roman boxing-match. (Sanzogno, Colosimo: Lazzari, Panerai.) More recently, Bucchi has made with very simple musical means an effective stage-work out of Tchekov's *Contrabbasso*. (Florence 1954: Perlea, Pavlova, Franchetti: Sakharoff: Beltrami, Tajo.)

Dallapiccola's *Prigioniero* was probably the most important post-war Italian operatic event, and took place at Florence in 1950. (Scherchen, Horowicz, Rossi: Laszlo, Colombo, Binci.) Dallapiccola disarmed criticism by describing it merely as ' un prologo e un atto.' The reaction, from both critics and public, was cordial. There was a universal tendency to see the composer as the prisoner of his ' stylistic fanaticisms '—as his enemies put it— or more broadly of his own artistic ideals. D'Amico, for instance, found a sort of formal paralysis which had not been the case with *Volo di Notte*. Many well-wishers were disconcerted by the static, introspective stage-form, and Mila, although considering it a valid opera, found the physical presence of the actors almost an encumbrance because all the dramatic substance has passed into the music: perhaps the most pertinent observations of all. *Job* (Amfiparnaso 1950) was also frequently found to be static and unsatisfying in stage realization, but to have achieved music more expressive and immediate than *Il Prigioniero*. (Previtali, Fersen, Casorati: Laszlo, Pirazzini, Colombo.)

Petrassi's encounter with the operatic world fared badly when it concerned a comic opera, *Il Cordovano* (Scala 1949), and reasonably well when the Amfiparnaso commissioned a tragic opera, the one-act *Morte dell'Aria* (Rome 1950). The real trouble with the first, based on a brilliantly-translated intermezzo of Cervantes, seems to have been a fatal discrepancy between the libretto and the nature of his comic music, too ' serious ' for the subject. The fact that the real dramatic quality lay in the orchestral writing was, in itself, no guarantee of failure. The performance was repeatedly praised. (Sanzogno, Strehler, Coltellacci: Tegani, Gardino, Gatta, Corena.) *Morte dell'Aria*, paired with Savinio's clever *Orfeo Vedova* and Tomassini's *Tenore Sconfitto*, found more than one critic exclaiming at Petrassi's power of lyric exaltation faced with a doubtfully effective libretto (Tito Scialoja) which dramatizes the dilemma of the contemporary artist. The choral and madrigalistic parts were by general accord the most successful. (Previtali, Scialoja: Annaloro, Modesti, Borriello.)

Pizzetti's position as the older statesman has been substantially unaltered by a prolific operatic production beginning with *L'Oro* (Scala 1946), *Vanna Lupa* (Florence 1949), *Ifigenia* (Maggio 1951) and *Cagliostro* (Scala 1952). He assumed a more down-to-earth tone for the latter—a radio opera in origin—forsaking what is generally described as his personal, noble and austere style. Malipiero's ill-fated *Favola del Figlio Cambiato* had a *succes d'estime* at the Scala in 1950. Ghedini's *Baccanti* was given a fine performance at the Scala in 1948, and showed a certain artificiality of language which earned him the accusation of attitudinising. This had disappeared in *Billy Budd* (Venice 1949). Though often nostalgically poetic, it failed to do dramatic justice to the subject, and left those in the know guessing about Britten. (Previtali, Pavolini, Guttuso.)

With his *Uragano*, by a rare chance staged almost simultaneously at the Scala and Rome (1952), Rocca scored a powerful theatrical success with a good opera which did not, however, reach the level of the *Dibuk*. (Ghione, Erhardt, Benois: Petrella, Elmo, Campora.)

So the story is finished, at least for a week or two. For whether or not opera is a dying form, in Italy, at least, the patient is lively; and the public, as is beginning to appear, has a strong mind of its own about the manner of its survival.

III. Opera in America

The Opera Scene in America

by JAMES HINTON Jnr.

I : The Financial Situation

IT has been said, and in round, authoritative tones too, that the Metropolitan Opera is not really, in any complete sense, a national institution. Evidence can certainly be adduced to show that Metropolitan performances are primarily events that take place in New York, for the benefit of and supported by a smallish, select group of subscribers; to show that (tour performances and radio broadcasts aside) the company does not really have much to do with the people of the country as a whole.

There is, to be sure, merit in this view—but the people of the country as a whole do not seem to agree with it. To them the Metropolitan is a national possession. It is *the* opera company in the United States. Furthermore (since it is a national possession), it is the greatest opera company in the world.

A statement like this makes the American public (in the sense of the United States public) out as being terribly arrogant. I don't think that it really is. There is a difference between arrogant chauvinism and prideful faith in the excellence of one's own possessions. Here, whatever may be its reputation elsewhere, the Metropolitan is a sort of operatic touchstone. Opera at its best equals the Metropolitan ; conversely, the Metropolitan equals opera at its best.

Not that the Metropolitan cannot be criticized. It can be—and often is, severely. But it is criticized for not having maintained some imagined perfection, not because most people are ready to believe seriously that any other company could really be better. Especially now, since recordings of fine European performances can be come by quite easily, members of the cognoscenti, and semi-cognoscenti—and would-be cognoscenti—are quite joyous in rushing to attack the management of the Metropolitan because it has not nailed Maria Callas or Renata Tebaldi, or whomever, to the roster; or because *La Traviata* was taken on tour rather than *Elektra*; or because, say, *Oberon* was not produced instead of *The Rake's Progress*. Some such attacks represent honest disagreements; some are merely underinformed; but all stem from a fundamentally possessive wish to take pride in the Metropolitan.

The point is this: for better or worse, the United States tends to regard itself as a one-opera-house nation. All operatically inclined ears (those not irreparably twisted in the direction of a new high-fidelity loudspeaker) tend to wiggle in the direction of New York. And there is good reason why they should, for the Metropolitan (again for better or worse) is the only company in this country, or on this continent, to give a full-scale season of repertory opera.

There is the New York City Opera Company (Europeans should not jump too quickly at the implications of the title), which gives seasons early in the fall and late in the spring—and whose box-office receipts dwindle dangerously when its schedule overlaps that of the Metropolitan. There are companies (some of them no more than names hopefully chosen to look impressive on programmes) in other cities, which sponsor seasons either shorter or more sporadic. There are semi-professional, semi-amateur, college and conservatory, and 'workshop' productions, which range from the very good to the abysmally incompetent. But, so far as live (as opposed to electronically-transmitted) opera performances are concerned, the Metropolitan, as long as it is able to maintain its schedule in the face of financial reverses, is likely to remain, in fact, and in public regard, *the* opera company in the United States.

The question of operatic finances is much too knotty to treat here in anything like adequate detail; however, it is so important that it would be wrong not to indicate its existence. In view of the vast quantities of money that the United States has expended abroad in recent years (and whatever unsympathetic view one may take of the nation's motives, apportionings, and achievements in this connection), it may seem strange to indicate that there actually are financial difficulties in the field of opera. But there are, and they are so stringent that many people in a position to know all of the facts have substantial doubts that an institution like the Metropolitan will be able to survive many more seasons. This is no cry of 'Wolf!'. 'Wolf!' has been cried, and the wolves have answered. When the light is right, they can be seen, sitting expectantly on their haunches at 39th Street and Seventh Avenue, outside the executive office entrance to the Metropolitan. The European reader may well wonder why they are allowed to stay there. The answer is simple: no one seems to be able to drive them away. Yet, why should a wealthy nation like the United States have any difficulty at all in financing at least one opera company of really major status? The answer is complex, and to understand it fully the trans-Atlantic reader must be willing to admit into the explanation some concepts to which he is not accustomed, along with some that he may have forgotten.

In the first place, opera, produced on a grand scale, never has really been a paying proposition anywhere. There have been exceptions, so ephemeral as to be almost surely mere accidents, but, in general, the most salient question about any large opera company always has been : who pays the deficit?

As a case in point, the Metropolitan never has made money. It has always had to be supported. By whom? By rich men, mostly. It was founded by rich men, and it has been paid for by rich men. Whether or not these rich men really knew how to evaluate what they were paying for is quite beside the point. The bills were paid. After all, if the question were whether to pay a million dollars for a zoo or a million dollars for an opera company, it could at least be argued that the opera company would be a greater social asset.

In the late 1920's and early 1930's, Giulio Gatti-Casazza directed some Metropolitan years that were (at least technically) not losing ones. Otherwise, there has always been a deficit. Some of the red ink has in the last few years been cancelled out by contributions made through the Metropolitan Opera Guild by listeners to the weekly broadcasts of Saturday matinées; the rest has still had to be met by the wealthy few.

Now, with taxes astronomically high, private fortunes are not as fat as they once were, and (whether one privately considers the reasons nefarious or altruistic) much money has gone out of the country, a great deal of it, very likely, to stay. Yet production costs continue to rise. Materials are more expensive by far than they were twenty years ago. Each time one of the many union contracts comes up for renewal negotiations, the Metropolitan has to meet demands that are higher than before. Perhaps the most honest statement would be this: None of the contracting unions wants the Metropolitan to go under. If it did, too many jobs would be lost. But all of the contracting unions are willing to drive as hard a bargain with the Metropolitan as they can.

When Rudolf Bing became general manager of the Metropolitan—and he has just finished his fourth season in office—he stipulated that it would be his job to produce opera as well as possible (within certain financial limitations), while it would be up to the board of directors to find the money (if they could). Still, he has not been able to escape the problem entirely—if at all—and it was impossible not to sense the wistful regret he felt as he refused, last fall, the wealthy Berlin intendancy.

And why? In Berlin he would have at his disposal public money; in New York he has only such money as the board of directors can donate themselves or beg and cajole from other private citizens. For the Metropolitan receives no subsidy from national, State, or city government; it is a public institution, but without public funds. Private citizens and journalists (and I do not except myself) tend to regard the general manager of the Metropolitan as the administrator of a public utility, which, in fact, he most certainly is not.

This odd, dichotomous situation can be explained only with reference to what writers on this side of the Atlantic (again, I do not except myself) have an unpleasant way of calling 'the American tradition,' or, if pressed, 'the democratic tradition.' Whatever that may be, support of artistic institutions out of tax funds is not part of it. The United States has many symphony orchestras; it has one great opera company and several of lesser magnitude; it has other musical manifestations. But, traditionally, these have been privately founded and privately maintained—not by individuals, for profit, but by groups of substantial citizens either convinced that they wanted to hear music, convinced of the therapeutic value of art, or convinced that since City X had an orchestra City Y could not hold up its corporate civic head until it, too, had one.

In any case, there is no precedent in the United States for government subsidy of a performing artistic organization like the Metropolitan. To Europeans, used to the idea of Imperial opera-houses, Royal opera-houses, State opera-houses, and

Municipal opera houses, the American lack of government subsidy may seem simply barbaric and silly. And to explain this phenomenon (or non-phenomenon) in terms of the American love of ' free enterprise ' both fails to really explain and risks serious misunderstanding. In fact, it is easy to imagine that an Englishman, unconvinced that what Americans call free enterprise is either good or quite free, however enterprising it may obviously be, might find such an explanation merely fatuous and offensive. Yet the kernel of truth is there. Many—it might almost be possible to say ' most '—Americans (in the sense, as above, of ' citizens of the United States ') shrink from the idea of a government subsidy of the arts. Certainly many members of the Metropolitan's board of directors do. It has never been; therefore it should not be.

The reason for this, it is possible to guess, is partly an ingrained conservatism, a feeling that there is *per se* something wrong with a government that takes too solicitous an interest in the private pleasures of the individual (so long as he breaks no laws). Partly it is that the idea is an unaccustomed one. And partly— especially at this time, when irresponsible and violent Congressional investigations are the extremely embarrassing news of the day—it is an actual fear that if an institution like the Metropolitan received government money it might be subjected to interference and artistic disruption by politicians in search of headline space. But for whatever reasons, many are dead set against government subsidy in any form.

So, production costs mount season by season; no significant increase in ticket prices can be made (they are higher than any other theatre tickets, as it is); and each year it becomes more difficult to find wealthy purses out of which the deficit can be met. How long can it go on ? How often can the Metropolitan go to the same doorways, asking for a handout ? Estimates vary, but if opera is seriously regarded, this situation must be seriously regarded.

The financial plight of the Metropolitan, and of opera producers generally, is no laughing matter. However, it was brought to public notice this year by an affair that was not entirely lacking in comic relief. A year ago last spring, a well-to-do Philadelphia man died. His name was McNair Ilgenfritz. He loved opera. For years he had been a boxholder at the Metropolitan. He also liked to compose a bit. Ten years before, he had submitted two opera scores to Edward Johnson—a one-acter called *Le Passant* and a three-acter based on *Phédre*. The Metropolitan took no action; Mr. Ilgenfritz brought no pressure; the scores rested on a shelf. But in his will, Mr. Ilgenfritz bequeathed a part of his estate—the rounded figure given out was $150,000—to the Metropolitan, *provided* the company produced one of his operas. Rudolf Bing had the scores taken down and dusted. They turned out to be piano scores only, but competenly factured, post-Debussy in style.

Problem: To produce or not to produce. Everyone argued the pros and cons. The Metropolitan certainly could use $150,000, and if *Le Passant* were to be produced (nobody seemed to even mention producing *Phédre*) only a small part of the bequest would be used up—orchestration, a setting, rehearsals, and all. Reactions ranged from white-hot indignation at the very idea of anyone (even a deceased putative composer) attempting to suborn the World's Greatest Opera Company to cheerful assent, that so much money would be cheap at the price of a couple of performances of an Ilgenfritz opera. At first, it was understood that the company was willing to meet the terms, then that it was not, then that the problem was being reconsidered, then that the answer was definitely ' No.' The period within which the Metropolitan must decide is two years, then it must implement an affirmative decision within another two. At that point, other first-class houses get in the act. As matters stand, it seems wildly improbable that *Le Passant* will ever be heard at the Metropolitan. In fact, there is no record of anyone having expressed a desire to *hear* it anywhere. But $150,000 are $150,000, and these particular Ilgenfritz dollars are waiting to be spent. A nice problem in artistic morality. Really, the nut of the question is this : What if Mr. Ilgenfritz had left, say, a million ? Or, what *is* the price of virtue ?

II : THE SEASON IN NEW YORK

The 1953-54 Metropolitan season opened with an entirely new—and controversial—production of Gounod's *Faust*. The controversy was over departure from period, for this was no vaguely medieval *Faust* but *Faust* circa 1830, a sort of E. T. A. Hoffmann *Faust*. At their best, Rolf Gérard's costumes and settings were very handsome to look at, and most of the audience seemed to adjust to the change in period without much difficulty. In general, there seemed not to be any real reason why such a production should be called wrong. However, Mr. Gérard (and the stage director, Peter Brook) left themselves needlessly vulnerable to attack. For example, in the garden of Marguérite there is no house. No house, no windows. No windows, no possibility of realizing the very shrewd and explicit theatrical calculation of the people who made the opera. It is unfortunate when a fresh and imaginative production is so vitiated by either carelessness or cynicism. However much one may want to defend the main idea, he cannot but admit failings of this kind, and his case is weakened.

Nicola Rossi-Lemeni made his début as Mephistophélès but did not make as strong an impression as had been expected. In this role (and as Boris and as Don Giovanni) he was always a powerful, vital personality, but he did too much rough, uneven singing to gain a great public success. All respected him, but he simply did not draw a following. In other parts, his story might have been different. Victoria de los Angeles sang beautifully as Marguérite, and Jussi Bjoerling did the same as Faust, but added to the already acute shortage of tenors by being indisposed a large part of the time, leaving the role to Eugene Conley. The finest thing about the production was Pierre Monteux's masterly conducting.

Another revival, and an ill-fated one, was Wagner's *Tannhäuser*. The settings and costumes, also by Mr. Gérard, were not nearly as handsome as pictures of them. In the opera-house, they looked mainly old-fashioned and not very well painted. Herbert Graf's staging was soundly conventional. Disputes over authority and rehearsals led to the explosive resignation of George Szell, who had been brought in to conduct, and the opera dropped out of the repertory, reappearing only near the end of the season to fill in subscription commitments. Really, it was just as well, for the work revived not. Ramon Vinay sang the title role with coarse, unfocused, bumpy tone, and although Margaret Harshaw made her vocal points as Elisabeth she created no illusion at all. Astrid Varnay, not ideally cast as Venus, sang well; George London sang away earnestly as Wolfram, and all the minor knights did their bits, but the old score—done, incidentally, in the Dresden version—resolutely refused to come alive.

With one formal, full-dress revival a failure and one controversial, the season got away to a slow start. *Pelléas et Mélisande* had new low-budget scenery (by Horace Armistead) that was acceptable and understandable, but little more. Again, the saving musical grace was provided by Mr. Monteux. Vocally, the performances were variable, but never entirely satisfactory. Theodor Uppman looked quite striking as Pelléas and sang with intelligence and good style, but with a dry voice. Both Nadine Conner and Victoria de los Angeles sang Mélisande; their performances were quite different, but both had merits, and Miss de los Angeles's tower scene was almost unbearably lovely to hear. But only Martial Singher as Golaud really seemed at home in the peculiar text-music milieu of Debussy, and even he was undeniably an ex-Pelléas grown older. Jerome Hines and Lorenzo Alvary both sang Arkel, not very interestingly. *Rigoletto* (in the fine settings commissioned by Mr. Bing from Eugene Berman) had a number of performances, but early in the season, with Robert Merrill in the title role, they were dull enough. Hilde Gueden and Roberta Peters both continued to improve as Gilda, and the Duke is perhaps Jan Peerce's best role, but the production as a whole seemed to have lost snap. The Gérard and Tyrone Guthrie's *Carmen* continued much as before, except for early performances conducted by Mr. Monteux, with his wonderfully broad tempi and ability to make the orchestra sing. Otherwise, the Metropolitan *Carmen* is fundamentally an artificial, opportunistic, tricked-up affair with little stylistic consistency and very little stylistic relevance to French opera— certainly not with Fedora Barbieri in the title role, or Risë Stevens, or Nell Rankin.

Then there was a surprise restaging of *Don Giovanni* in a unit setting that had nothing but cheapness to recommend it. Mr. Rossi-Lemeni sang the Don, semi-parlando much of the time, but was strong and masculine, if not notably charming. His ideas of Mozart style most certainly did not coincide with those of his Leporello, Erich Kunz, whose adroit Viennese performance verges on the over-done. They made an oddly assorted pair. Margaret Harshaw sang Donna Anna, and although she did give her music impact she looked dowdy, and in *fiorature* she seemed always about to run her voice off the tracks. Eleanor Steber and Lisa della Casa both sang Elvira competently and with good style, but made curiously negative impressions. Cesare Valletti sang Ottavio as his début role, and had a substantial personal success. Roberta Peters was a perfectly delightful Zerlina. It remained, though, for Cesare Siepi and Fernando Corena (making his début as Leporello) to bring the production alive, and Lucine Amara sang a stunning Elvira in the same performance. Max Rudolf's conducting was variable from performance to performance—sometimes crisp and decisive, sometimes ragged and seemingly preoccupied.

About the first of the year, there suddenly seemed to be an improvement all along the line. What had begun as a dull, run-of-the-mill kind of season all at once began to sparkle. Leonard Warren came back from La Scala, and although he arrived in something less than his best voice he soon rounded into form. His coming was opportune, for although the Metropolitan shortage of tenors during the season was somewhat artificial and had more to do with contractual tantrums than with supply, the shortage of good baritones for the Italian repertory is very real. Two new ones had made their débuts earlier—Ettore Bastianini, whose powerful dramatic voice and good diction more than made up for a certain youthful diffidence as an actor, and Josef Metternich, who made a fine impression before running into a stretch of uneven singing.

The real strength of the roster was in the bass and bass-baritone department, with Nicola Rossi-Lemeni, Cesare Siepi, George London, and Jerome Hines all available for the title role in *Boris Godunov*—an amazing display for any opera company. Each in his own way was impressive, but there is no space for analysis. Otherwise, the performances were spotty, except for Charles Kullman's Shuisky, which was a constantly reliable element. Other impersonations ranged from good (without enthusiasm behind it) to terrible, and the casting of Giulio Gari as Dmitri was inexcusable in a major opera-house. Still, this production—in spite of criticism of settings, of Fritz Stiedry's conducting, of the Rathaus-reconstituted " original " Mussorgsky score, and of John Gutman's English text—is building an audience.

Dolores Wilson returned to this country to make her début in *Lucia di Lammermoor*, and made a generally good impression with her clean, well-schooled singing, and Lily Pons, in the same role, was in excellent fettle. Jan Peerce and Brian Sullivan (a new role for him) sang Edgardo, and Renato Capecchi and Frank Valentino were stylistically excellent as Ashton, although neither voice sounded attractive, and Fausto Cleva's conducting was vital and alert. The production of *La Forza del Destino*, new last season, was revised again by its conductor, Mr. Stiedry. Still no inn scene; still the omnibus second act, but with Preziosilla now cut to almost nothing; still pretty much a mess. But Zinka Milanov continued to sing Leonora with great breadth of line and almost always, in the course of an evening, produced enough beautiful sound to make the performance memorable. Finally, at the end, Herva Nelli got to sing a performance. For the rest: various tenors, various baritones, including Richard Tucker and Mr. Metternich, who made his début as Carlo. Arriving in February, Gino Penno promptly became indisposed and finally made his début as Alvaro instead of on schedule as Radames. He subsequently sang in *Aida*, in *Il Trovatore*, and in *Norma*. Competent, accurate, and possessed of a big solid voice with a fine ring of B's and B flats, he did not seem very interesting otherwise, and there was certainly no mass defection from the ranks of admirers of Mario del Monaco.

Near the end of the season came two more revivals in new productions—*Il Barbiere di Siviglia* and *Norma*. The first was a success, and a delightful one; the second was a soggy travesty of the work it purported to represent. The Berman settings for *Barbiere* had grace and charm, and so did both Roberta Peters and Miss de los Angeles as Rosina, Mr. Valletti as Almaviva, Mr. Siepi and Jerome Hines as Basilio, and Renato Capecchi and Frank Guarrera (but *not* Robert Merrill) as Figaro. The hit of the production, though, was Mr. Corena's characterization as Bartolo. Alberto Erede conducted flexibly and well.

The *Norma* was a shambles, and not even Mr. Cleva's conducting could salvage much Bellini. It was *Norma* down a tone and badly sung at that, for Zinka Milanov, a pre-war Norma of striking gifts but uneven performances, sang cautiously and solved all problems in terms of present limitations, and Fedora Barbieri went back to Italy, leaving Blanche Thebom as the Adalgisa. It was all quite painful. Mr. Penno made a thoroughly uninspired Pollione, and Mr. Siepi seemed to have given up in advance any idea of doing more than go through the motions as Oroveso.

Yet, all told, it was not a bad season, in spite of the fact that there was much to deplore and some little to grow venomous about. The greatest disgrace actually belonged to the Press, or part of it, for wantonly destroying *The Rake's Progress* at the Metropolitan without, apparently, feeling any responsibility at all to allow a new and craftsmanlike work to find its audience. One way and another, enough good singing added up to enough good performances to make the season, in spite of its fallings-short, a respectable success. Actually, there was not much really *bad* singing, and Mr. Bing achieved his best average so far in the engagement of new artists, for none failed outright, and several had authentic triumphs. Nicola Rossi-Lemeni did not make as big a splash as he might have done, but no one could question his right to high status. Perhaps the most successful of the lot were Fernando Corena and Cesare Valletti. Looking to the future, both are fine additions to the company. Also looking to the future, Ettore Bastianini is already an exciting singer, and he is still in his formative years as an artist. Of the ladies, Irmgard Seefried was already known here, and fulfilled expectations as a Mozart singer. Lisa della Casa was puzzling, because in the roles she sang—Elvira and the Countess Almaviva—the total effect she made did not quite seem to add up to her reputation; but she was in no way a non-success, either. Josef Metternich seemed more a lyric baritone than his repertoire would indicate, and he was not at his best in dramatic Verdi roles such as Carlo in *Forza*; but, then, all the

Two scenes from Hans Werner Henze's opera 'Boulevard Solitude' at the Rome Opera, with MAGDA LASZLÒ and AGOSTINO LAZZARI

Photographs by Oscar Savio

THE SEASON IN ITALY

Right:

SENA JURINAC as the *Composer* in 'Ariadne auf Naxos', which she sang at Glyndebourne in 1953 and 1954

Photograph by Guy Gravett

Below left:

NICOLA ROSSI-LEMENI as *King Philip* in 'Don Carlo', which he sang at the Scala, Milan, in 1953 and 1954

Below right:

BORIS CHRISTOFF as *Mephistophélès*, which he sang at the Scala and recorded for His Master's Voice

Photographs by Piccagliani

PERSONALITIES OF THE YEAR

baritones, including even Renato Capecchi, were pressed into service for heavy roles like Ashton.

Of singers already in the company, some made notable progress—most notably, perhaps, Lucine Amara, who suddenly seemed no longer a little girl with a naturally lovely voice.

Younger, less experienced débutants had few chances to really make themselves heard. James McCracken gave good evidence of a strong, ringing dramatic tenor voice, but little of knowing much about being on a stage. Charles Anthony sang a smooth, attractive Peppe (in a *Pagliacci* restored to old-fashioned settings after three years of experiment with modernity), and Maria Leone was appealing as Clotilde in *Norma*. Sandra Warfield sang a Maddalena, but otherwise had a page-and-peasant-girl kind of season, and Heidi Krall had not much chance to show off her very good lyric voice, although she did sing frequently in small roles.

The conducting assignments, aside from the Szell rift and the engagement of Mr. Monteux, were not radically altered. Fausto Cleva and Alberto Erede shared the bulk of the non-*Forza* Italian repertory, with Fritz Stiedry retaining his control of works in which he is presumed to have special expertise. Max Rudolf took time off from administrative duties to conduct Mozart. In the course of the season, Kurt Adler the chorus master, Renato Cellini, Tibor Kozma, who took over the post-Monteux *Carmen* performances, and Pietro Cimara were more active than in the past. No one really took the place of Fritz Reiner; Rudolf Kempe is to come in 1954-55.

The policy of bringing in stage directors from outside the company was continued, with Cyril Ritchard coming for *Il Barbiere* and Peter Brook coming for *Faust*. However debatable some of the Bing productions have been, this policy has given a certain freshness to the repertory. But the final result of having had so many directors passing through has yet to be assessed. One repercussion was visible on the surface in an oddly ambiguous system of programme credits. For instance, *Aida* was still listed as ' production by Margaret Webster,' but Dino Yannopoulos, who returned from outer darkness to stage *Boris Godunov* the season before last, was listed as ' stage director '—a credit that in this country generally implies full producing responsibility. So whose staging of *Aida* did the audience see—Miss Webster's or Mr. Yannopoulos's? Such nuances are hard to evaluate, and one can only assume that both cooks named had ladles in the pot. Three stage directors are named on the staff—Désiré Defrère, Herbert Graf, and Mr. Yannopoulos—but there are a number of productions now in the repertory originally staged by guest directors, and as time goes by it may become extremely difficult to discover just who is, at a given time, responsible for what features of which production. Over a period of years this might easily result in stagings as unco-ordinated, if not as ' traditional,' as those that they replaced.

At any rate, the season began and ended without any of the newer productions really disintegrating, although some tended to lose their original precision as casts changed, and there were several surprises. The *Faust*, *Tannhäuser*, and *Barbiere* productions were announced in advance as new. No fuss was made over the revivals of such works as *Pélleas*, *Don Giovanni*, and *Figaro*, but they, too, turned up in new or extensively retailored dress. It was not necessary to like everything about such productions to take heart in the fact that the management was devoting time, energy, and at least some money to the whole repertory, and not resting its reputation merely on a few widely publicized prestige productions.

What will come next season, of course, remains to be seen. The 1954-55 repertory lists *Carmen*, *Andrea Chenier* (in a new production, presumably with Mario del Monaco and Renata Tebaldi), *Orfeo*, *Faust*, *Cavalleria* and *Pagliacci*, *Manon*, *Don Giovanni*, *Figaro*, *Bohème*, *Butterfly*, *Tosca*, *La Gioconda*, *Barbiere*, *Arabella* (new production; première here), *Salome*, *Aïda*, *Ballo in Maschera*, *Don Carlo*, *Otello*, *Traviata*, *Meistersinger*, *Parsifal*, *Tannhäuser*, and *Tristan*. Of these, *Tosca*, *Traviata*, *Manon*, and *Gioconda* have perhaps the most raggle-taggle old settings, and may be in line for at least partial interim refurbishing.

The New York City Opera, biologically speaking, is a sport. One thing is sure: it is not what it sounds to a European as if it would be, for it is not supported by a municipal subsidy. Yet it is not quite an independent enterprise, either. A detailed history would become much too involved; suffice it to say that the company came into being almost fortuitously, when the city acquired a big, ugly, pseudo-Moorish auditorium called Mecca Temple in a tax-lien action. No one actually wanted it, so a decision was made to use it as a sort of city-owned culture-container.

One cultural element it was destined to contain was opera, and in February, 1944, Laszlo Halasz, who had put on opera in St. Louis, brought in scenery and props and staged performances of *Tosca*, *Carmen*, and *Martha*. That was the beginning of the New York City Opera. The city allowed it to use the renamed auditorium—the City Center—but supplied no public moneys; Mr. Halasz continued in control, under a board of directors, and, one way or another, the company survived to give some mediocre performances, some bad ones, and a number of very good ones, and to produce off-the-beaten-path works like *Werther*, *Eugen Onegin*, *The Love for Three Oranges*, William Grant Still's *Troubled Island* (now called unkindly—when it is called at all—'Forgotten Island'), David Tamkin's *The Dybbuk*, *Turandot*, *I Quattro Rusteghi*, and so on. But. Mr. Halasz had made enemies, and in 1952, a *coup de théâtre* led to his removal by the board and the naming of Josef Rosenstock as artistic director.

The basic problem that any City Center opera administration must face is that of operating in the shadow of the Metropolitan, with which it cannot compete on equal terms yet with which it seems to be unable to avoid competition. The main tactic of disengagement has been a split season—early in the fall and late in the spring. This has worked only to an extent at the box office, and tends to impair continuity of effort on the part of the members of the company, who must go out and hunt engagements at just the time when other opera singers are most actively engaged. Thus young singers are willing to make their careers at the City Center only so long as they either can fill in the middle of the season with recital engagements or cannot find longer and more profitable engagements elsewhere.

In the ten years of its existence, the New York City Opera has hired an amazing number of singers. Some have gone on to the Metropolitan ; some have returned to Europe; some, born in this country, have gone to Europe to make their careers; but more, many more, have sung a performance or two and then disappeared, presumably whence they came. For whatever reason, each new roster is a real gold mine of unfamiliar names, and it is almost impossible for even the most diligent listener to hear all of a season's débuts. A young soprano will be given a single performance as Violetta—and no more. Next week, another will sing the same role—and similarly drop from sight. A young tenor will sing a couple of performances as Peppe (or maybe just one), and disappear. Without going into other possible pros and cons, this kind of thing leads to the development of neither reliable ensemble nor individual talents. And from the audience point of view—assuming that an audience is wanted—only the hardy minority made up of those insatiably curious about singers and operas is likely to buy a seat to hear the latest batch of newcomers try out in *La Bohème*, especially if the last performance heard was patchy and tentatively sung. The moral is simply this: If a company is going to undertake standard repertory, and if it wants audiences to come, it really ought to make sure that it has, and uses, people who are professionally qualified; or if a company is going to turn itself into a charitable institution devoted to open auditions, it ought to stop selling tickets. But if an inexperienced singer *is* deemed talented enough to be given a chance to sing Violetta, the people who chose her ought to back up their decision with more than one lone performance, or admit publicly that they were guessing to begin with.

However that may be, it is much easier to criticize than it is to produce, and the New York City company has managed to stay afloat for ten years, subsisting mainly on standard repertory items, not very well done, usually, with a constant stream of novelties passing in and out of the repertory. The company now has funds from a private foundation, contingent on the production of new works. But if only new works are paid for, and they fail to have public success, the operating base cannot be said to be very solid. Last season—or seasons—saw productions of Einem's *The Trial* (in English) and Aaron Copland's *The Tender Land*. Neither had a success. Other new productions were *Hansel and Gretel* and *Falstaff*, both in English, and an experiment whereby Jerome Kern's *Show Boat* was introduced into the opera season.

III : Opera Outside New York

Aside from the Metropolitan, the biggest-scale formal opera productions in the United States are those presented by the San Francisco Opera. This has been so since the demise of the Chicago Opera. The San Francisco company, founded over thirty years ago by Gaetano Merola, leads a peculiar kind of existence. Its stage and auditorium (the War Memorial Opera House) are better than those of the Metropolitan; it has in some ways been more enterprising than the Metropolitan—partly because it has a shorter season and, in consequence, a lower deficit potential. Its season comes early in the fall (partly because of habit; partly to avoid conflict with the Metropolitan over singers engaged by both) and lasts about a month. It gives performances in other West Coast cities—Los Angeles, Sacramento, San Diego, Pasadena, Fresno—with first-class casts. It can hardly be called a second-class company, yet it cannot, without qualification, really be called a first-class one.

As at the Metropolitan, the bulk of the repertory is bread-and-butter; but the departures are often fascinating, and many interesting European singers appear in San Francisco before coming to the Metropolitan, while others come and go without being heard at all in New York. When Mr. Merola died last year, there was much talk of engaging an outsider as director, but after a good deal of parrying and thrusting, Kurt Herbert Adler (not the Metropolitan Kurt Adler), who had been chorus master and Mr. Merola's assistant, was named artistic director.

Meanwhile, the 31st season had proceeded as planned. The unusual items in the repertory were *Werther* (with Giulietta Simionato and Cesare Valletti making their American débuts and Tullio Serafin conducting), *Mefistofele* (revived especially for Nicola Rossi-Lemeni, with Jan Peerce and Licia Albanese, and with Fausto Cleva conducting), *Elektra* (with Inge Borkh, Margarete Klose, and Ludwig Suthaus making their American débuts, Ellen Faull, Paul Schoeffler, and Georg Solti—also making his American début—conducting), and *Turandot* (with Miss Borkh, Licia Albanese and later Dorothy Warenskjold, Roberto Turrini, and Italo Tajo, with Mr. Cleva conducting). The problem of covering performances of *Turandot* on the West Coast of North America was solved by scheduling Wagner: *Tristan und Isolde* (with Gertrud Grob-Prandl, Miss Klose, Mr. Suthaus, and Mr. Shoeffler) and *Die Walküre* (with Miss Grob-Prandl as Brünnhilde, Miss Borkh as Sieglinde, Miss Klose, Mr. Suthaus, Dezsö Ernster, and local Valkyries; Mr. Solti conducted both operas. Mr. Rossi-Lemeni also sang the title role in *Boris Godunov* (in Russian) for the second season running and the title role in *Don Giovanni* (with Mr. Tajo as Leporello, Miss Faull as Donna Anna, and a débutant Elvira in Beverly Sills), both with Mr. Serafin conducting. The rest of the repertory was standard, with casts drawn from the Metropolitan, local sources, and the national pool of free-lance opera singers.

The 1954 San Francisco season will be the 32nd; it is scheduled to begin in September and last a month. The announced repertory includes *Rigoletto*, *Forza*, Cherubini's *The Portuguese Inn* (new production; première here; in English) in a double bill with *Salome*, *Manon*, *Tosca*, *The Flying Dutchman* (new production), *Turandot*, *The Marriage of Figaro*, *Il Tabarro* in a double bill with Honegger's *Joan of Arc at the Stake* (with Greer Garson—fancy—as Joan), *La Bohème*, *Lucia*, and *Madama Butterfly*.

The roster announced—and it is not difficult to fill in casts and covers when the repertory is given—is as follows. Licia Albanese, Inge Borkh, Rosanna Carteri (American début), Dorothy Kirsten, Carla Martinis (who sang at the New York City Opera as Dragica Martinis—in *Turandot*), Mado Robin (American début), Dorothy Warenskjold, Claramae Turner, Elinor Warren, Rosalind Nadell, and a newcomer called Lola Casselle; Charles Kullman, Jan Peerce, Brian Sullivan, Richard Tucker, Roberto Turrini, and Giacinto Prandelli; Lorenzo Alvary, Salvatore Baccaloni, Frank Guarrera, Ralph Herbert, Hans Hotter, Nicola Moscona, Cesare Siepi, Leonard Warren, Robert Weede, and Alexander Welitsch (American début); Alessio de Paolis, Cesare Curzi, Virginio Assandri, George Cehanovsky, and Colin Harvey. Conductors: Kurt Herbert Adler, Ernesto Barbini, Fausto Cleva, Pierre Monteux (who refused to conduct opera in San Francisco during his years as conductor of the symphony there), Karl Kritz, and Eugen Szenkar (American début).

The stage departments, which lost Armando Agnini, principal producer-designer in the past, during the 1953 season, list Harry Horner as both designer and stage director, and Carlo Piccinato and Paul Hager as stage directors, with William Christensen as ballet master.

After San Francisco comes Cincinnati, which gives a month-long season of opera each summer at the city Zoological Gardens, on a covered stage, with the audience in the open air. The stage is small, but for many years the performances have had a good reputation for musical quality, with Fausto Cleva as artistic director. The repertory is prevailingly standard; the casts generally strong; the orchestra (made up of Cincinnati Symphony players) good.

The 1954 repertory, spread over a month, ending the first of August, listed *Lucia di Lammermoor*, *La Traviata*, *Tosca*, *Andrea Chenier*, *Rigoletto*, *Un Ballo in Maschera*, *Carmen*, *La Bohème*, *The Bartered Bride*, *Faust*, *The Barber of Seville*, *Aida*, and *Madama Butterfly*. The roster: Roberta Peters, Lucia Evangelista, Dorothy Kirsten, Herva Nelli, Brenda Lewis, Jarmila Novotna, Dorothy Warenskjold, Dolores Wilson, Tomiko Kanazawa, Claramae Turner, Helen George, and Mary Kreste; Giorgio Bardi, David Poleri, Eugene Conley, Jan Peerce, Charles Kullman, Rudolf Petrak, and Costanzo Gero; George Chapliski, Cesare Bardelli, Frank Guarrera, John Brownlee, Richard Torigi, Salvatore Baccaloni, William Wilderman, Nicola Moscona, and Lorenzo Alvary. As has been pointed out before, this is about as close as any company here comes to duplicating the level of reputable provincial European opera-houses.

In many other cities there are opera companies, at least so-called, but most of them do not actually exist; they are sponsoring organizations which provide local orchestra players and chorus members (sometimes comprimario-level singers) and import principals for a few performances scattered over a season. How good the productions and performances are depends largely on how good a job the entrepreneur does in keeping himself from being bilked by, say, the owner of the theatrical warehouse with which he is dealing—and upon whom he is likely to rely for advice.

These putative opera companies fill, more or less, a vacuum left by the withering of the old San Carlo Opera Company, which Fortune Gallo used to take on season-long tours across the country, presenting excellent repertory performances—almost entirely of proven repertory staples, but excellent performances nonetheless. But Mr. Gallo grew older as touring and production costs climbed higher, and when the Center Theatre in New York (which used to be the recouping station, in event the tour had been unlucky) was turned to television, he quit. Results: No San Carlo tours; no steady employment and repertory training for twenty-five or thirty good singers. With no opera in Chicago, and only sporadic activity elsewhere, the lot of the free-lance opera singer in the United States is a rat-race business of skipping from pick-up performance to pick-up performance, from short season to short season, scrounging for engagements, and hoping that the next three months will bring in enough to pay the rent. This is not to intimate that all free-lance singers are great but abused artists, yet enough of them are very good to make the waste rather appalling.

There are opera performances in New Orleans, many in Philadelphia, a short season in Pittsburgh, one in San Antonio, performances in Miami, and so on. The Charles L. Wagner management sends out packaged productions of single operas. But the United States—despite the fact that it really is an opera-conscious country—simply does not have a healthy provincial operatic life on the professional level. Opera workshops dot the country, and seem to be increasing. All over the nation people reserve their Saturday afternoons to listen to the Metropolitan broadcasts. Opera recordings are big business. But there is—tot it all up—not enough regular, professional opera given in the country to take care of the singers of other than Metropolitan status, much less to allow any but the most talented (or most fortunate) younger singers to develop into soundly trained singing actors.

The young would-be opera singer has an unpleasant prognosis. If he wants to remain in his native country, he must make the New York City Opera, then the Metropolitan, or else. Take a case in point, familiar to British readers. If Jess Walters had remained in this country, and failed to win a Metropolitan contract—which he well might have, since Robert Weede, who is regraded within the profession as at least the equal of any baritone on the Metropolitan roster, bar none, has had an in-again-out-again career there—where would he be now? Perhaps singing at the City Center and filling in the midseason as best he could; competing with Mr. Weede for the upper-bracket dates available to an unencumbered baritone. Much of interest operatically happens in America, but, in spite of the fact that there is a large, enthusiastic opera public, despite the status of the Metropolitan, the roots are none too healthy.

Television Opera in the U.S.A.

by MILES KASTENDIECK

AFTER five years of experimentation, of production, and of performance, Television Opera has qualified as a major achievement in its field. Beyond a doubt it has proved television to be an excellent medium for opera, and opera to offer a great deal in artistic significance to television. With the advent of colour, opera can possibly become more of a synthesis of the arts than ever before.

These thoughts arise from seeing as well as hearing performances given by the National Broadcasting Company's Television Opera Theatre during the past season. This organisation dominates television opera activity in the United States. With seven productions to its credit it has concluded its fifth season amidst wide critical approval and enthusiastic endorsement by its growing audience. The experience of other years brought notable gains in techniques. Though highly praised for its productions of Britten's *Billy Budd*, Puccini's *Sister Angelica*, Strauss's *Rosenkavalier*, N.B.C. Television Opera Theatre has advanced considerably beyond these high points of previous seasons.

The productions offered by the N.B.C. group included: Bizet's *Carmen*, Verdi's *Macbeth*, Menotti's *Amahl and the Night Visitors*, Mozart's *The Marriage of Figaro*, Giannini's *Taming of the Shrew*, Debussy's *Pelléas and Mélisande* and Strauss's *Salome*. Except for *Carmen* and *Figaro*, none of these operas would qualify as a popular item in the repertory. Giving them thus became a challenge to the audiences as well as to the producers. It is quite possible that these unfamiliar works have already extended the horizons of many opera goers who would be lured to the opera house only for more staple items of the operatic repertory.

Of these offerings three were produced in colour: *Carmen*, *Amahl* and *The Taming of the Shrew*, in that order. In each case the ' compatible colour,' as it is called, created a new sense of dimension and a naturalness of environment quite striking. *Carmen* was the least successful, but nevertheless it provoked exciting speculation as to the future of TV opera in colour. This achieved reality much more quickly than anticipated in the production of *The Taming of the Shrew*, which aroused spontaneous enthusiasm among those few privileged to see it.

With the prospect that many of the Opera Theatre's productions will be telecast in colour next year, the importance of opera in the whole field of television may be more fully appreciated. If it will attract commercial sponsorship, which is necessary to any long-range programme of activity in this country, then its place will be assured. Current costs of operation can perhaps be charged off to research and to pioneering. The cost of a regular season may depend, a great deal however, on how attractive the productions in colour are.

Usually the performances have been timed to last an hour and a half. This limitation frequently caused some kind of condensation, some good and some less satisfactory. It was not necessary of course for *Salome*; it curtailed very little the performances of *Pelléas and Mélisande* and *The Taming of the Shrew*. To solve the dilemma presented by *The Marriage of Figaro*, the producers offered it in two consecutive performances a week apart: Acts I and II for one session; Acts III and IV for the other. For this, precedent had been set by *Rosenkavalier* which had been similarly presented the year before.

Brief comment on three of this year's productions may be in order: Considerable scepticism surrounded the presentation of *Pelléas and Mélisande*. To subject such an elusive work especially to the literal aspect of a TV black-and-white performance was indeed courageous. That the treatment did not jar the sensibilities meant that there were compensations elsewhere for values otherwise lost. These came in a remarkably plastic English translation that not only clarified meaning but actually strengthened the tragedy of the story, and a distinguished interpretation of the score by Jean Morel who conducted. Colour will undoubtedly soften the pictorial element. More experienced singers would have deepened the impression of this particular performance. Nevertheless, the outcome was most successful.

To the Opera Theatre fell the honour of giving a first New York performance of Vittorio Giannini's *The Taming of the Shrew*. While not outstanding, either in originality or quality, the work is well integrated. It sings and plays smoothly. Shakespeare's comedy emerges persuasively through expert craftsmanship and apt characterization in the libretto by the composer and Dorothy Fee. That it appeared most suitable for television may also be attributed to the superior work done by the Opera Theatre group. Again, the conductor synchronized the whole show. Without Peter Herman Adler's musical and artistic perspicacity the performance would not have risen above the frankly romantic style and lush use of strings inherent in the score.

The boldest and, as it turned out, the most brilliant venture of the season was *Salome*. The extraordinary success of the performance emanated again from the English translation, some ingenious staging, and exceptional camera work. Two innovations solved two most difficult problems connected with the performance of this opera. The first concerned the Dance of the Seven Veils which has always made excessive demands on the singer of the title role. In this case an exchange between a singer and a dancer took care of this matter most cleverly. Parallel performances of an actor on-stage and a singer off dramatized the role of Jokanaan impressively. This device was also used for the role of the Page. What practices may result from this experiment can provoke considerable argument.

That television places the accent on opera as theatre is the nature of the medium. For well over a decade in operatic production such emphasis has come more and more into focus. During the past season TV opera has been notably production conscious. The show as well as the music is the thing. It took *Salome*, however, to reveal how extensively the theatre can exert itself through the innovations already noted. Whether miming a part can become dangerous practice has become an immediate question.

Television opera has made necessary an operatic singer who is also a first-class actor or actress. Singing for itself alone will not suffice. It is only a means to complete performance. Stage action is as much a prerequisite as accomplished vocalism. Again *Salome* made this situation clear in the person of Elaine Malbin, whose performance in the title role was as important dramatically as it was vocally. Through her acting ability she not only made the part believable but intensified all the action of the performance. Furthermore a new close-up technique made facial expression a vital part of the opera. It is not surprising, therefore, to find that casts have been recruited from young singers not necessarily too well known but adaptable to the medium.

Since all these operas are presented in English, practical translations have become a necessity. Where the individual translator may not have been completely successful, the N.B.C. Opera Department has undertaken to fashion a version as workable as it is singable. The final version has usually been the product of ironing out the language from rehearsal to rehearsal. The fetish of rhyme has been discarded and the policy of direct communication adopted. This in itself is an important advance in translated opera.

Physical handicaps have occurred in blending the stage and musical performances. At times the orchestra has been out of hearing of the singers so that only the conductor and the engineers could bring the two together. Such a situation creates an artificiality and a basic insecurity foreign to our present art form. The construction of appropriate studios instead of this kind of make shift must of course await further general acceptance for television opera itself.

In the meantime this year's telecasts received five major awards, including a testimonial dinner by the New York Music Critics Circle to honour Samuel Chotzinoff, the producer of the N.B.C. Opera Theatre and the man chiefly responsible for its marked progress. Working closely with him has been Peter Herman Adler as both music and artistic director to whom must be attributed much of the synthesis of the performances. Three other men have made imaginative contributions to the productions: Kirk Browning as director, Charles Polacheck as associate producer, and John Block as a second director. These five are most active in shaping the course of television opera today. If they carry still further the advances made in this one season, T.V. opera will be an even bigger story a year from now.

Monteverdi's "Orfeo"

by DAVID HERMGES

AT last we have positive proof that Vienna's legendary 'Romantic' conservatism is something of a myth! This year's *Festwochen* provided the Viennese with extremes of the musical scale. In the programme of the enterprising Konzerthaus-Gesellschaft could be heard, on practically succeeding evenings, works by Claudio Monteverdi and by Alban Berg. Symbolic in itself of this extremism was the Monteverdi work. His opera, *Orfeo* (first performed in 1607) had, in this instance, been revived under the guiding genius of that great exponent of modern music, Paul Hindemith. The latter himself supplied the performing edition of the work and conducted a stage performance of it in the large hall of the Konzerthaus at the beginning of June.

Since the present writer took part in the production, entirely objective criticism may prove somewhat difficult but some useful facts may fairly be given. The three principal difficulties to be faced if, as Hindemith wanted, an attempt were to be made to present the opera in its original form, may be summed up under the following headings: instruments, voices, scenery. Old instruments, even if they could be found and played, would not necessarily sound as they did in Monteverdi's time when techniques were, putatively, different; the singers, however excellent, could never be sure that they were imitating seventeenth-century practice in inflexion and decoration (not to mention the present-day impossibility of using *castrati*); the scenery—although in this case it was possible to follow a seventeenth-century Viennese precedent—had to adapt itself to an overlarge twentieth-century concert hall, which had only a short time before the performance been given an acoustic 'face-lift,' the success of which was still uncertain. Perfection, itself an unknown quantity, could not, then, be attained, but each of the difficulties was squarely tackled and brought some rewarding results.

The confusion existing in the matter of the instrumentation is illustrative of the whole. All writers on the subject of the early operas are agreed on the fact that Monteverdi's use of the orchestra is the most striking feature of *Orfeo*. It is, however, open to question whether he was the first to compose what we would nowadays call an opera or, for that matter, the first to write for a specified band of instrumentalists. Certain it is, that he was an important innovator in each of these fields. The question was dealt with at length by J. A. Westrup (himself responsible for one of the most authentic of the numerous modern performances) some time ago in an article for the magazine *Music and Letters*. Further comment here would be superfluous, if it were not for several misleading statements made about the Vienna production in a normally highly reliable London journal, where an admiring review appeared, but one particularly misinformed in relation to the instrumentation. In fact, the following instruments were used in Vienna: two harpsichords; one five-stringed double bass; two *pardessus de viole* (an upper member of the viol consort, tuned a fourth higher than the *dessus* or treble viol); one harp; two eighteenth-century violins, two double-strung lutes, each with eleven strings; two chamber organs, one of them specially built for this performance; three violas da gamba; three trombones; one regal (a small portable organ with reed pipes only); four recorders (two descant and two sopranino); and two trumpets; in addition, it had been planned to use two cornetts, but the difficulties of playing these obsolete instruments (they are members of the woodwind family but have a trumpet mouthpiece and are related to the well-known serpent) and their unreliability, made substitution (in this case by cors anglais) essential. The strange and beautiful tone colours, produced by this unusual orchestra, proved one of the main attractions of the evening and completely took the Viennese public and press by storm.

As we have already pointed out, the problem of the voices was not easily, or completely, to be solved. However, the name part (for whom, after all, this opera is a show-piece) was outstandingly well sung by Gino Sinimberghi (Rome). Quite clearly a good actor anyway, he was also completely at home in the original Alessandro Striggio libretto which was used (that is to say, as far as Monteverdi himself used it). He was backed by a cast of varying abilities, amongst whom the *Plutone* of Frederick Guthrie (a splendid bass, *kolossal* in every respect), Uta Graf (*Euridice*), and two members of the Staatsoper—Dagmar Hermann (*Primo Pastore*) and Waldemar Kmentt (Apollo)—call for special mention.

The scene-designing had been entrusted by the producer, Leopold Lindtberg, to the famous Burgtheater *Buhnenbildner*, Sepp Nordegg. The latter constructed a striking set always in full view of the audience. This also provided an apt, if necessarily somewhat cramped, setting for the dances arranged by Rosalia Chladek. To indicate change of scene a bare minimum of movable ' props ' were used—potted trees for the Arcadian fields, a ship's prow and willows for the River Styx, and short columns with black wreaths for the underworld. Alas, there was no cloud for the descent of Apollo, but then we did not have the resources of the Staatsoper at our disposal!

All in all it was a courageous attempt on the part of the Konzerthaus-Gesellschaft to widen our musical experience and one can only hope that it will lead to further (and even more authoritative) performances, either of the same opera, or of the works of some of Monteverdi's near-contemporaries—Cavalieri, Peri, Caccini, and Landi. Only in that way may this year's undoubtedly large financial outlay (certainly not recovered in spite of the *Ausverkauft* notices) be really justified.

Strauss's Operas Reassessed

by WILLIAM MANN

THE Editor's suggestion was that I should consider whether Richard Strauss's operas were likely to be compared by posterity with those of Verdi or those of Meyerbeer. Taken literally, neither comparison is apposite; Strauss's operas follow the aesthetic of neither composer—he was more of a thinker than Meyerbeer, and a more accomplished natural craftsman than Verdi. In any case Verdi and Meyerbeer are not themselves to be compared, for the first would hardly have attained his greatness without the example of the second.

What the Editor meant was this; are Strauss's operas liable to fall out of circulation after some decades, as Meyerbeer's seem to have, or will they grow in glory like Verdi's ? A glorious bonfire or an incandescent, unquenchable brightness ? Even this speculation would be dangerous: how could 18th century Germany guess that in 200 years Bach would be more esteemed than Telemann ? We cannot foresee what our great-grandchildren's tastes will be like; equally, the 19th century could not know that Meyerbeer's vocal parts would be too much for the opera-houses of a century later (for that is the real problem with Meyerbeer today; many people who dismiss his music have hardly heard any of it).

What I can attempt here is to assess the chances of popularity for Strauss's operas in our own time, and to consider why it is that, five years after his death, they are more prized than ever before. Strauss himself attributed his operatic success to a flair for drama and the theatre, but that is not the whole of the matter. It is true that many of the thrilling moments in his operas attack eye and ear—and so the formal and sensual parts of the intellect—simultaneously: the descent of Jokanaan into the cistern, the entry of Klytemnestra, the Presentation of the Rose, Arabella's last entry, the transformation of Daphne, etc., etc., are scenes that would lose the greater part of their vividness and impressiveness if heard for the first time *en oratorio;* and the reason why they continue to impress when we hear them on gramophone records is that at the back of the mind a remembered visual image is assisting the receptive faculties.

The comparison that Strauss himself proposed was with Wagner: "I have a complicated mind; someone like me had to come after him, so as to make his position clear.' Yet he was not a latterday Wagner. For all his knowledge of history and painting, Greek and Roman art, philosophy and so on, he was not a pamphleteering dilettante, nor an aesthetic revolutionary. He was a plain musician and, whereas Wagner had to set down his theories on paper before he could see his musical road (sometimes not the road previously marked on his map), Strauss's changes were musical and internal: the horrors of the *Elektra* score happened naturally, and were not coaxed. Wagner was a self-reliant artist (not to say an

128

egotist); he was able to plan and carry out his new road alone. Strauss was more human, and more co-operative; thus he was able to work with such a questing, fertile writer as Hoffmannsthal, and able to adapt his style to the needs of the subject. And so it was that Strauss responded in some measure to Hoffmannsthal's pleas, and moved away from a post-Wagnerian idiom, though he did not quit it altogether, as pages in *Die Frau ohne Schatten* and *Die Liebe der Danae* testify.

If Strauss was an heir of Wagner, he was also an heir of the great classics: Mozart to some extent, and Gluck even more. The intuitive ease of his invention brings him close to Mozart whom he above all adored but his Olympian stretches and his adaptability descend from Gluck, as does his manner of approaching classic stories in a personal manner. For this quality, Strauss became partly indebted to Hofmannsthal who favoured a classic dignity but never left a subject as he found it. It is noteworthy, too, that Strauss was fortunate in the brand-new inventions of his librettists: *Rosenkavalier, Frau ohne Schatten, Arabella, Friedenstag,* and *Capriccio,* as well as *Intermezzo,* were all ' new ' stories, originally conceived by their authors; of the others, after *Salome* (and Oscar Wilde's drama was original enough, for that matter), *Elektra* was re-illumined by Hofmannsthal's lurid characterization, *Ariadne* endued with a Thorne Smith-like extravagance by its commixture with the *commedia del arte* (but also lifted on to a new and more sublime plane by this very, apparently degrading, translation), *Helen* and *Danae* viewed from new angles and redecorated, *Daphne* shrouded in a pastoral and symbolic mist.

To these librettos Strauss brought his own personality as musician and man of theatre and—simply, man. He was a virtuoso craftsman, a practised and zealous musician, a theatre-lover, and something of a stylist, as has been suggested—since he could embrace the very different worlds of *Friedenstag, Daphne* and *Capriccio* within a few years (or, if you like, of the second *Ariadne, Die Frau ohne Schatten,* and *Intermezzo*), without loss of his own musical personality. But he was also a perceptive human being, and a warm-hearted man; and so it is that human sympathy flows through the music of his operas, and that in every one the effect of the music is to spotlight the predicament and the feelings of a woman or women: the sex-crazed Salome and the sexless Elektra, the wistful Marschallin, the distraught Empress and the desirous Dyer's wife, the hesitant Arabella and the yearning Zdenka, and in the end the Countess Madeleine burning between two fires; they are all ringed with heartfelt lyrical music, so that each man must share the love their composer gave them (Strauss's letters suggest that the later heroines owe much to Pauline Strauss-de Ahna; he once proposed writing ten miniature operas, each on a single aspect of his wife's character). The men in Strauss's operas, and expecially the tenors, are less gratifyingly catered for (Julius Patzak taxed Strauss with this in congratulating him on his 70th birthday); *Friedenstag* and, to a lesser extent, *Arabella* offer a realizable character to their principal baritone, and it is significant that the best-rounded sympathetic male role in all these operas is that of Jupiter in

Die Liebe der Danae, the least favoured of Strauss's later operas, like *Parsifal* only fully appreciated by the composer's most faithful disciples.

It is sometimes said that a composer was 'born out of his time,' and Strauss himself has been named as the last of the German romantics in contrast with Mahler as the first of the German modernists. Yet Strauss would have been no greater, no lesser an artist in whatever age he had lived. His works, at all stages of his career, reflect a part of their time, nor can that be called a reactionary part because *Capriccio* is less harmonically advanced than the works of Strauss's thirties and forties. It is true that many people enjoy Strauss's music who stop their ears at *Wozzeck* and *Billy Budd* and *Leonore* 40/45. Strauss's operas are of their time because of the ideas they convey, and because of their authors' approaches to those ideas. The time may come when Puccini's heroines will be considered nauseatingly sentimental; and the same age will strike a blow at Arabella and her sisters. But Strauss's posterity will prove hasty if they overlook the treatises on materialism, possessiveness, chastity, the death wish, pacifism and, above all, the one on humanity (in *Die Frau ohne Schatten*), which are argued under cover of those heroines and their actions.

There is a wide range of ideas, and a wide range of human feelings here. They are conveyed in music which may vary in aptitude and in inevitability (as the texts themselves do) but which is at one in its fluency, in the rightness of the melodic movement, and in the sonorous felicity of the harmony and the scoring. There are weaknesses of emphasis, of emotional level, of evaluation. But people who admit admiration of *Die Liebe der Danae*, the end of *Death and Transfiguration* and even the *Japanese Festival Music*, confess that it is above all the sound of the music, the Straussian style, that captivates them. Strauss found himself most fully in his 15 operas; which is why we love them most of all his works.

Boulevard Solitude

by ERWIN STEIN

H ANS WERNER HENZE'S opera is neither a failure nor a success, though it has the making of either, and both success and failure have accompanied its various productions. The violent reaction of the audience in Rome last spring, is explicable less by the artistic qualities of the work than by the very definite ideas on opera of the Italian public who were incensed because their expectations had been disappointed. It is quite true that some of opera's normal attributes are missing in *Boulevard Solitude;* its positive artistic qualities, on the other hand, are perhaps beyond the grasp of the naive opera-goer. There are many fine, and genuinely operatic, details, but the opera as a whole is not sufficiently consistent.

The faults are largely with the libretto. Two acts comprise seven fairly short scenes, few of which are well constructed. The language rarely has distinction and is often beside the point. And the story seems not to have sufficiently matured in the author's mind.

It is roughly a modernized version of Abbé Prévost's novel *l'Histoire du Chevalier des Grieux et de Manon Lescaut.* The undergraduate Armand (the des Grieux of the opera) meets Manon at a railway station. They fall in love and, instead of travelling to her Swiss boarding school, Manon goes with Armand to Paris. The subsequent idyll in Armand's attic ends when money is short and her brother Lescaut procures a rich, old lover, M. Lilaque. He, however, turns her out when Lescaut plunders his safe. Manon flies back to Armand, but their happiness is short : Armand turns to drugs, and Manon becomes the mistress of Lilaque's son. Lilaque's father discovers Manon, Armand and Lescaut in his house, misses a picture Lescaut has stolen and calls the police. Lescaut thrusts a revolver in Manon's hand, and she kills Lilaque. The last scene shows Armand brokenhearted before Manon's prison.

Whether the title *Boulevard Solitude* or the story of the heroine was the primary idea, the two conceptions are at variance with each other, and the attempts to integrate them remain superficial. Manon is not a lonely person but social with a vengeance. As for her lover, Manon's fickleness, which is the sole apparent cause of his *Weltschmerz*, hardly justifies the opera's ambitious title. The name Manon invites comparison : whether or not we like the sweetness of Massenet's music, the figure he presents has vitality and style. The Manon of *Boulevard Solitude* has neither. Her character is not defined enough to become alive, nor is the scope of the opera wide enough to promote her to a symbol. The figure of Lulu springs to mind, but there is little of Wedekind's dynamism in the plot.

Musically, there is a certain likeness to Berg's Lulu, and not only because both operas are dodecaphonic. Manon's part is less dramatic than Lulu's, but the lyrical treatment of her vocal line reminds one of Lulu's graceful phrases. The method of deriving the entire music of an opera from a basic set of twelve notes secures the homogeneity of the musical material, but needs much ingenuity if monotony is to be avoided. Henze is very resourceful in obtaining a great diversity of melodic and harmonic shapes from his note row. His scoring is delicate and refined. By making much use of solo instruments he keeps the sound lucid, and its transparency allows the singer easily to dominate. The music abounds in lovely details, but the larger forms are less satisfactory.

Form, however, is opera's central musical problem. Confronted with the long stretches of scenes and acts the composer must group the music in distinct sections in order to make sure that the details become comprehensible and the whole remains surveyable. Length and character of the musical sections depend on the lay-out of the libretto which ought to allow for self-contained pieces. But the libretto of *Boulevard Solitude* is not sufficiently clear-cut for this purpose. Looking at certain clumsy passages one realizes the difficulties the composer had to contend with, and one cannot help wondering why he has not asked the librettist to rewrite and extend such lines that need lyrical expansion, and to abridge, on the other hand, some recitatives that are styled in rhymed verbosity. The libretto is the framework of the musical form and its deficiencies can be fatal to an opera.

The build-up of operatic scenes needs careful planning. Both similar and contrasting elements are to be combined so that they complement each other and, by their dovetailing, form higher unities. The first scene, when Manon and Armand meet at a railway terminus, is formally excellent. Starting with a rhythmically organized clatter of percussion instruments the music becomes gradually articulate and gains shape in a well defined theme of twelve bars. Subsequently there are variations on the theme, or rather on the row from which the theme is derived. The scene is thus built as a set of variations. They are separated from each other by pauses, and the clear-cut form is rounded off by a recapitulation of the theme.

There is another admirable scene—perhaps the most accomplished of the opera—which is satisfactory from the musical as well as from the dramatic point of view. Armand, deserted by Manon, has resumed his studies, and we find him in the university library. Against the background of a male chorus murmuring lines from Catullus, he converses with a friend. When Manon enters, the duet of the friends gives way to a duet of the lovers : they in turn now sing the lines from Catullus which have an odd relevancy to their own love experience. Composer and librettist have here achieved a measure of stylization that is both new and convincing. The music is well shaped and is remarkable by its calm atmosphere.

The other scenes that proceed at a livelier dramatic pace are less successful. Consistency of style is lacking in the music where conflicts arise and contrasts are juxtaposed. The characters of Armand and of Manon's brother Lescaut are antagonistic—but even the greatest contrasts need the ties of stylistic unity if there is to be consistency in a work of art. Great composers have created a new style with each of their operas, marked by certain traits of melody, harmony, rhythm

THE METROPOLITAN, NEW YORK, 1953-1954

Scene from the new production of 'Pelléas et Mélisande'. MARTIAL SINGHER as *Golaud*, NADINE CONNER as *Mélisande*, JEROME HINES as *Arkel*. Setting by Horace Armistead.

Photographs by Sedge Leblang

Act II, scene ii, of 'Così fan tutte' with BLANCHE THEBOM as *Dorabella* and FRANK GUARRERA as *Guglielmo*

THE METROPOLITAN, NEW YORK, 1953-1954

TELEVISION OPERA IN THE U.S.A.

Right:

SUSAN JAGAR (*Kate*) and JOHN RAIN (*Petruchio*) in N.B.C.'s 'The Taming of the Shrew' (Giannini)

Below:

A scene from the N.B.C. 'Marriage of Figaro'

TELEVISION OPERA IN THE U.S.A.

Right:
DAVIS CUNNINGHAM as *Pélleas* and VIRGINIA HASKINS as *Mélisande*

Below left:
ELAINE MALBIN as *Salome*

Below right:
PATRICIA NEWAY as *Lady Macbeth*

All N.B.C. photographs

and colour. The music of *Walküre* is easily distinguishable from that of *Tristan:* and the melodies of *Trovatore* and *Traviata* are no less distinct from each other. As far as style is concerned, the figure of Lohengrin is closer akin to his opponent Telramund than to his father in the opera *Parsifal*. But Armand has no stylistic traits in common with the other male characters, and though this may seem motivated from the psychological angle, it is aesthetically wrong. It causes an abruptness that often impedes the music's flow. Henze has made his task no easier by his avoidance of clear-cut themes. He relies on his note row to yield whatever musical structures he needs. He handles the row with ingenuity, but expects too much formal consistency from what is, in fact, only form's raw material.

There are interludes—or intermezzi, as Henze calls them—between the scenes, in order to gain time for the change of scenery without interrupting the performance and leaving the audience sitting in the dark. But the insertion of orchestral pieces in an opera involves obligations both in musical and dramatic respects. Only the last interlude of *Boulevard Solitude* is striking enough to hold the listener's attention, without flagging after the curtain has dropped. A violent *ostinato* in 3/8 + 4/8 + 5/8 time (it is rather 12/8 time with stresses on the first, fourth and eighth beats) pictures the drama's catastrophe more effectively than the preceding events on the stage had done. The other interludes are lacking in interest. They are neither mere transitions between the scenes nor are they sufficiently worked out to be a part of the opera's architecture. Interludes need not always be as substantial as those of *Peter Grimes*. In *Wozzeck* most of the scenes are linked only by short transitions, which necessitate very quick changes of scenery, but keep the opera going. *Wozzeck* is an example of how formal problems can be solved : its multitude of scenes urged the composer to write a great variety of neatly defined forms. Henze's opera, on the other hand, lacks the necessary thoroughness of formal organization which composition with twelve notes cannot alone provide.

Boulevard Solitude presents the Manon story in a stylized fashion that makes illogicalities appear plausible. The stylization does not work, however, in the last scene when Manon and Armand are duplicated, with several Manons and Armands growing out of their bodies—if it is supposed to symbolize that their case is everybody's experience, the idea just does not come off. In several scenes the action is accompanied by dance movements. This suits the quiet atmosphere of the library scene, but is distracting on other occasions. Surely, the difference between dramatic and dance music is fundamental. By the very balance of its forms dances cannot increase the dramatic tension or gather such momentum as the drama may require. Compared with opera's dynamism dance music is static and tends to relaxation. Dancing is a dubious means of opera production unless it is part of the action. The dancing stationmasters, signalmen and porters in the first scene look like a joke and detract from the opera's exposition. The dancing in the bar scene, while more to the point, weakens the drama's climax. And the dancing pandemonium of the final scene is confused and confusing—it is the worst part of the opera.

The House of Ricordi

by PETER DRAGADZE

IN nearly every home where there is a musician—in nearly every library where there is music—and of course in every opera house in the world the name ' Ricordi ' is to be found. Yet to how many people has it occurred that this is any more than a name of a shop that sells music? Without Ricordi much of the music that is heard in the opera-house might have been lost to posterity.

The Ricordi tradition and publishing house started in Milan in 1808; to be exact, on January 16th. Its founder Giovanni Ricordi, was a poor violinist earning a few lire a day playing incidental music for the marionette shows in the Teatro Gerolamo. Giovanni was also a copyist of manuscripts at La Scala, and one day whilst he was writing out some orchestral parts in this theatre noticed that large quantities of manuscripts of operas that had been performed perhaps once or twice were being used to prop up the scenery, or being put under the leg of a rocky chair or piano to keep it steady. It crossed his mind that it seemed wrong to throw away the results of the labour of so many composers who had perhaps received 50 lire as their reward for months of intense work. One day in Milan (and in those days Milan was a very small city and it was easy to see everybody) he was seen no more. He had run away to Lipsia and had obtained employment with Breitkopf & Hartel, the great printers of German music. Young Ricordi was learning the business.

After a period he returned to Milan armed with a small printing press and enormous courage, and printed his first piece of music—a song for voice and guitar. He also returned to his copying work at the Scala where he took, in part salary, all the old scores and manuscripts that were lying around and which formed the nucleus of his publishing house. He then formed a partnership with a certain Felice Festa who after five months withdrew his share of the capital (100 lire!) because business was going badly. Giovanni was not down-hearted about this, and soon found another, more reasonable, financier. Things began to look up and by 1813 there were already 800 publications. Up to that time Giovanni Ricordi had done all of the editorial work himself, in his house in Via Ciovasso, where he also copied, printed, engraved. The work became too great for him alone and in addition to his son Tito, who was to succeed him, he took in Francesco Lucca and Pietro Clausetti, both editors in their own right.

The prosperity of the House grew, and Rossini, Bellini, Donizetti and Pacini were by the side of Giovanni—in 1838 he published his first grand catalogue printed in Italian, French and German, and which stated ' In addition to being publisher for the Imperial Conservatory of Music and of all the works used in the Imperial Theatres of Milan and Naples, I am publisher of works for piano-forte and voice, quartets, quintets and other searched-for works by Mr. Rossini, Donizetti and many others, including Asioli, Herz, Pollini, Liszt, Kalkbrenner, Hunten, Bertini, Pixis, Czerny, Schoberlachner, Rolla, etc.—I have more than 10,000 pieces of music available.'

Tito succeeded his father, and frequently visited Germany and England to acquire more and more printing machinery and to learn the latest techniques. He in his turn was helped by his own son, Giulio, who was to become the best known of the Ricordi family. Giovanni was, above all, a sincere friend to all of his musicians, and it was this policy that was responsible for the eventual great success of his enterprise. Many operas were born and many libretti modified following discussions between the editor and composer. The libretto of *Bohème* came to life in the office of Giulio Ricordi. Ilica, one of the four librettists of *Bohème*, records how, when they were discussing this matter, Puccini became so agitated that he had to immediately go to have his hands manicured after the meeting because he had bitten all his finger nails down to the quicks. The relationship however between Ricordi's and Verdi was quite different. Verdi was a man who knew his own value and who was sure of himself and who asked no help from anybody, but only requested that his wishes were entirely followed. Just before the first performance of *Forza del Destino*, Verdi wrote to Tito Ricordi

' Dear Tito, I will come to Milan myself to direct the rehearsals of *Forza del Destino*, to change the finale and one or two other small points of the opera. I do not want to have anything to do with the Director of La Scala. I only want to put my opera on the stage and to then go away from Milan after the first night. I give you the rights to this new opera, and only ask that, if it should be asked for, you will give a copy to the Teatro di St. Petersburg.
In compensation I require:

(1) Author's rights as you gave me for *Don Carlo*.

(2) Pay me 15,000 lire in cash.

If you agree with my proposition, very well—if not, without formality tell me so, and the whole matter will be closed.'

With Verdi, there were no alternatives and Tito realized the greatness of the Maestro, and sent him an open contract to dictate his own terms. It was the House of Ricordi that established ' performance rights ' for composers, in spite of enormous opposition from the theatres and impresarios.

And so time passed, and the direction came into the hands of yet another Tito Ricordi who died in 1933. It was he who expanded his firm all over the world and now in every corner of the globe one can find a ' Casa Ricordi ' which offer 125,000 pieces of music, amongst which are 2,000 operas and 500 symphonies.

Complete Opera Recordings

by ANDREW PORTER

THE purpose of this article is to indicate briefly the extent to which the operatic repertory is represented, in Great Britain, on the gramophone. This country still lags behind France, and far behind America, in the production of long-playing records. All the same, complete operas pour from the record presses just about as fast as a listener can keep pace with them. Since most of the big artists are under contract to the big companies, the best-cast and best-conducted performances tend to come from Decca and from the E.M.I. group (H.M.V. and Columbia). Their policy, on the whole, has been to aim at producing best-sellers of the popular repertory. Smaller companies, Vox and Nixa, have wisely concentrated on not-so-standard operas, where we may be prepared to lower standards a little in order to hear unfamiliar music. Occasionally these companies have ventured into direct competition with the big firms, but (except in the case of the Vox *Heure Espagnole*), so far without success. Supraphon, who distribute in Great Britain discs manufactured in Prague, have issued a splendidly vital performance of *The Bartered Bride*, and *Dalibor* is impending. Monarch, a division of the same firm which manufactures, from Russian tapes, in England, has announced the U.S.S.R. *Sadko*. At the time of writing (August, 1954) two large sources of recorded opera still remain untapped in this country: the Cetra and Deutsche Grammophon catalogues. Philips, who are affiliated to American Columbia, have started operations here: so far only a *Salome* has appeared, while a *Bastien und Bastienne* is announced. These are both from their European catalogue ('Epic' in America).

ITALIAN

IN the Italian field Decca led the LP repertory with their series of Puccini recordings with Renata Tebaldi as soprano : *Bohème*, *Butterfly* and *Tosca* (1952). These were followed by *Aida*, with Tebaldi and Mario del Monaco, and since then nothing has been added to the company's Italian catalogue except *Cavalleria Rusticana* and *Pagliacci*, with Mario del Monaco in both and Elena Nicolai and Clara Petrella as the two heroines. All of these except *Cavalleria* are Rome performances, carefully prepared by Alberto Erede ; *Cavalleria*, with an anonymous orchestra under France Ghione, is considerably coarser in execution. Meanwhile Columbia, co-operating with E.A. Teatro alla Scala, has started another notable series of Italian recordings, with Maria Callas as the star. Only one set comes into direct competition with Decca ; *Tosca* (although a Callas *Cavalleria* is also on its way). Fans of the two great prima donnas may argue happily or fiercely about their respective merits. The Columbia version has wonderfully exciting orchestral playing under Victor de Sabata—his first operatic recording. These two *Toscas* tend to steal the limelight from yet a third version, the 1938 H.M.V. set republished on LP ; this, however, has the best tenor of all, Gigli. The Columbia tenor is Giuseppe di Stefano, who also partners Callas in *I Puritani* and *Lucia* (this last not a Scala recording) ; in these operas he is robust, but far from elegant. Serafin conducts both these and the Callas/Filippeschi *Norma*, which is announced as the third production of the Columbia/Scala series.

H.M.V.'s contribution to the Italian repertory, apart from the *Tosca* already mentioned, consists chiefly of six American (Victor) recordings, three made under Toscanini and three with Metropolitan Singers under Renato Cellini. Toscanini's *Traviata* and *Bohème* both have casts led by Licia Albanese and Jan Peerce, neither of them—in England we speak from recorded evidence only—particularly attractive artists. They have comparatively little chance to blossom, however, since Toscanini's rigid tempi holds them relentlessly to the letter of the score (and critics have fairly complained that the spirit is often lacking). The tremendous vitality of the orchestral playing is compensation. Toscanini's *Otello* is more successful, not because it is notably better sung, but because the intensity of Toscanini's reading, his breathtaking realization of the drama in the score, do not abide question. The three sets conducted by Cellini are a middling *Rigoletto* (Erna Berger, Peerce, Leonard Warren) and *Trovatore* (Milanov, Barbiere, Björling, Warren), and a fine back-to-back coupling of *Cavalleria* and *Pagliacci* (with Björling in both, and Milanov and De los Angeles as the respective heroines). This easily outclasses the Decca rival sets ; each opera is sung with the sort of artistry that dissolves scales formed during a hundred hard-boiled routine performances.

In addition to these, H.M.V. have issued an *Elisir d'Amore*, delicately sung by Margherita Carosio and Nicola Monti, but too heavily by Tito Gobbi. The baritone (this time Gino Becchi) is again the weak point in the H.M.V. *Barbiere*, but De los Angeles also makes a too mature-sounding Rosina ; Monti is an agreeable Almaviva. More enjoyable than either of these is Nixa's *Don Pasquale*, a carefully prepared performance under Argeo Quadri, sung by Lina Aimaro, Juan Oncina, Scipio Colombo and Melchiorre Luise. Nixa have also issued Donizetti's *Betly* and three little-known Rossini operas : *Il Cambio della Valigia*, *La Cambiale di Matrimonio* and *La Scala di Seta*, none too well performed by the Rome Comic Opera company. Another Rossini one-acter, *Il Signor Bruschino*, rather better cast, comes from Vox.

Nixa have four other Italian operas in their catalogue, all cast with well-known if not quite front-rank singers : *Mefistofele* (Noli, Poggi, Neri), *Lucia* (Dolores Wilson, Poggi), *Andrea Chenier* (Franca Sacchi, Gino Sarri) and *Gioconda* (Anita Corridori, Campora). In the last resort, however, none of them reaches that much-better-than-average level which—with so many records now on the market—we are entitled to demand.

GERMAN AND AUSTRIAN

Elisabeth Schwarzkopf is the star of a series of opera and operetta recordings which were made after the break between English and American Columbia. These ' Angel ' discs (as the American branch of English Columbia is called), recorded in London with the Philharmonia Orchestra, set a very high standard indeed. Two Lehár operettas, *The Merry Widow* and *The Land of Smiles*, present Schwarzkopf, Erich Kunz in the leading tenor roles, suitably transposed, Emmy Loose as second soprano and the young Swedish singer, Nicolai Gedda, as ' second ' tenor. Schwarzkopf as Gretel is heard with Elisabeth Grümmer's Hänsel in a Karajan performance of Humperdinck's opera; and Karajan is continuing this London series with an *Ariadne auf Naxos* (Schwarzkopf and Gedda, Rita Streich as Zerbinetta, Seefried as the Composer), *Così fan tutte* (with Seefried, Merriman and Lise Otto), and *Don Giovanni*.

Figaro and *Zauberflöte* appeared some years ago, with all-star Viennese casts under Karajan, on Columbia. Decca's contribution to the Mozart field has been an *Entführung*, with Wilma Lipp and Walter Ludwig under Krips. Nixa have the astonishing total of nine Mozart operas in their catalogue: *Bastien und Bastienne*, *La Finta Giardiniera*, *Il Rè Pastore*, *Zaïde*, *Idomeneo*, *Schauspieldirektor*, *Don Giovanni*, *Così*, and *La Clemenza di Tito*. Satisfying though it is to contemplate all this activity, it is less pleasing to reflect that not one of these sets equals, in standard of performance, the pre-war publications of the H.M.V. Mozart Opera Society (LP editions of these famous albums are long overdue in England). The two Columbia sets ought to have been good, since they offered, in the main roles, the most distinguished of post-war singers. But both belong to a period when Seefried (Susanna and Pamina) declined to sing sure, round notes to Mozart's phrases; and Karajan, conducting, drove both operas remorselessly hard. The Decca *Entführung* fails, in the last resort, because the singers are not up to the formidable demands of the music. Mariano Stabile's Don apart, the Nixa *Don Giovanni* and *Così* are not much better than provincial routine. The seven lesser-known operas are worth hearing mainly because of the unfamiliar and beautiful music they reveal.

H.M.V. have two notable recordings conducted by Furtwängler: *Fidelio* with Mödl and Windgassen, and *Tristan* with Flagstad and Suthaus. In the former it is possible to feel that the slowness of the great conductor's tempi rob the music of much dramatic power. The Fürtwangler/Flagstad *Tristan*, on the other hand, is one of those unforgettable performances such as to make one bless Edison's invention afresh. The other good Wagner recordings have come from Bayreuth via Decca: *Parsifal* in the 1951 performance, and *Lohengrin* in that of 1953. We have besides two *Meistersinger* (Columbia from Bayreuth 1951, and Decca recorded in Vienna under Knappertsbusch); the best things in both would make a fine set between them, but neither can be regarded as definitive. There are also two more *Lohengrins* (H.M.V. and Nixa) and a *Tannhäuser* (Nixa)—performances that it was hardly worth putting on record.

Three other outstanding Decca sets must be mentioned: a *Fledermaus* with Güden and Patzak under the late Clemens Krauss, which is one of the most delightful and high-spirited recordings ever made (a *Zigeunerbaron* with the same forces is slightly less enjoyable, and a *Wiener Blut* from Nixa decidedly less so); and two Richard Strauss operas: *Salome* with Christel Goltz in the title-role, superlatively conducted by Krauss; and *Rosenkavalier* conducted by Kleiber, with Reining, Güden, Jurinac and Weber, so good that it rivals the famous Lotte Lehmann/Schumann/Olcewszka set. For the rest we may note rivals to *Salome* and *Rosenkavalier* (from Philips and Nixa respectively the first is a very close rival), and a Decca *Freischütz* spoilt by Maud Cunitz's unsteady singing as Agathe.

Nixa have an interesting recording of Haydn's *Orfeo ed Euridice*, an opera composed for London. Vox present Haydn's short opera *Philemon und Baucis*, and have announced recordings of Handel's *Giulio Cesare* and Schubert's *Die Verschworenen*.

FRENCH

The successful *Carmen* has eluded the three companies (Decca, Columbia and H.M.V.) who have attempted it. *Les Pêcheurs de Perles*, however, is enjoyable in Nixa's set with Mattiwilda Dobbs as Léïla. H.M.V.'s *Faust*, with De los Angeles, Gedda and Christoff, will have appeared before these words reach print; Decca's *Roméo et Juliette*, with Janine Micheau and Raoul Jobin, and Nixa's *Thaïs*, with Geori Boué and Roger Bourdin, are on the usual level of present-day performances at the Opéra (a level to which the gramophone is cruel). *Lakmé* and *Manon*, both Decca, sound as they do at the Opéra-Comique when Mado Robin and Janine Micheau, respectively, are singing.

It will be seen that most French operas, so far, have come from Decca; and so does the best set of all here; *Pelléas et Mélisande*, which is given a transcendentally beautiful performance by Ernest Ansermet, with Suzanne Danco and Pierre Mollet in the title-roles. Ansermet and the same soprano have recorded Ravel's *L'Heure Espagnole*. The limpid orchestral playing is dreamlike in its beauty, and this performance proves more durable than that of Vox, under René Leibowitz, which has a more vivacious Conception in Janine Linde. A third, Columbia version, with Denise Duval as heroine, scores in neither respect.

Leibowitz also conducts, for Nixa this time, two sparkling performances of Offenbach opérettes: *Orphée aux Enfers* and *La belle Hélène*—both streets ahead of two *Contes d'Hoffmann*, a clumsy Opéra-Comique performance on Columbia and a Beecham-conducted one, taken from the sound-track of a film, which is our only LP example of opera translated into English.

Gluck should be mentioned. He is represented by a stylish *Orfeo*, with Margarete Klose in the title-role, and a lively performance of the comic opera *L'Ivrogne corrigé* (both Nixa).

MISCELLANEOUS

Great interest attaches to Kirsten Flagstad's singing of Dido in *Dido and Aeneas*, her last operatic assumption. But the recording (H.M.V.) is hardly successful in evoking the quality of those unforgettable performances in the little Mermaid Theatre in St. John's Wood. What is, on the whole, a more satisfying realization of Purcell's masterpiece is recorded by Nixa, with the young Australian soprano, Eleanor Houston, as Dido. This, and John Blow's *Venus and Adonis* (Oiseau-Lyre), are the only English operas we have on records. American opera is represented solely by Gian-Carlo Menotti's *The Consul*, in a badly-engineered recording. In the field of Spanish opera H.M.V. have issued *La Vida Breve* with Victoria de los Angeles; and Decca have embarked on a series of *Zarazuelas*, featuring Maria de los Angeles Morales and Ina Maria Iriarte. The first of these to appear, Vives's *Doña Francesquista*, is enchanting. In our first paragraph we spoke of Russian and Czech recordings. It remains only to mention *Boris Godunov* (H.M.V.), recorded in Paris, a magnificent performance sung by Boris Christoff (in three roles) and conducted by the late Issay Dobrowen.

CHRISTEL GOLTZ as *Elektra* at the Scala, Spring 1954. Setting by Ludwig Siewert

Photograph by Piccagliani

Below:

A scene from the Prologue to 'Ariadne auf Naxos' at Glyndebourne, 1953, with SENA JURINAC, SESTO BRUSCANTINI, MATTIWILDA DOBBS, MURRAY DICKIE

Photograph by Guy Gravett

RICHARD STRAUSS 1953-1954

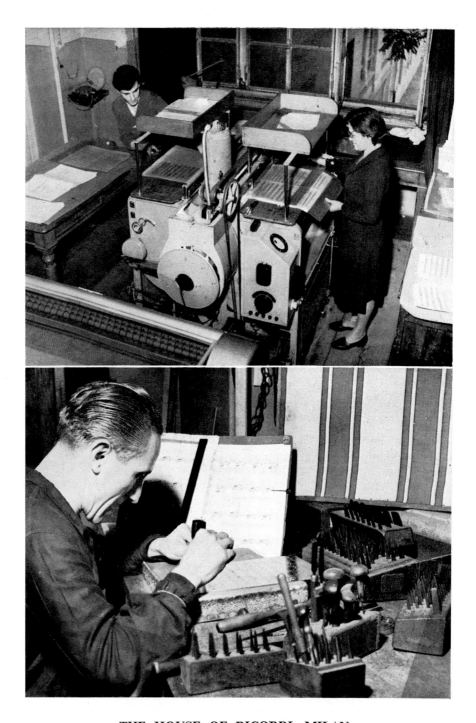

THE HOUSE OF RICORDI, MILAN

Two stages in the printing of the music

Photographs by Publifoto, Milan

APPENDICES

I. Opera Houses of the World
Their Artists and Repertories, 1953-4.

(Listing works performed, artists who appeared during last opera season, 1953-1954. This list does not pretend to be exhaustive but should give an overall picture of present-day operatic activity.)

Great Britain

ROYAL OPERA HOUSE COVENT GARDEN

General Administrator : David Webster

SEASON 1953-1954

REPERTORY

New Productions : Carmen, Le Coq d'Or, Der Freischütz, Der Ring des Nibelungen.

Already in Repertory : Marriage of Figaro, Fidelio, Lohengrin, Rigoletto, Traviata, Trovatore, Masked Ball, Aida, Bohème, Tosca, Madama Butterfly, Turandot, Elektra, Salome, Gloriana, Peter Grimes. (All operas were sung in English except Elektra and The Ring (in German), and Il Trovatore (in Italian)).

ARTISTS

Sari Barabas, Gré Brouwenstijn, April Cantelo, Edith Coates, Joan Cross, Gita de la Fuente, Gita Denise, Mattiwilda Dobbs, Sylvia Fisher, Ruth Guldbaek, Una Hale, Joan Hammond, Margaret Harshaw, Emily Hooke, Eleanor Houston, Janet Howe, Barbara Howitt, Valetta Iacopi, Maria von Ilosvay, Iris Kells, Anny Konetzni, Hilde Konetzni, Leonore Lafayete, Adele Leigh, Colette Lorand, Arda Mandikian, Leonne Mills, Elsie Morison, Rosina Raisbeck, Nell Rankin, Leonie Rysanek, Erna Schlüter, Constance Shacklock, Monica Sinclair, Victoria Sladen, Joan Stuart, Joan Sutherland, Marjorie Thomas, Hella Toros, Blanche Turner, Elfriede Wasserthal, Jean Watson, Ljuba Welitsch, Francis Yeend, Hilde Zadek.

Paul Asciak, Hans Beirer, Hugues Cuenod, Frederick Dalberg, Rhydderch Davies, Edmund Donlevy, Bryan Drake, William Edwards, Desző Ernster, Edgar Evans, Geraint Evans, Ferdinand Frantz, Nicolai Gedda, Forbes Robertson, Howell Glynne, Tito Gobbi, Thorstein Hannesson, Ludwig Hoffmann, Hans Hotter, James Johnston, Parry Jones, Rowland Jones, Ronald Jackson, Karl Kamann, Oreste Kirkop, Otakar Kraus, Paul Kuen, John Lanigan, Michael Langdon, Ronald Lewis, William McAlpine, Peter Markworth, Walter Midgley, Raymond Nillson, Marian Nowakowski, Julius Patzak, Peter Pears, Marko Rothmüller, Dennis Stephenson, Set Svanholm, Inia Te Wiata, David Tree, Günther Treptow, Hermann Uhde, Howard Vandenburg, Ramon Vinay, Jess Walters, Norman Walker, Erich Witte.

CONDUCTORS

Sir John Barbirolli, Edward Downes, James Gibson, Reginald Goodall, Rudolf Kempe, Clemens Krauss, Igor Markewitch, John Pritchard, Fritz Stiedry, Vilem Tausky, Emanuel Young.

PRODUCERS

Anthony Asquith, Basil Coleman, John Cranko, Tyrone Guthrie, Rudolf Hartmann, Robert Helpmann, Günther Rennert, Christopher West.

SADLER'S WELLS, LONDON

Director : Norman Tucker

SEASON 1953-1954

REPERTORY

New Productions : Luisa Miller, Don Pasquale, Hansel and Gretel, The Pearl Fishers.

Revivals : Carmen, Werther, The Snow Maiden, Katya Kabanova.

In the Repertory : Seraglio, Marriage of Figaro, Don Giovanni, La Traviata, La Bohème, Madama Butterfly, Pagliacci,

Cavalleria Rusticana, Eugen Onegin, Fledermaus, Bartered Bride, Samson and Delilah, Riders to the Sea, Hugh the Drover, The Immortal Hour, Romeo and Juliet (Sutermeister).

ARTISTS

Patricia Bartlett, June Bronhill, Edith Coates, Victoria Elliott, Glenice Halliday, Helen Hillier, Patricia Howard, Janet Howe, Eleanor Houston, Elsie Morison, Judith Pierce, Anna Pollak, Olwen Price, Sheila Rex, Elisabeth Robinson, Marjorie Shires, Amy Shuard, Victoria Sladen, Joan Stuart, Marion Studholme, Blanche Turner, Jennifer Vyvyan, Jean Watson.

Harold Blackburn, Owen Brannigan, Stanley Clarkson, Gerald Davies, Denis Dowling, John Faasen, Peter Glossop, John Hargreaves, James Johnston, Rowland Jones, Roderick Jones, John Kentish, Oreste Kirkop, Gwent Lewis, Arnold Matters, Alfred Orda, John Probyn, Frank Sale, Frederick Sharp, Thomas Round, Robert Thomas, David Ward.

CONDUCTORS

Richard Austin, Edric Cundell, Marcus Dodds, Alexander Gibson, Rafael Kubelik, Charles Mackerras, Leo Quayle, James Robertson, Vilem Tausky.

PRODUCERS

Dennis Arundell, Basil Coleman, John Donaldson, Gavin Gordon, Powell Lloyd, John Moody.

CARL ROSA OPERA COMPANY

Artistic Director: Mrs. H. B. Phillips

SEASON 1953-1954

REPERTORY

Barber of Seville, Rigoletto, Traviata, Il Trovatore, La Bohème, Madama Butterfly, Cavalleria Rusticana, Pagliacci, Carmen, Faust, Tales of Hoffmann, Tannhäuser (new production).

ARTISTS

Pauline Allen, Odetta Ansell, Gwen Catley, Julia Bouttell, Gita Denise, Alice Gange, Edna Graham, Una Hale, Sophia Katsarou, Ruth Packer, Betna Pontin, Elizabeth Theilmann, Estelle Valery.

David Allen, George Chitty, Arthur Copley, Charles Craig, Ivan Dixon, Hubert Dunkerley, Richard Golding, Redvers Llewellyn, John Heddle Nash, John Myrddin, Kenneth McKellar, Peter Piccaver, Stanislav Pieczora, Frank Sale, Joseph Satariano, Ernest Thomas, Arthur Wallington, Frederick Wood.

CONDUCTORS

Arthur Hammond, Maurits Sillem.

THE ENGLISH OPERA GROUP

General Manager: Basil Douglas

SEASON 1954

REPERTORY

The Turn of the Screw (Britten) (World première), A Dinner Engagement (Berkeley) (World première), The Beggar's Opera, Love in a Village, The Rape of Lucretia.

ARTISTS

April Cantelo, Joan Cross, Olive Dyer, Rose Hill, Emelie Hooke, Valetta Iacopi, Catherine Lawson, Martha Lipton, Arda Mandikian, Flora Nielsen, Gladys Parr, Margaret Ritchie, Marjorie Thomas, Gladys Whitred.

Trevor Anthony, John Ford, James Johnston, Otakar Kraus, Ronald Lewis, Norman Lumsden, Heddle Nash, Raymond Nilson, Peter Pears, Marko Rothmüller, Frederick Sharp, Alexander Young.

CONDUCTORS

Benjamin Britten, Norman de Mar, Vilem Tausky.

PRODUCERS

Basil Coleman, William Chappell, Michael Langham.

THE GLYNDEBOURNE FESTIVAL OPERA, ENGLAND

Artistic Director : Carl Ebert
General Manager : Moran Caplat

SEASON 1954

REPERTORY

Don Giovanni, Così fan tutte, Alceste, Il Barbiere di Siviglia, Le Comte Ory, Ariadne auf Naxos, Arlechino, The Rake's Progress.

ARTISTS

Lucine Amara, Sari Barabas, Noreen Berry, Fernanda Cadoni, Mattiwilda Dobbs, Marina de Gabarain, Margaret Harshaw, Mary Jarred, Sena Jurinac, Magda Laszlo, Elaine Malbin, Monica Sinclair. Elsie Morison, Alda Noni, Anny Schlemm, Graziella Sciutti, Maureen Springer, Halinka de Tarczynska.

Hervey Alan, James Atkins, Sesto Bruscantini, John Carolan, Antonio Cassinelli, Hugues Cuenod, Murray Dickie, Geraint Evans, Murray Dickie, Kurt Gester, Gwynn Griffiths, Thomas Hemsley, Benno Kusche, Richard Lewis, Fritz Ollendorff, Juan Oncina, James Pease, Marko Rothmüller, Leopold Simoneau, Raimondo Torres, Dermot Troy, Ian Wallace.

CONDUCTORS

Vittorio Gui, John Pritchard, Paul Sacher, Georg Solti.

ASSOCIATE CONDUCTOR

Bryan Balkwill.

PRODUCERS

Carl Ebert, Peter Ebert.

DESIGNERS

Hugh Casson, Osbert Lancaster, Oliver Messel, John Piper, Peter Rice.

CHOREOGRAPHER

Pauline Grant.

United States

THE METROPOLITAN OPERA, NEW YORK

General Manager : Rudolf Bing
Assistant Managers : Reginald Allen, Max Rudolf, John Cutman, Francis Robinson.
Administrator of Stage Departments : Horace Armistead.
Comptroller : Alfred Georger.

SEASON 1953-1954

REPERTORY

Aida, Barbiere di Siviglia*, La Bohème, Cavalleria Rusticana, Don Giovanni, La Forza del Destino, Lucia di Lammermoor, Norma*, Le Nozze di Figaro, Pagliacci, Rigoletto, Simon Boccanegra, La Traviata, Il Trovatore (all in Italian). Carmen, Faust*, Pelléas et Mélisande* (in French). Parsifal, Tannhäuser*, Die Walküre* (in German). Boris Godunov, Così fan tutte, Fledermaus, The Rake's Progress (in English).

*New productions.

SINGERS

Licia Albanese, Lucine Amara, Fedora Barbieri, Nadine Conner, Lisa della Casa, Victoria de los Angeles, Jean Fenn, Hertha Glaz, Hilde Gueden, Margaret Harshaw, Dorothy Kirsten, Heidi Krall, Brenda Lewis, Maria Leone, Martha Lipton, Virginia MacWatters, Jean Madeira, Zinka Milanov, Mildred Miller, Patrice Munsel, Herva Nelli, Elena Nikolaidi, Jarmila Novotna, Roberta Peters, Lily Pons, Nell Rankin, Regina Resnik, Irmgard Seefried, Margaret Roggero, Rise Stevens, Eleanor Steber, Blanche Thebom, Astrid Varnay, Thelma Votipka, Genevieve Warner, Sandra Warefield, Dolores Wilson.

Lorenzo Alvary, Charles Anthony, Salvatore Baccaloni, Ettore Bastianini, Kurt Baum, Jussi Bjoerling, Algerd Grazis, John Brownlee, Arthur Budney, Renato Capecchi, Gabor Carelli, George Cehanovsky, Eugene Conley, Fernando Corena, Lawrence Davidson, Alessio de Paolis, Desző Ernster, Paul Franke, Ferdinand Frantz, Giulio Gari, Frank Guarrera, Mack Harrell, Clifford

Harvout, Osie Hawkins, Thomas Hayward, Jerome Hines, Hans Hotter, Erich Kunz, Charles Kullman, James McCracken, Robert Merrill, Josef Metternich, Nicola Moscona, Jan Peerce, Gerhard Pechner, Gino Penno, Nicola Rossi-Lemeni, Martial Singher, Norman Scott, Cesare Siepi, Brian Sullivan, Set Svanholm, Richard Tucker, Theodor Uppman, Giuseppe Valdengo, Cesare Valletti, Frank Valentino, Lubomir Vichegonov, Ramon Vinay, Leonard Warren.

CONDUCTORS

Fausto Cleva, Alberto Erede, Pierre Monteux, Fritz Stiedry, George Szell, Kurt Adler (Chorus Master).

ASSOCIATE CONDUCTORS

Renato Cellini, Tibor Kozma.

PRODUCERS

George Balachine, Peter Brook, Desiré Defrère, Herbert Graf, Tyrone Guthrie, Garson Kanin, Alfred Lunt, Joseph Mankiewicz, Cyril Ritchard, Margaret Webster, Dino Tannopoulos.

BALLET

Zachary Solov, Choreography. Janet Collins, Prima Ballerina.

ORCHESTRA

John Mundy Manager. Felix Eyle, Leader.

THE SAN FRANCISCO OPERA ASSOCIATION

General Director : Gaetano Merola

(who died August, 1953 and was succeeded by)
Kurt Herbert Adler
Manager : Howard K. Skinner

SEASON AUTUMN 1953

REPERTORY

Don Giovanni, Il Barbiere di Siviglia, Un Ballo in Maschera, Traviata, Mefistofele, La Bohème, Madama Butterfly, Turandot*, Boris Godunov (all in Italian).

Die Walküre, Tristan und Isolde, Elektra (in German).

Carmen, Werther (in French).

*New production.

SINGERS

Licia Albanese, Inge Borkh, Elen Faull, Barbara Gibson, Gertrude Grob-Prandl, Lois Hartzell, Dorothy Kirsten, Margarete Klose, Janice Moudry, Margaret Roggero, Beverly Sills, Giulietta Simionato, Dorothy Warenskjold, June Wilkins.

Lorenzo Alvary, Virginio Assandri, Salvatore Baccaloni, Cesare Bardelli, George Cehanovsky, Alessio de Paolis, Deszö Ernster, Jan Gbur, Frank Guarrera, Colin Harvey, Desiré Ligeti, John Lombardi, Enzo Mascherini, Lawrence Mason, Jan Peerce, David Poleri, Nicola Rossi-Lemeni, Paul Schoeffler, Brian Sullivan, Ludwig Suthaus, Italo Tajo, Roberto Turrini, Cesare Valletti, Robert Weede.

CONDUCTORS

Kurt Herbert Adler, Fausto Cleva, Glauco Curiel, Tullio Serafin, Georg Solti.

PRODUCERS

Armando Agnini, Carlo Piccinato.

CHOREOGRAPHER

William Christensen.

Germany (Western Zone)

STÄDTISCHE OPER, BERLIN

General Intendant: Heinz Tietjen

SEASON 1953-1954

REPERTORY

New Productions: Tales of Hoffman, Der Prozess (Einem), Götterdämmerung, Arabella, Meistersinger, Fra Diavolo, Jenufa, Figaro, Peer Gynt (Egk).

In the repertory: Die Entführung aus dem Serail, Die Zauberflöte, Don Giovanni,

Fidelio, Zar und Zimmermann, Orpheus and Eurydice, Der Fliegende Holländer, Tannhäuser, Der Ring des Nibelungen, Tristan und Isolde, Boccaccio (Suppé), Wiener Blüt, Rigoletto, Trovatore, Forza del Destino, Don Carlo, L'Africaine, Carmen, Faust, Elektra, Salome, Rosenkavalier, Mona Lisa (Schillings), Die Schlaue Susanne (Lehner).

ARTISTS

Matthieu Ahlersmeyer, Hans Beirer, Herbert Brauer, Leopold Clam, Dietrich Fischer Dieskau, Gottlob Frick, Josef Greindl, Ernst Häffliger, Sebastian Hauser, Josef Hermann, Edwin Heyer, Fritz Hoppe, Otto Hüsch, Robert Koffmane, Herold Krauss, Helmut Krebs, Ernst Krukowski, Wilhelm Lang, Hans Heinz Nissen, Hans Pick, Ludwig Suthaus, Horst Wilhelm, Erich Witte, Erich Zimmermann.

Irma Beilke, Johanna Blatter, Inge Borkh, Elisabeth Grümmer, Emmi Hagemann, Elisabeth Hufnagel, Margarete Klose, Hedwig Müller-Bütow, Martha Musial, Lisa Otto, Maria Reith, Rita Streich, Elfride Trötschel, Sieglinde Wagner, Gertrude Walter, Helene Werth, Alice Zimmermann.

Guest Singers: Lisa Buckup, Valerie Bak, Anne Bollinger, Clara Ebers, Trude Eipperle, Aga Joesten, Annamarie Leben, Martha Mödl, Astrid Varnay, Gisela Vivarelli, Elfriede Wasserthal, Hertha Wilfert, Lore Wissman; Karl Dönch, Walter Giessler, Ludwig Hoffmann, Walter Kreppel, Benno Kusche, Walter Ludwig, Helmut Melchert, James Pease, Heinrich Pflanzl, Rudolf Schock, Heinz Sauerbaum.

CONDUCTORS

Karl Böhm, Richard Krauss, Arthur Rother, Hans Lenzer, Leopold Ludwig, Reinhard Peters, Arthur Rother, Heinz Tietjen.

PRODUCERS

Heinz Tietjen, Güthner Rennert, Adolf Rott, Kurt Rosenthal, Richard Strauss, Paul Sommer, Irma Neumann.

STAATSTHEATER, BREMEN
Intendant: Willi Hanke
Generalmusikdirektor: Paul van Kempen
SEASON 1953-1954
REPERTORY

New Productions: Idomeneo, Fidelio, Lustigen Weiber von Windsor, Das Rheingold, Götterdämmerung, Tristan und Isolde, Der Rosenkavalier, Die Schlaue Susanne (Lehner), The Rake's Progress, Tales of Hoffmann, Tosca, Traviata, The Sorceress (Tchaikowsky), Die Schwarze Spinne (Sutermeister).

In the repertory: Euryanthe, Hans Sachs (Lortzing), Der Glöckner von Notre Dame (Schmidt), Johanna auf dem Scheiterhaufen, Arabella, Die Liebe der Danae, Mathis der Maler, Carmina Burana, Die Kluge, The Consul.

ARTISTS

Marilyn Cotlow, Cilly Goedecke, Hanna Gruhnert, Gretel Hartung, Irmgard Huber, Paula Lechner, Irmgrad Meiners, Liselotte Thomamüller, Maria Treiber, Erika Wien.

Caspar Broechler, Ernst Ebeling, Hans Günther Grimm, Fritz Grumann, Otto Haupt, Heinz Herrmann, Willy Horsten, Heinz Imdahl, Herbert Lehmann, Erich Mussel, Hans Paweletz, Gert Rainer, Hugo Sieberg, Fritz Schlegel, Theodor Schlott.

CONDUCTORS

Paul van Kempen, Herbert Charlier, Hanns Eckerle, Theodor Holterdof, Hellmut Wuesst.

STÄDTISCHE BÜHNEN, COLOGNE
Intendant: Herbert Maisch
Generalmusikdirektor: Otto Ackermann
SEASON 1953-1954
REPERTORY

New Productions: L'Incoronazione di Poppea, Nozze di Figaro, Fidelio, Barbiere di Siviglia, Die Lustige Wieber von Windsor, Il Trovatore, La Forza del Destino, Der Fliegende Holländer, Tristan und Isolde,

Boris Godunov, Arabella, Prinzessin Brambilla (Braunfels), Mathis der Maler, Angélique, Orpheus in the Underworld, La Vie Parisienne (Offenbach), Der Vogelhändler.

In the repertory: Die Entführung, Don Giovanni, Così fan tutte, Zauberflöte, Der Freischütz, Zar und Zimmermann, Der Wildschütz, Der Waffenschmied, Martha, Don Pasquale, Rigoletto, Ballo in Maschera, Aida, Otello, Tannhäuser, Lohengrin, Meistersinger, Tales of Hoffmann, Carmen, Faust, Cavalleria Rusticana, Pagliacci, Manon Lescaut, La Bohème, Hänsel und Gretel, Salome, Der Rosenkavalier, Ariadne auf Naxos, Tiefland, Der Bettelstudent, Die Fledermaus, Die Zigeunerbaron, Der Opernball.

ARTISTS

Lilian Benningsen, Irmgard Gerz, Ursula Heyer, Charlotte Hoffmann-Pauels, Trude Eipperle, Helga Jenckel, Käthe Möller-Siepermann, Helene Petrich, Helmi Rau, Anny Schlemm, Else Veith, Walburga Wegner.

Frans Andersson, Georges Athána, Herbert Bartel, Heinrich Bensing, Robert Blasius, August Griebel, Gerhard Gröschel, Heiner Horn, Felix Knäpper, Matti Lehtinen, Peter Nohl, Wilhelm Otto, Karl Schiebener, Alexander Schödler, Albert Weikenmeier.

CONDUCTORS

Otto Ackermann, Wolf van der Nahmer, Hans Keller, Alfons Römer, Eugen Szenkar, Günter Wand.

PRODUCERS

Erich Bormann, Karl Bergeest, Günther Roth.

STÄDTISCHE BÜHNEN, DÜSSELDORF
Intendant: Walter Bruno Iltz
Generalmusikdirektor: Eugen Szenkar

SEASON 1953-1954

REPERTORY

New Productions: Così fan tutte, L'Elisir d'Amore, Il Trovatore, Tosca, Carmen, Der Rosenkavalier, Duke Blue-Beard's Castle, Giroflé-Girofla.

In the repertory: Martha, Traviata, Aida, Otello, Tristan und Isolde, Tales of Hoffmann, Orpheus in the Underworld, Fledermauss.

ARTISTS

Valerie Bak, Inge Borkh, Helene Braun, Martha Deisen, Erna Dietrich, Ilse Hollweg, Gertrud Jahoda, Hanna Ludwig, Hanni Mack, Martha Mödl, Hilla Oppel, Lizabeth Pritchett, Erna Schlüter, Anna Tassopulos.

Walter Beissner, Wilhelm Ernest, Helmut Fehn, Kurt Gester, Alfons Holte, Anton Imkamp, Walter Jenckel, Fritz Ollendorf, Gottfried Riedner, Heinz Sauerbaum, Set Svanholm, Kenneth Stevenson, Eugene Tobin, Willibald Vohla, Karl Maria Waldmeier.

CONDUCTORS

Eugen Szenkar, Arnold Quennet, Peter Maag.

PRODUCERS

Günther Roth, Walter Bruno Iltz, Werner Kelch.

STÄDTISCHE BÜHNEN, ESSEN
Intendant: Dr. Karl Bauer.
Generalmusikdirektor: Gustav König.

SEASON 1953-1954

REPERTORY

New productions: Der Freischütz, Macbeth (Verdi), Elektra, Carmen, La Vedova Scaltra (Wolf-Ferrari), Il Tabarro, Suor Angelica, Gianni Schicchi, Parsifal, Carmen, Tales of Hoffmann, Il Prigionniero (Dallapiccola), Antigone (Honegger).

In the repertory: Iphigénie en Aulide, Die Entführung aus dem Serail, Figaro, Don Giovanni, Fidelio, Rigoletto, Trovatore, Ballo in Maschera, Falstaff, Meistersinger, Tristan und Isolde, Il Barbiere di Siviglia, Palestrina, Bartered Bride, Salome.

ARTISTS

Tilla Briem, Paula Brivkalne, Gertie Charlent, Käthe Grauss, Helene Millauer, Hilde Plaschke, Trude Roessler, Helmy Rübsam, Anni Student, Erna Schlüter, Ruth Teitzel.

Hans-Walter Bertram, Karl-Maria Brucklacher, Robert L. Charlebois, Herbert Fliether, Jullius Jüllich, Wilhelm Lückert, Erwin Roettgen, Walter Reinhold Schaefer, Heinrich Semmetrath, Xaver Waibel, Peter Walter, Hugo Zinkler.

CONDUCTORS

Gustav König, Manfred Willfort, Josef Krepela, Mario Rossi.

HAMBURGISCHE STAATSOPER

Intendant : Dr. Günther Rennert
Generalmusikdirector : Leopold Ludwig

Season 1953-1954

REPERTORY

*New Productions :*Die Entführung aus dem Serail, Deidamia (Handel), Aroldo (1st performance in Germany), Parsifal, Andrea Chenier, Gianni Schicchi, The Marriage (Martinu), Volo di Notte (Dallopiccola).

In the Repertory : Der Freischütz, Fidelio, Der Wildschütz, Zar und Zimmermann, Barbiere di Siviglia, Traviata, Rigoletto, Otello, Forza del Destino, Tiefland, Tosca, Madama Butterfly, Cavalleria Rusticana, Pagliacci, Pique Dame, Il Campiello (Wolf-Ferrari), Walküre, Elektra, Rosenkavalier, Wozzeck.

ARTISTS

Valerie Bak, Oda Balsborg, Lisa Bischof, Anne Bollinger, Clara Ebers, Christine Görner, Hedy Gura, Gusta Hammer, Lore Hoffmann, Maria von Ilosvay, Ilse Koegel, Gisela Litz, Martha Mödl, Anneliese Rothenberger, Erna Schlüter, Elfriede Wasserthal, Helene Werth.

Mathieu Ahlersmeyer, Peter Anders, Heinrich Bensing, Toni Blankenheim, Caspar Broechler, Marcel Cordes, Johannes Drath, Walter Geisler, Fritz Göllnitz, Horst Günter, Theo Herrmann, Julius Katona, Fritz Lehnert, Peter Markworth, Kurt Marschner, Helmut Melchert, Adolf Meyer-Bremen, Josef Metternich, Arnold van Mill, Georg Mund, Karl Otto, James Pease, Jean Wilhelm Pfendt, Hermann Prey, Sigmund Roth, Rudolf Schock.

CONDUCTORS

Leopold Ludwig, Wilhelm Schleuning, Wilhelm Brückner-Rüggeberg, Horst Stein, Günter Hertel, Dr. Ludwig Schmitt de Giorgo, Herbert Sandberg, Hans Georg Ratjen.

GUEST SINGERS

Trude Eipperle, Christel Goltz, Ilse Hollweg, Erika Koth, Annelies Kupper, Ira Malaniuk, Melita Muzzély, Gerda Sommerschuh, Astrid Varnay ; Bernd Aldenhoff, Josef Greindl, Ludwig Suthaus, Erich Witte.

PRODUCERS

Dr. Günther Rennert, Wolf Völker, Werner Wiekenberg.

LANDESTHEATER, HANOVER

Intendant : Kurt Erhardt
Generalmusikdirektor : Johannes Schüler

Season 1953-1954

REPERTORY

New Productions : Il Matrimonio Segreto, Martha, Don Carlo, Der Fliegende Holländer, Boris Godunov, The Bartered Bride, Ariadne auf Naxos, Carmina Burana (Orff), Die Hochzeit (Strawinsky), Let's Make an Opera.

In the Repertory : Iphigénie en Tauride, Zauberflöte, Der Freischütz, Zar und Zimmermann, Tiefland, Hansel und Gretel, L'Elisir d'Amore, Ballo in Maschera, Aida, Barbiere di Siviglia, Madama Butterfly, Pique Dame, Meistersinger, Tristan und Isolde, Tales of Hoffmann.

ARTISTS

Margarethe Berg, Lieselotte Buckup, Sigrid Claus, Anita Gura-Dörnke, Gertrude Hutter, Grete Kraiger, Hilde Pickel, Irmgard Pipa, Ruth-Margaret Pütz, Wilma Schmidt, Dorothea von Stein, Milly Stolle-Garvens, Elfriede Weidlich, Hertha Wilfert.

Heinrich Bensing, Bert Bessmann, Karl Dieckmann, Alfred Frey, Curt Huxdorf, Otto Köhler, Walter Kreppel, Albrecht

Meyerolbersteben, Wilhelm Patsche, Walter Schneemann, Willy Schönweiss, Condi Siegmund, Hubert Weindel, Wenko Wenkoff, Theo Zilliken, Heinz Günther Zimmermann.

CONDUCTORS

Johannes Schüler, Ernst Richter, Gottfried Weisse.

PRODUCERS

Kurt Erhardt, Dr. Walter Jockisch, Karlheinz Streibing.

STAATSTHEATER KARLSRUHE

Intendant : Paul Rose
Generalmusikdirektor : Otto Matzerath

SEASON 1953-1954

REPERTORY

New Productions : Aroldo, The Kiss (Smetana), Tobias Wunderlich (Haas), Madame Bovary (Bondeville) (First performance in Germany), Johanna auf dem Scheiterhaufen, Die Pilger von Mekka (Gluck).

In the Repertory : Così fan tutte, Der fliegende Holländer, Tristan und Isolde, Undine, Otello, Götterdämmerung, Il Trovatore, Traviata, Tosca.

ARTISTS

Paula Baumann, Margrit Bollmann, Ingeborg Janzen, Jane Lawrence, Anneliese Mila, Ingeborg Möckel, Anke Naumann, Gudrun Neirich, Alice Oelke, Irmgard Stähle, Ilse Mengis, Hannelore Wolf-Ramponi.

Marcel Cordes, Edmund Eichinger, Josef Ellmauer, Gottfried Fehr, Willi Försterling, Carl-Heinz Graumann, Erwin Hodapp, Hans Hofmann, Robert Kiefer, Willy Müller, Hans Peter, Eugen Ramponi, Christoph Reuland, Bert Rohrbach, Hubert Türmer, Joseph Walden.

CONDUCTORS

Otto Matzerath, Walter Born, Heinz Hoffmann-Glewe.

PRODUCERS

Fritz Wiek, Gerhard Overhoff.

STAATSTHEATER, KASSEL

Intendant : Dr. Hermann Schaffner
Generalmusikdirektor : Paul Schmitz

SEASON 1953-1954

REPERTORY

New productions : Don Giovanni, Die Lustigen Weiber von Windsor, Don Pasquale, Fra Diavolo, Lohengrin, Ballo in Maschera, Tales of Hoffmann, Il Tabarro, Gianni Schicchi, Die Schweigsame Frau (Strauss), Sly (Wolf-Ferrari), Mathis der Maler.

In the repertory: Der Wildschütz, Barbiere di Siviglia, Tristan und Isolde, Rigoletto, Trovatore, Tosca, Peer Gynt (Egk.)

ARTISTS

Ruth Beheim, Dagmar Behrendt, Anneliese Calenberg, Carin Carlsson, Margarere Cremer-Bibica, Ingeborg Exner, Elffe Götz, Paula Jirka, Else Mühl, Hedwig Müller-Bütow, Ellen Pfitzner, Dorothea Schmidt-Harder, Marianne Soeldner.

Hermann Blasig, Hans Busch, Willi Domgraf-Fassbaender, Horst Ebersbach, Horst Euler, Werner Franz, Walter Habernicht, Rolf Heide, Egmont Koch, Eric Marion, Helmut Melchert, Michael Rhodes, Willy Schmidt, Kurt Schüfler, Willi Wolff.

CONDUCTORS

Paul Schmitz, Willy Krauss, Helmut Fellmer, Rudolf Ducke, Erwin Born.

PRODUCERS

Dr. Hermann Schaffner, Hanns Friederici, Dr. Sigmund Skraup.

NATIONALTHEATER, MANNHEIM

Intendant : Dr. Hans Schüler
Generalmusikdirektor : Prof. Herbert Albert

SEASON 1953-1954

REPERTORY

New Productions : Saul (Handel), Der Postillon von Longjumeau, Jenufa, Cavalleria Rusticana, Pagliacci, Otello, Falstaff, La Finta Giardiniera, Abstrakt Opera Nr. 1 (Blacher), Der Prozess, Angélique, Le Vin Herbé (Martin), Le Pauvre Matelot, Les Malheurs d'Orphée.

In the Repertory : Die Zauberflöte, Fidelio, Zar und Zimmermann, Hansel und Gretel, Lohengrin, Ballo in Maschera, Forza del Destino, Tosca, Bohème, Eugen Onegin, Carmen, Salome, Romeo und Julia (Sutermeister).

ARTISTS

Carin Carlsson, Irma Handler, Carla Henius, Natalie Hinsch-Gröndahl, Nora Landerich, Hedwig Müller-Bütow, Lore Paul, Grete Scheibenhofer, Hertha Schmidt, Eleanor P. Waldmann, Irma Wolff, Irene Ziegler.

Kurt Albrecht, Max Baltruschat, Hans Beck, Georg Fassnacht, Heinrich Hölzin, Hans Otto Kloose, Theo Lienhard, Bruno Manazza, Hans Rössling, Heinz Sauerbaum, Kurt Schneider, Walter Strecktuss, Erich Witte, Willi Wolff.

CONDUCTORS

Prof. Herbert Albert, Karl Fischer, Eugen Hesse, Joachim Popelka, Richard Laugs.

BAYERISCHE STAATSOPER, MUNICH

Staatsintendant : Professor Rudolf Hartmann
Generalmusikdirektor : Rudolf Kempe

SEASON 1953-1954

REPERTORY

New Productions: Carmen, Die Hochzeit des Jobs (Haas), Jenufa, Die Bernauerin (Orff), Die Frau ohne Schatten (Strauss), Falstaff, Der Freischütz, Der Wildschütz (Lortzing), The Rake's Progress.

In the Repertory : Orpheus and Eurydice, Così fan tutte, Don Giovanni, Die Entführung Die Zauberflöte, Don Pedros Heimkehr, Fidelio, Zar und Zimmermann, Der fliegende Hollander, Die Meistersinger, Der Ring des Nibelungen, Tannhäuser, Tristan und Isolde, Aida, Don Caro, Macbeth, La Forza Destino, Un Ballo in Maschera, Otello, Rigoletto, Trovatore, Traviata, Tales of Hoffmann, Pagliacci, Hänsel and Gretel, La Bohème, Madama Butterfly, Tosca, Turandot, Cavalleria Rusticana, Boris Godunov, Tiefland, Arabella, Capriccio, Rosenkavalier, Die Liebe der Danae, Salome, Elektra, Palestrina, Johanna auf dem Scheiterhaufen (Honegger), Antigonae (Orff), Angélique, Peer Gynt (Egk), The Consul. (All operas sung in German).

ARTISTS

Sari Barabas Irmgard Barth, Lilian Bennigsen, Inge Borkh, Helena Braun, Maud Cunitz, Lisa della Casa, Clara Ebers, Antonie Fahberg, Ina Gerhein, Uta Graf, Anny van Kruyswyk, Annelies Kupper, Elisabeth Lindermeier, Erika Köth, Wilma Lipp, Ira Malaniuk, Ruth Michaelis, Käthe Nentwig, Cäcilie Reich, Leonie Rysanek, Marianne Schech, Rosl Schwaiger, Erna Schlüter, Gerda Sommerschuh, Hertha Töpper, Astrid Varnay, Lucia Wehr, Ingeborg Weiss.

Bernd Aldenhoff, Kurt Böhme, Hans Braun, Walter Carnuth, Murray Dickie, Lorenz Fehenberger, Ferdinand Frantz, Gottlob Frick, Robert Hager, Walter Hesse, Hans Hopf, Richard Holm, Karl Hoppe, Hans Hotter, Adolf Keil, Franz Klarwein, Josef Knapp, Paul Kuen, Benno Kusche, Josef Metternich, Hans Hermann Nissen, Karl Ostertag, Albrecht Peter, Max Pröbstl, Karl Schmitt-Walter, Rudolf Schock, August Seider, Hermann Uhde, Howard Vandenburg, Georg Wieter, Ludwig Weber, Rudolf Wünzer.

CONDUCTORS

Rudolf Kempe, Hans Knappertsbusch, Erich Kleiber, Eugen Jochum, Robert Heger, Kurt Eichorn, Victor Reinshagen, Hans Gierster.

CHORUS MASTERS

Herbert Erwenlein, Alfred Leder.

PRODUCERS

Heinz Arnold, Rudolf Hartmann, Josef Gielen, Alfred Rott, Herbert List.

STÄDTISCHE BÜHNEN, NÜRNBERG-FURTH

Intendant : Karl Pschigode
Generalmusikdirektor : Alfons Dressels

SEASON 1953-1954

REPERTORY

New Productions : Le Nozze di Figaro, Oberon, Zar und Zimmermann, Mignon, Die Walküre, Ballo in Maschera, Turandot, Ariadne auf Naxos, Cardillac, Wozzeck, Comedy on the Bridge (Martinu), The Happy End (Winifried Wolf) (Première), Brüderlein Hund (Bresgen).

ARTISTS

Renate Gottschalk, Martha Hermann, Hildegard Jonas, Hannelore Ludwig, Grete Pense, Hella Ruttkowski, Lise Sorell, Gisela Vivarelli, Margot Weindel.

Günther Baldauf, Arthur Bard, Jonny Born, Jean Butzon, Heinrik Drost, Jacob Engels, Georg Goll, Max Kohl, Karl Kronnenberg, Hugo Kratz, Robert Licha, Hermann Sandbank, Alfred Stein, Josef Traxel, Albert Vogler, Hannsjoachim Worringen.

CONDUCTORS

Alfons Dressels, Max Loy, Konrad Peter Mannert.

PRODUCERS

Willi Domgraf-Fassbaender, Paul Hager, Georg Goll, Rudolf Hartmann.

WURTTEMBURGISCHE STAATS-THEATER, STUTTGART

Intendant : Dr. Walter Eric Schaffer
Generalmusikdirektor : Ferdinand Leitner

SEASON 1953-1954

REPERTORY

New Productions : Götterdämmerung, Titus, Euryanthe (new version by Kurt Honolka), Falstaff, La Bohème, Fra Diavolo, Die Frau ohne Schatten, Die Zaubergeige, The Rape of Lucretia, Oedipus Rex (Stawinsky), Les Noces (Strawinsky).

ARTISTS

Paula Bauer, Inge Borkh, Rosemarie Braun, Trude Eipperle, Res Fischer, Ellinor Junker-Giesen, Paula Kapper, Maria Kinasiewicz, Ira Malaniuk, Martha Mödl, Olga Moll, Hetty Plümacher, Marianna Radev, Leonie Rysanek, Friederike Sailer, Hilde Scheppan, Ilse Marie Schnering, Franzi Wachmann, Margrit Wieden, Lore Wissmann.

Hans Blessin, Hubert Buchta, Heinz Cramer, Englebert Czubock, Gustav Grefe, Walter Hagner, Gustav Neidlinger, Alfred Pfeifle, Otto von Rohr, Max Roth, Wilhelm Schirp, Karl Schmidt-Walter, Gerhard Schott, Stefan Schwer, Josef Traxel, Gerhard Unger, Alexander Wellitsch, Wolfgang Windgassen, Marcel Wittrisch.

CONDUCTORS

Ferdinand Leitner, Josef Dünnwald, Wilhelm Seegelken, Robert Heger.

PRODUCERS

Kurt Puhlmann, Heinz Arnold, Georg Hartmann, Wolf Völker.

HESSISCHES STAATSTHEATER, WIESBADEN

Intendant : Dr. Friedrich Schramm
Generalmusikdirektor : Karl Elmendorff

SEASON 1953-1954

REPERTORY

New Productions : The Rape of Lucretia, Das Rheingold, Così fan tutte, Die Walküre, Arabella, Johanna auf dem Schecterhaufen, Angélique, Eugen Onegin, I Quattro Rusteghi.

ARTISTS

Hannelore Bakrass, Helga Bierhoff, Elisabeth Friedmann, Eva Görgen, Trude Kortegast, Ilse Lehnert, Margarete Lüddecke Irmgard Meining, Erna Maria Müller, Dora Palludan, Aurelie Richter, Vera Schlosser, Elfriede Wild.

Ewald Böhmer, Dolf Dolz, David Garen, August Gschwend, Victor Hospach, Werner Jonas, Martin Kremer, Karl Liebel, Rolf

Sander, Friedrich Schlüter, Hans Schwarze, Georg Stern, Lothar Weber, Leonardo Wolkovsky.

CONDUCTORS

Karl Elmendorff, Ludwig Kauffmann, Bernard Stimmler.

PRODUCERS

Friedrich Schramm, Walter Pohl, Kurt Nachmann, Hubertus Moller.

Austria

VIENNA STAATSOPER
Theater an der Wien
SEASON 1953-1954

REPERTORY

New Productions: Julius Caesar (Handel), Fidelio, L'Elisir D'Amore, Un Ballo in Maschera, Don Carlo, Intermezzo (Strauss).

In the Repertory: Die Entführung aus dem Serail, Le Nozze di Figaro, Don Giovanni, Die Zauberflöte, Alceste, Der Fliegende Holländer, Lohengrin, Die Walküre, Tristan und Isolde, Die Meistersinger, Elektra, Salome, Der Rosenkavalier, Ariadne auf Naxos, Arabella, Daphne, Das Christelflein, Palestrina, Iwan Tarassenko, Der Prozess, Johanna auf dem Scheiterhaufen, Traviata, Trovatore, Forza del Destino, Rigoletto, Aida, Otello, Tosca, Bohème, Turandot, Carmen, Tales of Hoffmann, Manon, Boris Godunov, Pique Dame, Eugen Onegin, The Consul.

ARTISTS

Rosetta Anday, Polly Batic, Ruthilde Boesch-Loibner, Dagmar Herrmann Braun, Lisa della Casa, Anny Felbermayer, Dorothea Frass, Christel Goltz, Gertrude Grob-Prandl, Elisabeth Grümmer, Hilde Güden, Judith Hellwig, Ilse Hollweg, Elisabeth Höngen, Sena Jurinac, Mira Kalin, Margarita Kenney, Margarethe Klose, Anny Konetzni, Hilde Konetzni, Wilma Lipp, Emmy Loose, Liselotte Maikl, Carla Martinis, Aenne Michalsky, Georgine Milinkovic, Martha Mödl, Maria Reining, Hildegard Rössel-Majdan, Marta Rohs, Irmgard Seefried, Berta Seidl, Maureen Springer, Teresa Stich-Randall, Ljuba Welitsch, Hilde Zadek.

Herbert Alsen, Theo Baylé, Walter Berry, Hans Braun, Oscar Czerwenka, Anton Dermota, Murray Dickie, Karl Dönch, Otto Edelmann, Karl Friedrich, Gottlob Frick, Hermann Gallos, Josef Gostic, Ludwig Hoffmann, Hans Hopf, Hans Hotter, Alfred Jerger, Karl Kamann, Peter Klein, Endré Koreh, Erich Kunz, Max Lorenz, George London, Viktor Madin, Erich Majkut, Josef Metternich, Hugo Meyer-Welfing, Alfred Muzzarelli, Ljubomir Pantscheff, Julius Patzak, Alfred Poell, Harold Pröglhöf, Helge Roswaenge, Rudolf Schock, Paul Schoeffler, Hans Schweiger, Friedrich Sperlbauer, Karl Terkal, Günther Treptow, Adolf Vogel, Ludwig Weber, William Wernigk, Wolfgang Windgassen.

CONDUCTORS

Karl Böhm, Heinrich Hollreiser, Berislav Klobucar, Wilhelm Loibner, Rudolf Moralt.

GUESTS

Clemens Krauss, Rudolf Kempe, Franco Capuana.

PRODUCERS

Oscar Fritz Schuh, Josef Witt, Erich Wymetal.

Volksoper
SEASON 1953-1954

REPERTORY

New Productions: Zar und Zimmermann, Der Kuhreigen, Der Waffenschmied, Giroflé-Giroflá, Graf von Luxenburg.

In the Repertory: Der Freischütz, Die Lustigen Weiber von Windsor, Tiefland, Tannhäuser, Hansel und Gretel, Verkaufte, Braut, Notre-Dame, Die Kluge, Faust, Barbiere di Siviglia, Madama Butterfly, Fanciulla del West, Cavallaria Rusticana, Pagliacci, The Medium, Fledermaus, Wiener Blut, Tausend und eine Nacht, Nacht in Venedig, Zigeunerbaron, Lustige Witwe, Bettelstudent, Vogelhandler, Opernball, Boccaccio.

ARTISTS

Erika Feichtinger, Emmy Funk, Eva Görner, Sonja Knittel, Else Liebesberg, Gabriele Lupancea, Elfie Mayerhofer, Henny Henze, Ester Réthy, Gerda Schreyer, Maria Schiber, Dorothea Siebert, Lorna Sydney.

Franz Bierbach, Franz Böheim, Per Grunden, Walter Höfermayer, August Jaresch, Erich Kaufmann, Waldemar Kmentt, Fritz Krenn, Fred Liewehr, Erwin Nowaro, Georg Oeggl, Alois Pernerstorfer, Kurt Preger, Marjan Rus, Richard Sallaba, Josef Schmidinger, Emil Siegert, Laszlo Szemere, Eberhard Wächter, Hans Wrana.

GUEST ARTISTS

Willi Nerling, Josef Knapp, Maria Jeritza, Geraldine Katt, Lotte Lang and many singers from the Theater and der Wien Company for the opera performances.

CONDUCTORS

Anton Paulik, Felix Prohaska, Wilhelm Schönherr.

PRODUCERS

Adlof Rott, Heinz Haberland.

THE SCALA, MILAN

(Ente Autonomo)

Sovrintendente : Dr. Antonio Ghiringhelli
General Secretary : Signor Luigi Oldani

SEASON 1953-1954

REPERTORY

Le Nozze di Figaro, Alceste*, La Cenerentola*, Medea*, Rigoletto*, Don Carlo, Il Trovatore, Otello, La Wally*, Tosca, Arlecchino*, I Quattro Rusteghi*, Cyrano de Bergerac*, Amelia al Ballo*, La Figlia del Diavolo (Mortari) *(première), La Gita in Campagna* (Peragallo) (première).

Eugen Onegin*, Götterdämmerung (in German), Elektra*, Faust, Leonore 40/45*, Giovanna d'Arco al Rogo (Honegger)*, Bluebeard's Castle*.

(All operas sung in Italian unless otherwise stated).

*New production.

ARTISTS

Lina Aimaro, Maria Amadini, Fedora Barbieri, Clara Betner, Lina Bonello, Fernanda Cadoni, Anna Maria Canali, Margherita Carosio, Rosanna Carteri, Disma de Cecco, Dorothy Dow, Franca Duval, Cloe Elmo, Bruni Falcon, Jolanda Gardino, Dora Gatta, Christina Gayraud, Christel Goltz, Gertrude Grob-Prandl, Adriana Guerrini, Sena Jurinac, Magda Laszlo, Hilde Konetzni, Ilvia Ligabue Martha Luccioni, Wanda Madonna, Ira Malaniuk, Mafalda Masini, Maria Meneghini-Callas, Maria Minetto, Elena Nicolai, Rosetta Noli, Alda Noni, Clara Petrella, Elvina Ramella, Luisa Ribacchi, Elda Ribetti, Bruna Ronchini Senni, Anna Maria Rovere, Elisabeth Schwarzkopf, Renata Scotto, Irmgard Seefried, Giulietta Simionato, Antonietta Stella, Rise Stevens, Ebe Stignani, Renata Tebaldi, Emma Tegani Ebe Ticozzi, Angela Vercelli, Silvana Zanolli.

Wladimiro Badiali, Carlo Badioli, Aristide Baracchi, Attilio Barbesi, Ettore Bastianini, Gino Bechi, Aldo Bertocci, Amadeo Berdini, Augusto Beuf, Mario Borriello, Sesto Bruscantini, Franco Calabrese Enrico Campi, Giuseppe Campora, Renato Capecchi, Mario Carlin, Dario Caselli, Boris Christoff, Eraldo Coda, Fernando Corena, Luciano della Pergola, Mario del Monaco, Giuseppe di Stefano, Carlo Forti, Enzo Feliciati, Nicola Filacuridi, Renato Gavarini, Josef Greindl, Gian Giacomo Guelfi, Melchiore Luise, Silvio Maionica, Enzo Mascherini, Angelo Mercuriali, Giuseppe Modesti, Paolo Montarsolo, Nicola Monti, Gustav Neidlinger, Giuseppe Nessi, Mario Ortica, Rolando Panerai, Paolo Pedani, Gino Penno, Mario Petri, Antonio Pirino, Gianni Poggi, Giacinto Prandelli, Aldo Protti, Nicola Rossi-Lemeni, Giulio Scarinci, Paolo Silveri, Marco Stefanoni, Ludwig Suthaus, Carlo Tagliabue, Ferrucio Tagliavini, Italo Tajo, Giorgio Tozzi, Raimondo Torres, Cesare Valletti, Ramon Vinay, Nicolai Zaccaria, Giuseppe Zampieri, Antonio Zerbini, Leonard Warren.

CONDUCTORS

Leonard Bernstein, Carlo Maria Giulini, Herbert von Karajan, Dimitri Mitropoulos, Artur Rodzinski, Nino Sanzogno, Heinz Tietjen, Antonio Votto.

CHORUS MASTER

Vittorio Veneziani.

STAGE DIRECTOR

Nicola Benois.

PRODUCERS

Pierre Bertin, Otto Erhardt, Mario Frigerio, Herbert Graf, Herbert von Karajan, Tatiana Pavlova, Corrado Pavolini, Günther Rennert, Roberto Rosselini, Heinz Tietjen, Luchino Visconti, Federico Wolf-Ferrari, Margherita Wallmann, Franco Zeffirelli.

CHOREOGRAPHERS

George Balanchine, Serge Lifar, Leonide Massine, Jerome Robins, Margherita Wallmann.

BALLET MASTER

Ugo dell 'Ara.

ACTORS (for Giovanna d'Arco all Rogo).

Ingrid Bergmann, Memo Benassi.

TEATRO DELL'OPERA, ROME

(Ente Autonomo)

SEASON 1953-1954

REPERTORY

Iphigénie en Aulide (Gluck), Don Giovanni, La Cenerentola, La Favorita, Il Trovatore, Rigoletto, Don Carlo, Otello, Falstaff, La Bohème, Andrea Chenier, I Cavalieri di Ekebu (Zandonai), I Giojelli della Madonna (Wolf-Ferrari), Margherita da Cortona (Refice), Il Sistema della Dolcezza (Tosatti), Romulus (Allegra).

The Snow-Maiden, Chrisophe Colombe (Milhaud), Boulevard Solitude (Henze), Lohengrin.

(All sung in Italian).

Der Fliegende Holländer (in German).

ARTISTS

Guiseppina Arnaldi, Elisabetta Barbato, Fedora Barbieri, Ines Bardini, Maria Benedetti, Gianella Borelli, Fernanda Cadoni, Anna Maria Canali, Laura Carol, Rina Corsi, Loretta di Delio, Cloe Elmo, Fiorella Carmen Forti, Jolanda Gardino, Maria Huder, Magda Laszlo, Rina Malatrasi, Caterina Mancini, Carla Martinis, Maria Meneghini-Callas, Marinella Meli, Ruth Michaelis, Elena Nicolai, Alda Noni, Gianna Pederzini, Maria Pedrini, Clara Petrella, Amelia Pini, Miriam Pirazzini, Marcella Pobbe, Elena Rizzieri, Leonie Rysanek, Elisabeth Schwarzkopf, Giulietta Simionato, Antonietta Stella, Ebe Stignani, Gabriella Tucci, Renata Tebaldi, Eugenia Zareska.

Ettore Bastianini, Umberto Borghi, Mario Borriello, Sesto Bruscantini, Antonio Cassinelli, Mariano Caruso, Francesco Calabrese, Boris Christoff, Plinio Clabassi, Alfredo Colella, Franco Corelli, Raffaele de Falchi, Mario del Monaco, Gino del Signore, Vito de Taranto, Giuseppe di Stefano, Giuseppe Forgione, Nicolai Gedda, Tito Gobbi, Gian Giacomo Guelfi, Piero Guelfi, Josef Hermann, Hans Hopf, Giacomo Lauri-Volpi, Agostino Lazzari, Giampiero Malaspina, Silvio Maoinica, Guido Mazzini, Saturno Meletti, Petre Munteanu, Kenneth Neate, Giulio Neri, Juan Oncina, Giorgio Onesti, Mario Petri, Mirto Picchi, Gianni Poggi, Afro Poli, Giacinto Prandelli, Aldo Protti, Augusto Romani, Bruno Sbalchiero, Paolo Silveri, Mariano Stabile, Vito Susca, Italo Tajo, Karl Terkal, Giulio Tomei, Giuseppe Vertecchi, Ludwig Weber, Zbyzlaw Wosniak, Adelio Zagonara.

CONDUCTORS

Vincenzo Bellezza, Karl Böhm, Franco Capuana, Oliviero de Fabritiis, Gianandrea Gavazzeni, Vittorio Gui, Herbert von Karajan, Angelo Questa, Gabriele Santini, Nino Sanzogno, Ottavio Ziino.

CHORUS MASTER

Giuseppe Conca.

PRODUCERS

Carlo Azzolini, Enrico Colosimo, Peter Ebert, Giovacchino Forzano, Mario Frigiero, Herbert Graf, Herbert von Karajan, Alessandro Manetti, Gian Carlo Menotti, Leonide Massine, Riccardo Moresco, Bruno Nofri, Carlo Piccinato, Guido Salvini, Heinz Tietjen, Vieri Tosatti, Vittorio Viviani, Aldo Vassallo.

CHOREOGRAPHERS

Leonide Massine, Boris Romanoff.

TEATRO GIUSEPPE VERDI, TRIESTE

(Ente Autonomo)

SEASON 1953-1954

REPERTORY

Guglielmo Tell, L'Elisir d'Amore, Tosca, Bohème, Andrea Chenier, La Farsa Amorosa (Zandonai), Arlecchino (Busoni)

Thais, Macbeth (Bloch), Parsifal.

Two operas by ' I Cadetti della Scala.' L'Osteria Portoghese (Cherubini) and Il Maestro di Musica (Pergolesi).

ARTISTS

Maria Caniglia, Rosanna Carteri, Aurora Cattelani, Laura Cavalieri, Aurora Dean Guglia, Disma de Cecco, Renata di Margherita, Fiorella Carmen Forti, Lillana Hussu, Pili Martorel, Lucia Mattiussi, Maria Meneghini-Callas, Martha Mödl, Elena Nicolai, Alda Noni, Ondina Otta, Gianna Pederzini, Maria Luisa Nache, Alma Pezzi, Rita Pierobon, Bruna Ronchini, Giuseppina Sani.

Bernd Aldenhoff, Carlo Badioli, Ettore Bastianini, Umberto Borso, Raimondo Botteghelli, Piero Cappuccilli, Virglio Carbonari, Franco Corelli, Boris Christoff, Nicola Filacuridi, Mario Filippeschi, Ettore Geri, Tito Gobbi, Fernando Li Donni, Miro Lozzi, Silvio Maoinica, Giampiero Malaspina, Antonio Massaria, Guido Mazzini, Rodofo Moraro, Enzo Mucchiutti, Giuseppe Nessi, Ugo Novelli, Alois Pernerstorfer, Ugo Savarese, Glauco

Scarlini, Ottavio Serpo, Paolo Silveri, Carlo Tagliabue, Hermann Uhde, Ludwig Weber.

CONDUCTORS

Herbert Albert, Francesco Molinari-Pradelli, Argeo Quadri, Luigi Toffolo, Antonino Votto.

CHORUS MASTER

Adolfo Fanfani.

PRODUCERS

Enrico Frigiero, Livio Luzzatto, Carlo Piccinato.

CHOREOGRAPHER

Nives Poli.

TEATRO SAN CARLO, NAPLES

(Ente Autonomo)

Sovrintendente : Comm. P. Di Constanzo

SEASON 1953-1954

REPERTORY

Le Nozze di Figaro, Cenerentola, Lucia di Lammermoor, Rigoletto, La Forza del Destino, La Wally, Madama Butterfly, Tosca, Andrea Chenier, Il Segreto di Susanna, I Pescatori (Napoli), (première), Turandot (Busoni), Debora e Jaele, La Leggenda di Sakuntala (Alfano), Carmen, Eugen Onegin, Mozart and Salieri (Rimsky-Korsakov), News of the Day (Hindesmith), Boulevard Solitude (Henze), Giovanna d'Arco al Rogo (Honegger), Der Prozess (Einem), Tristan und Isolde.

ARTISTS

Freda Adamo, Anna Maria Borrelli, Fernanda Cadoni, Maria Caniglia, Gilda Capozzi, Margherita Carosio, Maria Grazia Ciferri, Olga Constanzo, Anna de Cavalieri, Lisa della Casa, Orelia Dominguez, Agnese Dubbini, Mercedes Fortunati, Elisabetta Fusco, Dora Gatta, Leyla Gencer, Rina Gigli, Gertrude Grob-Prandl, Henny Herze, Rita Jorio, Sena Jurinac, Wilma Lipp, Luara Macario, Ira Malaniuk, Margherita Melato, Mafalda Micheluzzi, Maria Minazzi,

Orietta Moscucci, Alda Noni, Fiorella Ortis, Vittoria Palombini, Clara Petrella, Luisa Perlotti, Amalia Pini, Miriam Pirazzini, Marcella Pobbe, Vera Presti, Florence Quartararo, Guiliana Raymondi, Ornziella Rivere, Patrizia Rutelli, Guilietta Simionato, Teresa Stich-Randall, Renata Tebaldi, Pina Ulisse, Anna Vovola, Lucretia West.

Giovanni Amodeo, Raffaele Ariè, Gianni Avolanti, Carlo Badioli, Gino Bechi, Mario Borriello, Giuseppe Campora, Dario Caselli, Antonio Cassinelli, Plinio Clabassi, Alfredo Collella, Scipione Colombo, Franco Corelli, Piero di Palma, Mario del Monaco, Vito de Taranto, Wilhelm Ernest, Willy Ferenz, Renato Gavarini, Gerardo Gaudioso, Giuseppe Gentile, Enzo Guagni, Giangiacomo Guelfi, Endré Koreh, Max Lorenz, Erich Majkut, Antonio Manca Serra, Saturno Meletti, Giuseppe Micucci, Giuseppe Modesti, Petre Munteanu, Giulio Neri, Juan Oncina, Luigi Paolillo, Gino Penno, Gianni Poggi, Afro Poli, Giacinto Prandelli, Aldo Protti, Iginio Ricco, Otto van Rohr, Augusto Romani, Silvio Santarelli, Paul Schoeffler, Guiseppe Taddei, Carlo Tagliabue, Ferrucio Tagliavini, Italo Tajo, Aldo Terrosi, Roberto Turrini, Gaetana Valentini.

CONDUCTORS

Gianandrea Gavazzeni, Paul Hindemith, Jonel Perlea, Angelo Questa, Ugo Rapalo, Artur Rodzinski, Gabriele Santini, Tullio Serafin.

CHORUS MASTER

Michele Lauro.

STAGE DIRECTOR

C. M. Cristini.

PRODUCERS

Alessandro Brissoni, Vladimiro Cecchi, Max de Rieux, Enrico Frigiero, Livio Luzzatto, Carlo Piccinato, Roberto Rossellini, Adolf Rott, Ciro Scafa, Vittorio Viviani, Pietro Sharoff.

CHOREOGRAPHER

Bianca Gallizia.

TEATRO LA FENICE, VENICE

(Ente Autonomo)

1954 SEASON

REPERTORY

Il Conte Ory (Rossini), Medea (Cherubini), Lucia di Lammermoor, Don Carlo, Tosca, Il Tabarro, Pagliacci, La Luna dei Caraibi (Lualdi), Amahl and the Night Visitors. Die Meistersinger, Thaïs.

ARTISTS

Sari Barabas, Fernanda Cadoni, Maria Caniglia, Gina Consolandi, Rina Corsi, Mercedes Fortunati, Ina Gerhein, Mafalda Masini, Marinella Meli, Maria Meneghini-Callas, Clara Petrella, Amelia Pini, Miriam Pirazzini, Elena Rizzieri, Antonietta Stella, Ebe Stignani, Ebe Ticozzi, Gabriella Tucci, Hertha Wilfert.

Francesco Albanese, Bernd Aldenhoff, Ettore Bastianini, Umberto Borso, Sesto Bruscantini, Renato Capecchi, Mariano Caruso, Boris Christoff, Fernando Corena, Carl Dönch, Giovanni Fiorovanti, Renato Gavarini, Beniamino Gigli, Rudolf Gonzar, Heinz Imdahl, Luigi Infantino, Peter Klein, Agostino Lazzari, Melchiorre Luise, Giovanni Malipiero, Enzo Mascherini, Sante Messina, Nicola Monti, Cesare Masini-Sperti, Kenneth Neate, Giulio Neri, Heinrich Nillius, Rinaldo Pelizzoni, Giacinto Prandelli, Afro Poli, Camillo Righini, Giorgio Santi, Ugo Savarese, Marco Stefanoni, Mariano Stabile, Stefan Schwer, Paolo Silveri, Giorgio Tozzi, Giuseppe Zampieri, Arnold van Mill.

CONDUCTORS

Hugo Balzer, Bruno Bartoletti, Franco Capuana, Umberto Cattini, Vittorio Gui, Adriano Lualdi, Francesco Molinari-Pradelli, Angelo Questa.

CHORUS MASTER

Sante Zanon.

PRODUCERS

Sandro Bolchi, Augusto Cardi, Maria Lualdi, Gian Carlo Menotti, Frank de Quell, Carlo Maestrini.

II. Operatic Premières, 1939–1954

This list will, it is hoped, serve in some small measure to bring Lowenberg's " Annals of Opera " up to date. Owing to difficulties of space it has not been possible to give details of any but first performances, and as much archive material was destroyed in Germany during the war, there must naturally be some gaps. It has also been impossible to collect, at the time of going to press, details of productions from Eastern Europe and Russia, but it is hoped that it will be possible to rectify this omission in future issues of this Annual.

1939

11 February. Städtische Theater, Leipzig.
Die Pfiffife Magd. Comic opera in three acts by Julius Weismann.

29 March. Staatstheater, Kassel.
Elisabeth von England. Opera in four acts by Paul von Klenau. Given under the title of *Die Königen* at the Berlin Staatsoper and elsewhere in Germany during the war.

28 April. Teatro Comunale, Bologna.
Re Lear. Opera in three acts by Vito Frazzi.

17 May. Städtische Bühnen, Düsseldorf.
Die Nachtigall. Opera in four scenes by Alfred Irmler. Text by Rudolph Gahlbeck, based on the story of Hans Andersen.

7 October. Royal Opera, Stockholm.
Kathrin. Opera in three acts by Erich Korngold. Text by Ernst Decsey.

7 October. Royal Flemish Opera, Antwerp.
Medée. Opera in three acts by Darius Milhaud. Text by Madeleine Milhaud.

24 November. Royal Opera, Stockholm.
Königen Elisabeth. Opera in three acts by Fried Walter. Text by Christof Schulz-Gellen.

9 December. Teatro Comunale, Bologna.
Fabiano. Opera in a prologue, two acts and an epilogue, by Pratella. Text by A. Beltramelli.

23 December. Teatre Reale dell'Opera, Rome.
Monte Ivnor. Opera in three acts by Lodovico Rocca. Text by Cesare Meano.

1940

11 February. Scala, Milan.
Ghirlino. Opera in three acts by Luigi Ferrari-Trecate. Text by Elio Anceschi.

15 February. Carlo Felice, Genoa.
L'Intrusa. Opera in one act by Guido Pannain. Text by Romualdo Giani, based on the drama by Maurice Maeterlinck.

15 February. Carlo Felice, Genoa.
La Pulce d'Oro. Opera in one act and three scenes by Giorgio Federico Ghedini. Text by Tullio Pinelli.

27 February. Teatro Giuseppe Verdi, Trieste.
Il Revisore. Opera in one act by Amilcare Zanella. Text by A. Lega.

29 February. Teatro San Carlo, Naples.
Medusa. Opera in three acts by Bruno Barilli. Text by Schanzer.

—March. Teatro del Casino, San Remo.
Enrico di Mirval. Opera in three acts by Pietro Canonica. Text by C. Bernardi.

16 March. Royal Opera, Stockholm.
Singoalla. Opera in three acts by Gunnar de Frumerie. Text by Ella Byström-Baeckström.

13 April. Staatsoper, Dresden.
Romeo und Julia. Opera in two acts by Heinrich Sutermeister. Text by the composer, adapted from Schlegel's translation of Shakespeare.

5 May. Staatstheater, Stuttgart.
Kampfwerk. Scenic cantata by Marc André Souchay.

18 May. Teatro della Pergola, Florence.
Volo di Notte. Opera in one act by Luigi Dallapiccola. Text by the composer, based on *Vol de Nuit* by Antoine de Sainte-Eupery.

4 October. Staatsoper, Dresden.
Orpheus. New realization of the Monteverdi opera by Carl Orff.

17 October. Opéra-Comique, Paris.
Nele Dooryn. Opera in three acts by

Antoine Mariotte. Text by Camille Mauclair.

17 November. Opernhaus, Nürnberg.
Hille Bobbe. Opera by Hans Ebert.

19 December. Staatsoper, Berlin.
Andreas Wolius. Opera in three acts by Fried Walter.

1941

13 January. Teatro Reale dell' Opera, Rome.
Ecuba. Opera in three acts by G. Francesco Malipiero. Text by the composer after Euripides.

1 February. Scala, Milan.
Gli Orazzi. Opera in one act by Ennio Porrino. Text by the composer after Livy.

25 February. Staatstheater, Kassel.
Der Uhrmacher von Strassburg. Opera in three acts by Hans Brehme. Text by Paul Ginthum.

5 March. Teatro La Fenice, Venice.
Lo Standardo di S. Giorgio. Opera by Mario Peragallo.

18 March. Royal Opera, Stockholm.
Aladdin. Opera in three acts by Kurt Atterberg. Text by Bruno Hardt-Warden.

4 April. Vienna, Staatsoper.
Joanna Balk. Opera in three acts by Rudolf Wagner-Regény. Text by Caspar Neher.

12 May. Städtische Theater, Leipzig.
Die Windsbraut. Opera in three acts by Winfried Zillig. Text by Richard Billinger.

27 May. Opéra-Comique, Paris.
Comme ils s'Aiment. Opera in two acts by André Lavagne. Text by Marcel Belvianes.

—June. Teatro Colon, Buenos Aires.
Lin Calel. Opera in one act by Arnaldo d'Esposito. Text by Victor Mercante.

15 September. Royal Opera, Stockholm.
Lipps. Opera in two acts by Peter Kreuderk. Text by Hans Martin Kremer.

11 October. Städtische Bühnen, Düsseldorf.
Die Hexe von Passau. Opera in four scenes by Ottmar Gerster. Text by Richard Billinger.

22 November. Staatstheater, Brunswick.
Das Dreinarrenspiel. Opera by Hans Ulldahl.

1942

10 January. Royal Opera, Stockholm.
Birgitta. Opera in three acts by Natanael Berg. Text by the composer.

13 January. Städtische Bühnen, Frankfurt-am-Main.
Columbus. Opera in twelve scenes by Werner Egk. Text by the composer.

7 February. Philadelphia Academy of Music.
Ramuntcho. Opera in three acts by Deems Taylor. Text by the composer after Pierre Loti's novel.

20 February. Metropolitan Opera, New York.
The Island God. Opera in one act by Gian-Carlo Menotti. Text by the composer.

21 February. San Carlo, Naples.
Beatrice Cenci. Opera by Guido Pannain.

10 March. Opéra-Comique, Paris.
Mon Oncle Benjamin. Opera in three acts by Francis Bousquet. Text by Georges Ricou after the novel by Claudie Tillier.

5 May. Opéra-Comique, Paris.
Le Rossignol de Saint Malo. Opera in one act by Paul Le Flem. Text by Jean Grandrey-Réty.

16 May. Landestheater, Hamburg.
Das Königliche Opfer. Opera by Georg Vollerthun.

13 June. Stadttheater, Zürich.
Johanna auf dem Scheiterhaufen. Dramatic oratorio in a prologue and eleven scenes by Arthur Honegger. Text by Paul Claudel.

20 June. Städtische Bühnen, Düsseldorf.
Die Geschichte von Schönen Annerl. Dramatic Ballad in nine scenes by Leo Justinus Kauffmann. Text by Brentano von E. Reinacher and E. Bormann.

25 July. Opéra-Comique, Paris.
Ginevra. Opera in three acts by Marcel Delannoy. Text by Julien Luchaire after Boccasccio.

9 October. N.B.C., New York.
L'Incantesimo. Opera in one act by Italo

Montemezzi. Text by Sam Benelli. (First stage performance 9 August 1951, Verona Arena.)

24 October. Teatro Reale dell' Opera, Rome.
I Capricci di Callot. Opera in a prologue and three acts by G. Francesco Malipiero. Text by the composer. Revised version presented 11 September 1951, at Städtische Oper, Berlin.

28 October. Staatsoper, Munich.
Capriccio. A conversation piece in one act by Richard Strauss. Text by the composer and Clemens Krauss.

31 October. Staatsoper, Dresden.
Die Zauberinsel. Opera in two acts by Heinrich Sutermeseister. Text by the composer.

1 November. Städtische Theater, Leipzig.
Der Garten des Paradieses. Dramatic Rhapsody by Felix Petyrek. Text by Hans Reinhardt.

3 November. Broadway Theatre, New York.
The Opera Cloak. Opera in one act by Walter Damrosch. Text by Gretchen Damrosch Finletter.

1943

14 January. San Carlo, Naples.
La Vita e Sogno. Opera by Francesco Malipiero.

28 January. San Carlo, Naples.
Un Curioso Accidente. Opera by Jacopo Napoli. Text by Mario Chisalberti.

18 February. Städtische Bühnen, Frankfurt-am-Main.
Die Kluge. Fable in one act by Carl Orff.

27 May. Staatstheater, Oldenburg.
Die Kluge Wirtin. Opera in three acts by Hajo Hinrichs. Text by Friedrich Lindemann.

5 June. Landestheater, Hanover.
Der Kuckuck von Theben. Opera by Ermanno Wolf-Ferrari.

20 June. Opernhaus, Nürnburg.
Signor Formica. Opera by Hans Grimm.

6 November. Städtische Theater, Leipzig.
Catulli Carmina by Carl Orff.

7 November. Städtische Theater, Leipzig.
Das Kalte Herz. Opera by Norbert Schulze. Text by Kurt E. Walter.

25 November. Royal Opera, Stockholm.
Fredlös. Opera in three acts by Oskar Lindberg. Text by Fritz Tutenberg.

1944

25 January. Opéra-Comique, Paris.
Amphytrion 38. Opera by Marcel Bertrand. Text by Alexandre Guinle after Jean Giradoux.

10 March. Opéra-Comique, Paris.
Fantaisie Nocturne. Opera in two acts by Alfred Bachelet. Text by Mme. Machelet.

2 July. Staatsoper, Dresden.
Die Hochzeit des Jobs. Opera in seven scenes by Joseph Haas. Text by Ludwig Andersen.

4 July. Opéra-Comique, Paris.
La Gageure Imprévue. Opera in one act by Henry Sauguet. Text by Pierre Bertin after Sedaine.

1945

1 February. Royal Opera, Stockholm.
Lycksalighetens O. Opera in three acts by Hilding Rosenberg. Text by P. D. A. Aterboms.

26 March. San Carlo, Naples.
Miseria è Nobilta. Opera in three acts by Jacopo Napoli. Text by Vittorio Viviani, from the play by Edward Scarpetta.

7 June. Sadler's Wells, London.
Peter Grimes. Opera in a prologue and three acts by Benjamin Britten. Text by Montague Slater.

1946

7 January. Royal Theatre, Copenhagen.
The Travelling Companion. Opera in three acts by Ebke Hamerik. Text by the composer, based on Hans Andersen.

—March. Teatro La Fenice, Venice.
La Matrona di Efeso. Opera by Sante Zanon.

— April. Teatro Puccini, Milan.
Alba Eroica. Opera in three acts by Cinque.

22 June. Stadttheater, Zürich.
Niobe. Opera in one act by Heinrich Sutermeister. Text by Peter Sutermeister.

12 July. Glyndebourne.
The Rape of Lucretia. Opera in two acts by Benjamin Britten. Text by Ronald Duncan.

12 November. Staatsoper, Berlin.
Postmeister Wyrin. Opera in three acts by Florizel von Reuter. Text by the composer after Pushkin.

20 December. Radio Berlin.
Die Flut. Chamber Opera in one act by Boris Blacher. (First stage performance 7 March 1947, Dresden Staatsoper.)

1947

2 January. Scala, Milan.
L'Oro. Opera in three acts by Ildebrando Pizzetti. Text by the composer.

11 January. Metropolitan, New York.
The Warrior. Opera in one act by Bernard Rogers. Text by Norman Corwin.

6 February. San Carlo, Naples.
Il Borghese Gentiluomo. Opera in one act by Assunto Gargiulo. Text by Vittorio Viviani.

22 April. Teatro Verdi, Florence.
Vindice. Opera in one act by Mo. Morini.

3 June. Opéra-Comique, Paris.
Les Mamelles de Tiresias. Opera in two acts by Francis Pullenc. Text by Guillaume Appolinaire.

15 June. Staatstheater, Stuttgart.
Die Bernauerin. A Bavarian Play, with music by Carl Orff.

20 June. Glyndebourne.
Albert Herring. Comic Opera in three acts by Benjamin Britten. Text by Eric Crozier, based on the Maupassant Story.

6 August. Festspielhaus, Salzburg.
Dantons Tod. Opera in two parts by Gottfried van Einem. Text by the composer after Georg Büchner.

31 August. Landestheater, Hanover.
Luzifer. Opera by Max Peters. Text by the composer.

25 October. Royal Opera, Stockholm.
Genoveva. Opera in three acts by Natanael Berg. Text by the composer after the drama by Friedrich Hebbels.

31 December. Städtische Bühnen, Cologne.
Die Nachtigall. Opera in three acts by Hans Schanazara. Text by Herbert Hennies, from Hans Andersen.

1948

31 January. Théâtre Municipal, Mulhouse.
Roxelane. Opera by Henri Büsser.

8 February. Hamburgichse Staatsoper.
Trotz Wider Trotz. Opera by Arthur Grüber.

21 February. Scala, Milan.
Le Baccanti. Opera in a prologue and three acts by Giorgio Federico Ghedini. Text by Tullio Pinelli from Euripides.

29 February. Städtische Theater, Leipzig.
Die Nachtschwalbe. Opera by Boris Blacher.

17 March. Sadler's Wells, London.
Lady Rohesia. Opera in two parts by Anthony Hopkins. Text by the composer, based on the Ingoldsby Legends.

28 April. Teatro dell' Opera, Rome.
Salammbo. Opera in four acts by Franco Casavola. Text by Emidio Mucci from the novel by Flaubert.

7 May. Scala, Milan.
Gli Incatenati. Opera in two scenes and an Intermezzo by Renzo Bianchi. Text by the composer.

8 May. Théâtre Municipal, Strasbourg.
Judith. Opera in four acts by Fr. Adam. Text by Charles Hellem and Pol d'Estoc.

2 June. Opéra-Comique, Paris.
La Carrosse du Saint Sacrement. Opera in one act by Henri Büsser. Text by the composer after Prosper Merimée.

26 June. Opéra-Comique, Paris.
La Farce de Maitre Patelin. Opera in one act by Henri Barraud. Text by Gustave Cohen.

15 July. Indiana University.
Down in the Valley. Opera in one act by Kurt Weill. Text by Arnold Sundgaard.

15 August. Landestheater, Salzburg.
Le Vin Herbé Opera by Frank Martin. Text by the composer from Joseph Bedier's novel.

11 September. Teatro La Fenice, Venice. *L'Incubo.* Opera in one act by Riccardo Nielsen. Text by Elsa Pradella.

19 September. Royal Opera, Stockholm. *Stormen.* Opera in three acts by Kurt Atterberg. Text by the composer from Shakespeare's *The Tempest.*

14 October. Royal Opera, Stockholm. *Raskolnikoff.* Opera in three acts by Heinrich Sutermeister. Text by Peter Sutermeister.

22 October. Städtische Bühnen, Cologne. *Des Simplicius Simplicissimus Jugend.* Chamber opera by Karl Amadeus Hartmann. Text by Wolfgang Petzer and the composer from an idea and scenario by Hermann Scherchen, after H. J. Chr. Grimmelshausen.

5 November. Teatro Comunale, Bologna. *Buricchio.* Opera in three acts and an epilogue by Luigi Ferrari-Trecate. Text by Elio Anceschi.

18 December. Städtische Oper, Berlin. *Circe.* Opera in three acts by Werner Egk. Text by the composer from Calderon's *El Mayor Encanto Amor.*

1949

18 January. Opéra-Comique, Paris. *Guignol.* Opera in three acts by André Bloch. Text by Henri Fabert and Justin Godart.

29 January. Théâtre Municipal, Strasbourg. *Puck.* Opera in three acts by Marcel Delannoy.

5 February. Teatro Giuseppe Verdi, Trieste. *Trittico.* Opera in three acts by Antonio Illersberg. Text by Morello Torrespini.

12 February. Teatro Massimo, Palermo. *Millesima Seconda.* Opera in one act by Giuseppe Savagnone. Text by Cesare Meano.

13 February. Théâtre Municipal, Bordeaux. *L'Homme de Poupre.* Opera by Roger Gayral.

15 February. Théâtre Municipal, Mulhouse. *Rocio.* Opera by Maurice Perez.

2 March. Stadttheater, St. Gallen.

Die Schwarze Spinne. Opera in one act by Heinrich Sutermeister. Text by Albert Roesler from the novel by Jeremias Gotthelf.

17 March. Scala, Milan. *Regina Uliva.* Opera in three acts by Giulio Cesare Sonzogno. Text by Renato Simoni.

31 March. New York City Centre. *The Troubled Island.* Opera in three acts by William Grant Still. Text by Langston Hughes.

26 March. Teatro del Casino, San Remo. *Terra Santa.* Opera in one act by Paolo Salviucci. Text by Michele Franci.

30 April. Teatro dell' Opera, Rome. *Il Dottor Antonio.* Opera in three acts by Franco Alfano. Text by Mario Ghisalberti, from the novel by Giovanni Ruffini.

4 May. Teatro Comunale, Florence. *Vanna Lupa.* Opera in three acts by Ildebrando Pizzetti. Text by the composer.

7 May. Städtische Oper, Berlin. *Das Wundertheater.* Opera in two scenes by Hans Werner Henze. Text by the composer from an Intermezzo by Cervantes.

12 May. Scala, Milan. *Il Cordovano.* Opera in one act by Goffredo Petrassi. Text by the composer from Cervantes.

28 May. Stadttheater, Zürich. *Die Schwarze Spinne.* Opera in two acts by Willy Burkhard. Text by Robert Faesi and Georgette Boner from the novel by Jeremias Gotthelf.

21 June. Opéra-Comique, Paris. *Le Oui des Jeunes Filles.* Opera in three acts by Raynaldo Hahn. Text by René Fauchois.

25 June. Städtische Bühnen, Wuppertal. *Das Verzauberte Ich.* Opera in four acts by Ottmar Gerster. Text by Paul Koch from Raimund's *Apelkönig und Menschenfeind.*

15 July. Staatstheater, Bremen. *Die Bremer Stadtmusikanten.* Opera in two acts by Richard Mophaut. Text by Theo Phil.

9 August. Felsenreitschule, Salzburg. *Antigonae.* Opera by Carl Orff. Text by Friedrich Hölderlin from Sophocles.

8 September. Teatro La Fenice, Venice.
Billy Budd. Opera in one act by Giorgio Federico Ghedini. Text by Salvatore Quasimodo from the novel by Melville.

17 September. Städtische Oper, Berlin.
Spanische Nacht. Opera by Eugen Bodart.

29 September. Covent Garden, London.
The Olympians. Opera in a prologue and three acts by Arthur Bliss. Text by J. B. Priestley.

30 October. Städtische Theater, Leipzig.
Die Laune des Verliebten. Opera in one act by Erwin Dressel. Text by the composer from Goethe.

31 October. Broadway Theatre, New York.
Regina. Opera in three acts by Marc Blitzstein. Text by the composer, based on the novel *The Little Foxes* by Lillian Hellman.

23 November. Landestheater, Coburg.
Der Spielmann. Opera by Kurt Striegler.

26 November. Teatro Comunale, Bologna.
L'Arcangelo. Opera in three acts by Guido Guerrini.

17 December. Théâtre Municipal, Mulhouse.
Jeanne d'Arc. Opera by Paul Bastide.

1950

7 January. Royal Theatre, Copenhagen.
Susanne. Burlesque opera in one act by Knudage Riisager. Text by Mogens Lorentzen.

14 January. San Carlo, Naples.
La Badarna. Opera in one act by Alfredo Sangiori. Text by Alberto Colantouni.

21 January. Städtische Bühnen, Munster.
Liebe ist Teuer. Opera by Hans Brehme.

28 January. Teatro La Fenice, Venice.
Il Ponte delle Maravegia. Opera in one act by Bianchini.

28 January. Strasburg Opera.
Noé. Opera in three acts by Claude Arrieu. Text by André Obey.

28 January. Strasbourg Opera.
Hannele Mattern. Opera in five scenes and an epilogue by Camille Erlanger. Text by Gerhart Hauptmann.

29 January. Deutsches Theater, Göttingen.
Das Spiel von König Aphelius. Opera by Heinrich Kaminski.

8 February. La Scala, Milan.
L'Oso Re. Opera in three acts by Luigi Ferrari-Trecate. Text by E. Aneschi and M. Corrado Cervi.

12 February. Städtische Oper, Berlin.
Die Fusse im Feuer. Opera in one act by Heinrich Sutermeister. Text by the composer.

12 February. Städtische Oper, Berlin.
Das Fingerhutchen. Opera in one act by Heinrich Sutermeister. Text by the composer.

24 February. Théâtre Municipal, Mulhouse.
Wanda. Opera in three acts by Emile Goué.

25 February. Stadttheater, Regensburg.
Wozzeck. Opera in three acts by Kurt Pfister.

1 March. Philadelphia.
The Consul. Opera in three acts by Gian-Carlo Menotti. Text by the composer.

7 May. Grand Théâtre, Bordeaux.
La Main de Gloire. Opera in four acts by Jean Francaix. Text by Gerard de Nerval.

12 May. Opéra, Paris.
Bolivar. Opera in three acts by Darius Milhaud. Text by Madeleine Milhaud, from the play by Supervielle.

13 May. Royal Flemish Opera, Antwerp.
De Nachtwacht. Opera in three acts by Henk Badings.

14 May. Staatstheater, Stuttgart.
Don Juan und Faust. Opera in three acts by Hermann Reutter.

16 May. Smetana Theatre, Prague.
Krutnava. Opera in three acts by Eugen Suchom.

18 May. Indiana University.
The Jumping Frog. Opera in one act by Lukas Foss. Text by Jean Karsavina, from Mark Twain's story *The Jumping Frog of Calaveras County.*

18 May. Indiana University.
The Veil. Opera in one act by Bernard Rogers. Text by Robert Lawrence.

20 May. Teatro Comunale, Florence.
Il Prigioniero. Opera in a prologue and one act by Luigi Dallapiccola. Text by the composer.

May. La Scala, Milan.
L'Allegra Brigata. Opera in three acts by Gian Francesco Malipiero. Text by the composer.

23 June. Netherlands Opera, Amsterdam.
Philomela. Opera in three acts by Hendrick Andriessen. Text by Jan Engelman.

9 August. Festspielhaus, Salzburg.
Romeo und Julia. Opera in one act by Boris Blacher. Text by the composer.

20 September. Royal Theatre, Copenhagen.
Rosaura. Opera in three acts by Knud Jeppesen. Text by the composer from the comedy by Carlo Goldini.

4 October. Teatro Nuovo, Bergamo.
Bersabea. Opera in a prologue and three acts by Livio Maise Luzzatto. Text by the composer.

13 October. Fortune Theatre, London.
Mr. Bellamy Comes Home. Opera in three acts by Hill Rivington. Text by Martin R. Holmes.

20 October. Teatro Nuovo, Bergamo.
La Croce Deserta. Opera in one act by Sandro Fuga. Text by Tullio Pinelli from the novel by J. P. Jacobsen.

23 October. Teatro Eliseo, Rome.
Orfeo Vedovo. Opera in one act by Alberto Savinio. Text by the composer.

23 October. Teatro Eliseo, Rome.
Morte dell 'Aria. Opera in one act by Goffredo Petrassi. Text by Toti Scialoja.

23 October. Teatro Eliseo, Rome.
Il Tenore Sconfitto. Opera in one act by Vincenzo Tommasini. Text by Vitaliano Brancati.

October. Teatro Eliseo, Rome.
Job. A Scared 'representation.' by Luigi Dalappicola. Text by the composer.

3 November. Teatro dell 'Opera, Rome.
Ecuba. Opera in one act by Bruno Rigacci. Text by Vittorio Martino.

14 November. Teatro Liceo, Barcelona.
Lola la Piconera. Opera in a prologue, three acts and an epilogue by Conrado del Campo. Text by José Maria Peman.

21 November. Paddington Town Hall, London.
The Corn King. Opera in a prologue and two acts by Brian Easdale. Text by Naomi Mitchison.

30 November. Teatro Massimo, Catania.
Zelia. Opera in three acts by Francesco Paolo Neglia. Text by Alessandro Cortella.

1951

19 January. Théâtre Municipal, Mulhouse.
Le Rire de Nils Halerius. Opera in three acts by Marcel Landowski. Text by the composer and Gerard Caillet.

19 January. Théâtre Municipal, Mulhouse.
La Farce du Contrebandier. Opera in one act by Claude Pascal.

3 February. Städtische Bühnen, Düsseldorf.
Troilus und Cressida. Opera in six scenes by Winfried Zillig. Text by the composer.

11 February. Opernhaus, Nürnberg.
Lady Hamilton. Opera in three acts by Robert Heger.

9 March. Opéra-Comique, Paris.
Il était un petit Navire. Opera in three scenes by Germaine Tailleferre. Text by Henri Jeanson.

13 March. Städtische Oper, Berlin.
Amphitryon. Opera in a prologue and three acts by Robert Oboussier. Text by the composer from Molière and Kleist.

17 March. Staatsoper, Berlin.
Das Verhör des Lukullus. Opera in thirteen scenes by Paul Dessau. Text by Bert Brecht.

6 April. Opéra, Paris.
Kerkeb. Opera in one act by Marcel Samuel-Rousseau. Text by Michel Carré from the novel by Elissa Rhaiss.

26 April. Covent Garden, London.
The Pilgrim's Progress. A Morality in a prologue, four acts and an epilogue by Ralph Vaughan Williams. Text by the composer founded on Bunyan's allegory of the same name.

2 May. Bovard Auditorium, Los Angeles.
Dark Waters. Opera in one act by Ernst Krenek. Text by the composer.

15 May. Hippodrome, Bristol.
John Socman. Opera in three acts by George Lloyd. Text by William Lloyd.

9 May. Teatro Comunale, Florence.
Ifigenia. Opera in one act by Ildebrando Pizzetti. Text by the composer and A. Perrini.

1 June. Opéra-Comique, Paris.
Madame Bovary. Opera in three acts by Emmanuel Bondeville. Text by René Fauchois after the novel by Flaubert.

9 June. Staatstheater, Stuttgart.
Phaedra. Opera in three acts by Marcel Mihalovici. Text by Yvan Goll.

27 June. Staatstheater, Wiesbaden.
The Duenna. Opera in three acts by Roberto Gerhard. Text by Peter Cresswell from the play by Sheridan. (Concert performance only).

5 July. Opernhaus, Graz.
Stella. Opera by Waldemar Bloch.

9 July. Opera House, Cheltenham.
The Sleeping Children. Opera in three acts by Brian Easdale. Text by Tyrone Guthrie.

20 July. Chapterhouse, Canterbury.
The Man from Tuscany. Opera in two acts by Anthony Hopkins. Text by Christopher Hassall.

28 July. Arts Theatre, Cambridge.
The Mayor of Casterbridge. Opera in three acts by Peter Tranchell. Text by the composer in collaboration with Peter Bentley from the novel by Thomas Hardy.

4 September. Moseley Institute, Birmingham.
The Mermaid. Opera in three acts by Margaret More. Text by Claudine Currey from the story by Hans Andersen.

4 September. Theatre Royal, Copenhagen.
Host. Opera in one act by S. v. Schultz. Text by Eyvind Falk-Ronne.

11 September. Teatro La Fenice, Venice.
The Rake's Progress. Opera in three acts and an epilogue by Igor Strawinsky. Text by W. H. Auden and Chester Kallman.

23 September. Teatro Nuovo, Bergamo.
Prometeo. Opera in three acts by Luigi Cortese. Text by the composer from the play by Aeschylus.

4 October. City Centre, New York.
The Dybbuk. Opera in three acts by David Tamkin. Text by Alex Tamkin, based on the play by S. Anstey.

9 October. Teatro Nuovo, Bergamo.
Noreia. Opera in three acts by Giuseppe Piazzi. Text by the composer.

12 October. Grand Théâtre, Bordeaux.
Ivan IV. Opera in four acts by Georges Bizet, revised by Henri Busser. Text by Francoise-Hippolyte Leroy and Henry Trianon.

25 October. Teatro Nuovo, Bergamo.
La Madre. Opera in one act by Donato di Veroli. Text by the composer.

25 October. Teatro Nuovo, Bergamo.
Il Sistema della Dolcezza. Opera in one act by Vieri Tosatti. Text by the composer from the story by Edgar Allan Poe.

13 November. Opernhaus, Nürnberg.
Der Igel als Bräutigam. Opera in five scenes by Cesar Bresgen. Text by the composer and Ludwig Adersen.

17 November. Opéra-Comique, Paris.
Marion. Opera in three acts by Pierre Wissmer. Text by Jean Goudal.

22 November. State Opera, Budapest.
Adventure in Huszt. Opera in three acts by Paul Kadosa.

23 November. Royal Opera, Stockholm.
Der Rote Stiefel. Opera in three acts by Heinrich Sutermeister. Text by the composer based on the story *Das Kalte Herz* by Wilhelm Haff.

5 December. Town Hall, Oxford.
Incognita. Opera in three acts by Egon Wellesz. Text by Elisabeth Mackenzie from the novel by Congreve.

6 December. Covent Garden, London.
Billy Budd. Opera in four acts by Benjamin Britten. Text by E. M. Forster from the novel by Hermann Melville.

1952

13 January. Opernhaus, Nürnberg.
Die Schlaue Susanna. Opera in nine scenes by Franz X. Lehner. Text by the composer from the German version by Hans Schlegel of the farce by Lope de Vagas.

19 January. Stadttheater, Zürich.
Don Pedros Heimkehr. Opera in three acts with music by Mozart and Hans Erismann. Text after Da Ponte and Varesco by Oscar Wälterlin and Werner Galusser.

9 February. Scala, Milan.
L'Uragano. Opera in three acts by Lodovico Rocca. Text by Eligio Possenti from the play by Ostrowsky.

17 February. Landestheater, Hanover.
Boulevard Solitude. Opera in seven scenes by Hans Werner Henze. Text by the composer.

— February. Staatstheater, Kassel.
König Lustig. Opera in three acts by Erich Riede.

23 February. Theatre Royal, Antwerp.
Malafonte. Opera in three acts by Angelo Francesco Lavagnino.

16 March. Teatro dell' Opera, Rome.
Antigonae. Opera in three acts by Lino Liviabella. Text by Mucci.

17 March. Scala, Milan.
Prosperpina e lo Straniero. Opera in three acts by Juan José Castro. Text by Omar del Carlo, adapted by Eugenio Montale.

26 March. Stadttheater, Basle.
Leonore 40/45. Opera semeseria in a prelude and seven scenes by Rolf Liebermann. Text by Heinrich Stobel.

27 March. Teatro Cagnoni, Vigevano.
Face di Liberta. Oper in three acts by Adama Biancardi. Text by Calogero Gilde.

— March. Städtische Bühnen, Cologne.
Kain. Opera in one act by Friedrich Schmidtmann. Text by the composer after Byron.

15 April. La Fenice, Venice.
I Misteri Gloriosi. Opera in three acts by Nino Cattozzo. Text by the composer.

19 April. San Carlo, Naples.
Maria Antonietta. Opera in three acts by Terenzio Gargiulo. Text by Vittorio Viviani.

27 April. Teatro Comunale, Florence.
Don Chisciotte. Opera in three acts by Vito Frazzi. Text by the composer.

2 June. Piccolo Teatro, Florence.
Aucassine Nicolette. A legend in music by Mario Castelnuovo-Tedesco.

12 June. Brandeis University, U.S.A.
Trouble in Tahiti. Opera in seven scenes by Leonard Bernstein. Text by the composer.

17 June. Staatstheater, Oldenburg.
Amati. Opera in three acts by Winfried Wolff. Text by the composer.

14 August. Festspielhaus, Salzburg.
Die Liebe der Danae. Opera in three acts by Richard Strauss. Text by Joseph Gregor from an indea by Hugo von Hofmannsthal.

31 August. Teatro Mediterraneo, Naples.
Romulus. Opera in three acts by Salvatore Allegra. Text by Emidio Mucci.

27 September. Teatro Nuovo, Bergamo.
Arlecchino Re. Opera in a prologue, three acts and an epilogue by Salvatore Orlando. Text by Luigi Bonelil from the Viennese drama by Rudolph Lothar.

5 October. Teatro Nuovo, Bergamo.
Il Ritorno. Opera in one act by Otello Calbi. Text by Mario Vitale from the poem by G. Pascoli.

5 October. Teatro Nuovo, Bergamo.
Suor Manuela. Opera in one act by Enzo de Bellis. Text by Tretotoli-Adami.

7 November. Opéra-Comique, Paris.
Dolores. Opera in three acts by Michel-Maurice Lévy. Text by Louise Marion.

22 November. Städtische Bühnen, Munster.
Claudia Amata. Opera in five scenes by Johannes Driessler. Text by Bettina Brix from Gottfried Keller's Legend *Eugenia*

29 November. Pfalztheater, Kaislerlauten.
Alles ist Kismet. Opera by Peter Thullen.

1953

24 January. Scala, Milan.
Cagliostro. Opera in four scenes by Ildebrando Pizzetti. Text by the composer.

31 January. Music Hall, Cincinnati.
The Taming of the Shrew. Opera in three acts by Vittorio Giannini. Text by Dorothea Fee.

7 February. NBC Television Theatre, New York.
The Marriage. Opera in one act by Bohuslav Martinu. Text by the composer based on Gogol's story.

(First stage performance was given at the Hamburg State Opera on 13 March 1954.)

7 February. Staatstheater, Brunswick.
Die Feuerprobe. Opera by Kurt Stiebitz.

11 February. Teatro Ponchielli, Cremona.
Mara. Opera in one act by Pasquale Benintende.

12 February. Peabody Conservatory of Music, Baltimore.
The Tenor. Opera in one act by Hugo Weisgall. Text by Karl Shapiro and John R. Allen from Frank Wedekind's *Der Kammersänger.*

13 February. Scala, Milan.
Trionfo d'Afrodite. Concerto scenico by Carl Orff. Words by Catullus, Sappho and Euripides, being the third part of the Trittico, *Trionfi.* (The other two parts of this work are *Carmina Burana* and *Catulli Carmina.*)

26 February. Landestheater, Graz.
Donna Miranda. Opera by Rudolf Kattnig.

29 February. Bovard Auditorium, Los Angeles.
Volpone. Opera in three acts by George Antheil. Text by Alfred Perry from the play by Ben Jonson.

5 March. Co-Operative Hall, Colchester.
Rapunzel. Opera in three acts by Tom Hammond. Libretto by the composer.

25 March. Scala, Milan.
Mas'Aniello. Opera in three acts by Jacopo Napoli. Text by Vittoria Viviani.

15 April. Wilshire Ebel Theatre, Los Angeles.
The Fall of the House of Usher. Opera in five scenes by Morris Hutchen Rugar. Text by Francis Millington, based on the story by Edgar Allen Poe.

4 May. New Theatre, Oxford.
Irmelin. Opera in three acts by Frederick Delius. Text by the composer.

4 May. Hartford, Connecticut.
The Mighty Casey. Opera in three scenes by William Schuman. Text by Jeremy Gury.

18 May. Theatre Royal, Copenhagen.
Prinsessen i det Fjerne. Opera in one act by Sv. Erik Tarp. Text by Enevold Hjejle after the novel by Hermann Sudermann.

25 May. Manhatten School of Music, New York.
The Harpies. Opera in one act by Marc Blitzstein. Text by the composer.

26 May. Hunter College, New York.
The Barber of New York. Opera in one act by Ashley Vernon. Text by Greta Hartwig.

27 May. Städtische Bühnen, Cologne.
Ein Landzart. Opera in one act by Hans Werner Henze.

27 May. Städtische Bühnen, Cologne.
Der Grossindustrielle. Opera in one act by Kurt Driesch. Text by Eric Bormann. (Given at the Dresden Staatsoper, 12 December 1953 under the title of *Der Indianer.*)

8 June. Covent Garden, London.
Gloriana. Opera in three acts by Benjamin Britten. Text by William Plomer.

16 August. Festspielhaus, Salzburg.
Der Prozess. Opera in two acts by Gotfried van Einem. Text by Boris Blacher and Heinz von Cramer from the novel by Kafka.

6 September. Städtische Theater, Leipzig.
Wat Tyler. Opera in a prologue and six scenes by Alan Bush. Text by Nancy Bush.

8 September. La Fenice, Venice.
Partita a pugni. An introduction and 'three rounds' by Vieri Tosati. Text by Luciano Conosciandi.

14 September. Teatro Giglio, Lucca.
La Figlia di Iefte. Opera in one act by Sebastiano Caltabiano. Text by Guiseppe Adami.

24 September. Teatro Nuovo, Bergamo.
Novella. Opera in one act by Cesare Brero. Text by Allessandro di Stefano and Cesare Brero from a story in the Decameron.

24 September. Teatro Nuovo, Bergamo.
La Guardia Vigilante. Opera in one act by Libero Granchi. Text by Mario Verdone, from the story by Cervantes.

24 September. Teatro Nuovo, Bergamo.
Don Ciccio. Opera in one act by Ottorino Gentilucci. Text by Margherita Gentilucci.

30 September. Rudolf Steiner Hall, London. *The Tinners of Cornwall*. Opera in three acts by Inglis Gundry. Text by the composer.

2 October. Opéra, Marseille. *Cadet Roussel*. Opera in three acts by Claude Arrieu. Text by André de la Tourasse.

15 October. Teatro Nuovo, Bergamo. *La Porta Verde*. Opera in four acts by Francesco Santoliquido. Text by the composer.

7 November. Sophia Gardens Pavilion, Cardiff. *Menna*. Opera in three acts by Arwel Hughes. Text by Wyn Griffith.

12 November. Opernhaus, Nürnberg. *Brüderlein Hund*. Children's opera in three scenes by Cesar Bresgen. Text by Ludwig Andersen.

1954

26 February. Théâtre Municipal, Mulhouse. *L'Atlantide*. Opera in four acts by Henri Tomasi. Text by Francis Didelot, from the novel by Pierre Benoit.

24 March. Scala, Milan. *La Figlia del Diavolo*. Opera in one act by Virgilio Mortari. Text by C. Pavolini.

24 March. Scala, Milan. *La Gita in Campagna*. Opera in one act by Mario Peragallo. Text by Alberto Moravia.

26 March. San Carlo, Naples. *I Pescatori*. Opera in three scenes by Jacopo Napoli. Text by Raffaele Viviani.

29 March. Curtis Institute, Philadelphia. *The Mother*. Opera in one act by Stanley Hollier. Text by the composer, from the story by Hans Christian Andersen.

1 April. New York City Centre. *The Tender Land*. Opera in two acts by Aaron Copland. Text by Horace Everett.

20 May. Teatro della Pergola, Florence. *Il Contrabbasso*. Opera in one act by Valentino Bucci. Text by Mario Mattolini and Mauro Pezzati, from the play by Chekov.

21 May. Teatre della Pergola, Florence. *Il Diavolo nel Campanile*. Opera in one act by Adriano Lualdi. Text by the composer, from the novel by Edgar Allen Poe.

23 May. Opernhaus, Nürnberg. *Das Glückliche Ende*. Opera in one act by Winfried Wolf.

27 May. Brander Matthews Hall, New York. *Malady of Love*. Opera in one act by Lehman Engel. Text by Lewis Allen.

27 May. Brander Matthews Hall, New York. *Hello Out There*. Opera in one act by Jack Besson. Text by the composer, from the tragedy by William Saroyan.

17 June. Jubilee Hall, Aldeburgh. *A Dinner Engagement*. Opera in one act by Lennox Berkeley. Text by Paul Dehn.

20 July. Aix-en-Provence. *Les Caprices de Marianne*. Opera in two acts by Henri Sauguet. Text by J. P. Gredy from the play by Musset.

17 August. Festspielhaus, Salzburg. *Penelope*. Opera semi-seria in two parts by Rolf Liebermann. Text by Heinrich Strobel.

14 September. La Fenice, Venice. *The Turn of the Screw*. Opera in a prologue and two acts by Benjamin Britten. Text by Myfanwy Piper from the story by Henry James.

22 September. Sadler's Wells, London. *Nelson*. Opera in three acts by Lennox Berkeley. Text by Alan Pryce-Jones.

III. Operatic Obituary

September 1939 to September 1954

Since many operatic artists died during the war years, and their deaths passed unnoticed in the British press, we have decided to publish as full a list as possible of singers, conductors and composers, whose deaths have occurred between September 1939 and the time of going to press.

(b) baritone; (c) contralto; (ms) mezzo-soprano; (s) soprano; (t) tenor; (comp) composer; (cond) conductor.

(The Editor wishes to express his appreciation to Mr. Leo Riemens, of Holland, who checked this appendix and rectified several important omissions.)

1939

Karl Hammes (b).   3 September.
Sofia Sedlmayer (s).   14 October.
Giulio Crimi (t).   29 October.
Borghild Bryhn (s).   2 November.
Artur Bodansky (cond).   23 November.
Charles Dalmores (t).   6 December.
Marcelle Mahieux (s).   Date unknown.

1940

Edward Lankow (bs).   29 January.
Giuseppe La Puma (b).   January.
Julius Lieban (t).   1 February.
Emma Redell (s).   2 February.
Thomas Meux (bs).   7 February.
Karl Muck (cond).   3 March.
Lola Beeth (s).   18 March.
Gustav Waschow (b).   25 April.
Luisa Tetrazzini (s).   28 April.
Dinh Gilly (b).   19 May.
Silvano Isalberti (t).   11 June.
Emma Nevada (s).   20 June.
Joseph Geiss (b).   22 June.
Albert Reiss (t).   29 June.
Claude Got (b).   June.
Lucy Weidt (s).   28 July.
Alessandro Bonci (t).   10 August.
Louis Dornay (t).   12 August.
Fritz Feinhals (b).   30 August.
Walther Zimmer (b).   25 September.
Ivar Andrésen)bs).   6 November.
René-Baton (cond).   9 October.
Alice   Guszalewicz (s).   26 November.
Constance Willis (c).   18 November.
Marie Dietrich (s).   14 December.
Blanche Marchesi (s).   15 December.

1941

Margaret Keyes (c).   6 January.

Luigi Rossi-Morelli (b).   January.
Anton Baumann (bs).   7 Feb.
Frida Felser (s).   16 February.
Edoardo Mascheroni (cond).   4 March.
Melanie Kurt(s).   11 March.
Angelo Bada (t).   24 March.
Hedy Iracema-Brugelmann(s).   9 April.
Julia Claussen (c).   1 May.
John Forsell (b)   30 May.
Milka Ternina (s).   26 May.
Charles Corri (cond).   8 June.
Giuseppe Borghetti (t).   5 July.
John Coates (t).   16 August.
Ernst Kraus (t).   September.
Paul Papfsdorf (t).   6 October.
Georgette Leblanc (s).   26 October.
Elise von Catopol (s).   10 November.
Gennaro Papi (cond).   30 November.
Georg Zottmayr (bs).   11 December.
Mary Lewis (s).   31 December.
William Anderson (bs).   Date unknown.
Léon Escalais (t).   Date unknown.
Philippe Gaubert (cond).   Date unknown.
Edmée Favart (s).   Date unknown.

1942

Charles Hackett (t).   1 January.
Emma Calvé (s).   6 January.
Foster Richardson (bs).   19 January.
Désiré Pauwels (t).   25 January.
Hans (Jean) Müller (bs).   26 January.
Robert Hutt (t).   5 February.
Gustav Werner (t).   16 March.
Felix Weingartner (cond).   7 May.
Helena Forti (s).   11 May.
Benno Haberl (t).   21 May.
Jean Vallier (bs).   June.
Laura Pasini (s).   30 June.
Elisabeth Feuge (s).   4 July.

Pasquale Amato (b).   13 August.
Alfred Hertz (cond).   17 August.
May Busby (s).   28 December.
Wilhelm Grünning (t).   2 December.
Josef von Manowarda (bs).   24 December.
Arthur Winckworth (t).   Date unknown.
Henri Sylvain (bs).   Date unknown.
Henri Seguin (bs).   Date unknown.
Anna Tanesy (s).   Date unknown.
Lise Landowsy (s).   Date unknown.
Jeanne Leclerq (s).   Date unknown.

1943

Renzo Rinolfi (b).   25 January.
Sigrid Arnoldson (s).   7 February.
Joseph Schmidt (t).   February.
Alice Nielsen (s).   8 March.
Johannes Reinhardt (t).   13 March.
Ben Davies (t).   28 March.
Raoul Lapara (comp).   4 April.
Henri Scott (bs).   4 April.
Frederic D'Erlanger (comp).   23 April.
Else Gentner-Fischer (s).   26 April.
Edoardo Garbin (t).   April.
Margaret Macintyre (s).   April.
Cesira Ferrani (s).   6 May.
Sigfrid Onegin (c).   18 June.
Jules Bledsoe (b).   17 July.
Carl Schiffeler (b).   22 July.
Maria Gay (ms).   29 July.
Helena Kugleman (s).   7 August.
Jane Osborne-Hannah (s).   13 August.
Jean Dickerson Bartlett (c).   14 August.
Berthold Sterneck (bs).   25 November.
Rafaelo Diaz (t).   12 December.
Georg von Tschurtschenthaler (b).   17 December.
Magda Spiegel (s).   Date unknown.
Juan Luria (b).   Date unknown.
Irene Minghini-Cattaneo (ms).   Date unknown.
Karl Armster (b).   Date unknown.
Maie Bouvet (c).   Date unknown.
Thomas Salignae (t).   Date unknown.
Ottilie Metzger-Lattermann (c).   Date unknown.
Mia Werber (s).   Date unknown.
Therese Rothauser (c).   Date unknown
Henrietta Gottlieb (s).   Date unknown.
Theodor Ritch (t).   Date unknown.

Richard Breiterfeld (b).   Date unknown.
(All German singers 'unknown' of this year were gassed in Jewish Concentration camps.)

1944

Maarjte Offers (c).   28 January.
Lina Cavalieri (s).   8 February.
Aroldo Lindi (t).   8 March.
Valentin Haller (t).   24 March.
Carl Schlegel (bs).   5 April.
Ethyl Smyth (comp).   8 May.
Paul Aumonier (bs).   27 May.
Hubert Paty (bs).   27 May.
Else Kochhann (s).   May.
Hermann Wiedemann (b).   2 June.
Riccardo Zandonai (comp).   20 June.
Aino Ackté (s).   8 August.
Willi Wörle (t).   13 August.
Artur Preuss (t).   20 August.
Angelo Canarutto (cond).   29 August.
Frederick Blamey (t).   29 September.
Erika Wedekind (s).   10 October.
Giuseppina Finzi-Magrini (s).   30 November.
Colette d'Arville (s).   16 December.
Marguerite Chambellan (s).   Date unknown.

1945

Enrico de Franceschi (b).   8 January.
Alfred Kase.   11 January.
Malcolm McEachern (t).   17 January.
Armando Borgioli (b).   20 January.
Luise Reuss-Belce (s).   12 February.
Blanche Arral (s).   3 March.
Roderick Lloydd (bs).   9 April.
Alois Burgstaller (t).   19 April.
Rosina Storchio (s).   10 June.
Björn Talen (t).   12 July.
Fanny Moody (s).   21 July.
Josefina Reinl (s).   22 July.
Elsa Stralia (s).   2 August.
Pietro Mascagni (comp).   2 August.
Gino Marinuzzi (cond).   17 August.
John McCormack (t).   16 September.
Bela Bartok (comp).   26 September.
Claudine Boons (s).   3 October.
Karl Alwin (cond).   16 October.
Oscar Seagle (b).   19 December.
Adelina Stehle (s).   24 December.
Alice Raveau (c).   Date unknown.
Germaine Cernay (ms).   Date unknown.
Francesco Daddi (t).   Date unknown.

Marius Chambon (bs). Date unknown.
Waldermar Henke (t). Date unknown.
Gustave Huberdeau (bs). Date unknown.

1946

Giuseppe Krismer (t). 6 January.
Adamo Didur (bs). 7 January.
Cornelia van Zanten (ms). 11 January.
Giuseppe Krismer (t). January.
Robert Burg (b). 9 February.
Ben Williams (t). 11 February.
Guerrina Fabbri (c). 21 February.
Susanne Strong (s). 11 March.
Juan Spiwaek (t). 15 March.
Alexander van Zemlinsky (cond). 16 March.
Otto Wolf (t). 28 March.
Tamaki Miura (s). 26 May.
Leo Slezak (t). 7 June.
Tillmann Liszewsky (b). 3 July.
Antonio Paoli (t). 26 August.
Maria Barrientos (s). September.
Antonio Paoli (t). September.
Carolina Lazzari (ms). 17 October.
Nicholas Gatty (comp). 10 November.
Francisco Granados (t). 23 November.
Ellen Gulbranson (s). 3 December.
Maria von Basilides (ms). December.
Claire Croiza (c). Date unknown.
Antonio Sabino (cond). Date unknown.

1947

Reynaldo Hahn (comp and cond). 22 January.
Grace Moore (s). 26 January.
Anna von Mildenburg (s). 27 January.
Marthe Chenal (s). 29 January.
Celestina Boninsegna (s). 14 February.
Robert Ainsworth (cond). 19 February.
Charles Friant (t). 22 April.
Gothelf Pistor (t). 27 April.
Louise Homer (ms). 6 May.
Marion Weed (s). 23 June.
Carlo Scattola (bs). June.
Corinne Rider-Kelsey (s). 10 July.
Carl Seydel (t). 17 August.
Lillian Blauvelt (s). 29 August.
Ellen Beach Yaw (s). 9 September.
Karl August Neumann (b). 18 September.
Hendrick Appels (t). 22 September.
Janet Fairbank (s). 26 September.
Eleanor Painter (s). 3 November.

Paul Bender (bs). 25 November.
William Wade Hinshaw (bs). 27 November.
Marguerite Carré (s). November.
Vernon Stiles (t). 10 December.
Aldo Sinnone (t). 16 December.
Cesare Sodero (cond). 16 December.
Karl Jörn (t). 19 December.
Franz von Hoesslin (cond). Date unknown.

1948

Richard Tauber (t). 8 January.
Ermanno Wolf-Ferrari (comp). 22 January.
John O'Sullivan (t). 9 February.
Lodovico Oliviero (t). 25 February.
Hermine Kittel (ms). 6 March.
Hedwig Francillo-Kauffmann (s). April.
Alois Hadwiger (t). 10 April.
Artur Fleischer (b). 11 April.
Marie Tiffany (s). 12 April.
Francisco Nuibo (t). April.
Janet Spencer (c). 19 May.
Francois Ruhlmann (c). 4 June.
Gertrud Rünger (s). 7 June.
Rena Vivienne (s). 8 June.
Muzio Giovagnoli (t). June.
Amilcare Pozzoli (t). 16 July.
Sergio Failoni (cond). 25 July.
Frank Wennerholm (b). 22 August.
Giuseppina Cobelli (s). 2 September.
Ferrucio Giannini (t). 17 September.
Bianca Scacciati (s). 15 October.
Umberto Giordano (comp). 12 November.
Josephine Jacoby (s). 13 November.
Louisa Edvina (s). 13 November.
Rosalia Chalia (s). 17 November.
Julius von Scheidl (b). 11 December.
Rosina Buckmann (s). 31 December.
Giuliano Biel (t). Date unknown.
Jean Bourbon (b). Date unknown.
Cesare Vezzani (t). Date unknown.

1949

Armida Parsi-Pettinella (s). 9 January.
Amadeo Bassi (t). 15 January.
Giovanni Zenatello (t). 11 February.
John Garris (t). 2 April.
Emilio de Gorgoza (b). 10 May.
Hans Pfitzner (comp). 22 May.
Maria Cebotari (s). 9 June.
Maurice d'Oisley (t). 18 June.

Germaine Féraldy (s). 30 June.
Hermann Weill (b). 6 July.
Riccardo Pick-Mangiagali (comp). 8 July.
Cesare Formichi (b). 21 July.
Walter Olitzki (b). 2 August.
Emilio Sagi-Barba (b). 7 August.
Hermann Devries (bs). 24 August.
Walter Widdop (t). 6 September.
Richard Strauss (comp). 8 September.
Guiseppe Reschiglian (t). 12 September.
Henri Rabaud (comp). 12 September.
Adolf Gröbte (t). 16 September.
Rosa Olitzka (c). 29 September.
Maria Galvany (s). 2 November.
Margit Bokor (s). 9 November.
Ludwig Ermold (bs). 15 December.
Zélie de Lussan (ms). 18 December.
Heinrich Rehkemper (b). 30 December.
Glanka Zwingenberg (s). Date unknown.

1950

Robert Ringling (b). 2 January.
Edyth Walker (s). 19 February.
Martha Atwood (s). 7 April.
Noel Eadie (s). 11 April.
Gemma Bellincioni (s). 23 April.
Paul Franz (t). April.
Arturo Lucon (cond). April.
Charles Rousselière (t). 11 May.
Gertrude Foerstel (s). 7 June.
Arnold Gabor (b). 17 July.
Giuseppe Agostini (t). 26 July.
Emanuel Salazar (t). 6 August.
Giuseppe de Luca (b). 24 August.
Giuseppe Borgatti (t). 18 October.
Francesco Cilea (comp). 2 November.
Giuseppe del Campo (cond). November.
Georg Hann (bs). 10 December.
Cristobal Altube (t). Date unknown.
Giuseppe Baroni (cond). Date unknown.
Giovani Ugolotti (t). Date unknown.
Eliette Schennemberg (ms). Date unknown.

1951

Giannina Russ (s). 28 February.
Walter Kirchoff (t). 29 March.
Olive Fremstad (s). 1 April.
Mme. Charles Cahier (ms). 14 April.
Desirée Ellinger (s). 30 April.
Lucy Gates (s). 30 April.
Hector Dufranne (b). 3 May.

Charles Marshall (t). 8 May.
Mario Valle (b). 14 May.
Quenna Mario (s). 28 May.
Serge Koussevitzky (cond). 4 June.
Lucia Mero (s). June.
Giannina Arangi-Lombardi (s). 9 July.
Giulio Fregosi (bs). 17 July.
Antonio Righetti (bs). 29 July.
Sophie Traubmann (s). 16 August.
Constant Lambert (cond). 21 August.
Georg Maikl (t). 22 August.
Fritz Busch (cond). 14 September.
Douglas Beattie (bs). 18 September.
Egisto Tango (cond). 5 October.
Paul Eisler (cond). 16 October.
Luciano Neroni (bs). 23 October.
Oscar Natzka (bs). 5 November.
Amy Castles (s). 19 November.
Gina Pinnera (s). 20 November.
Nino Ederle (t). November.
Léon Rothier (bs). 7 December.
Hermann Schramm (t). 11 December.
Francesco de Marchi (t). Date unknown.
Mila Kocova (s). Date unknown.
Walter Hyde (t). November.
Robert Parker (bs). Date unknown.
Felicia Kaschowska (s). Date unknown.
Josefina Huguet (s). Date unknown.

1952

Aureliano Pertile. 11 January.
Donald Dame (t). 21 January.
Max Altglass (t). 13 February.
Jeanne Gordon (ms). 21 February.
Oretse Luppi (bs). 24 February.
Giacomo Rimini (b). 6 March.
Octave Dua (t). 8 March.
Enzo de Muro Lomanto (t). 15 March.
Antonio Cortis (t). 2 April.
Frederick Austin (b). 10 April.
Margery Booth (c). 12 April.
Joy McArden (s). 12 April.
Elisabeth Schumann (s). 24 April.
Italo Montémezzi (comp). 15 May.
Aline Vallandri (s). 30 May.
Emma Eames (s). 13 June.
Heinrich Schlusnus (b). 19 June.
Medea Mei-Figner (s). July.
Riccardo Martin (t). 11 August.
Andreas Boehm (b). 12 September.
Francis Alda (s). 18 September.

Jeanne Pacquôt d'Assy (s).   6 October.
Berta Morena (s).   7 October.
Kay Peterson (s).   8 October.
Ettore Cesa-Bianchi (t).   October.
Jean Aquistapace (bs).   October.
Phoebe Strakosch (s).   6 November.
Antonio Guarnieri (cond).   25 November.
Bernadino Molinari (cond).   25 December.
Paul Breisach (cond).   26 December.
Vera Amerighi (s).   Date unknown.
Margarete Siems (s).   Date unknown.
Emilio Venturini (t).   Date unknown.
Jaques Ibos (t).   Date unknown.
Frida Ricci (s).   Date unknown.

1953

Ludwig Burgstaller (t).   1 January.
Lina Pacary (s).   3 January.
Gertrude Rennyson (s).   3 January.
Eduard Lichtenstein (t).   9 January.
Heinrich Knote (t).   12 January.
Andrés de Segurola (bs).   22 January.
Susanne Adams (s).   5 February.
Mariette Mazarin (s).   22 February.
Umberto Berrettoni (cond).   February.
Maria Labia (s).   February.
Hermann Marowski (bs).   3 March.
Serge Prokofiev (comp.).   4 March.
Max Dawison (b).   22 April.
Erik Schubert (bs).   April.
Jeanne Maubourg (ms).   12 May.
Hermann Jadlowker (t).   13 May.
Frank Mullings (t).   19 May.
Audrey Mildmay-Christie (s).   31 May.
Werner Faulhaber (b).   June.
Tita Ruffo (b).   6 July.
Friedrich Schorr (b).   14 August.
Margarete Slezak (s).   30 August.
Gaetano Merola (cond).   30 August.
Max Lohfing (bs).   9 September.
Reinald Werrenrath (b).   12 September.
Grete Kraiger (c).   14 September.
Louis Beydts (comp).   19 September.
William Boland (t).   September.
Virgilio Lazzari (bs).   4 October.
Kathleen Ferrier (c).   9 October.
Marguerite d'Alvarez (c).   19 October.
Käte Herwig (s).   27 October.
Carla Spletter (s).   29 October.
Maria Ranzow (c).   4 November.

Robert Büssell (b).   28 November.
Frederick Ranalow (b).   8 December.
Issay Dobrowen (cond).   9 December.
Albert Coates (cond).   11 December.
Ernesto Dominici (bs).   December.

1954

Irma Lozin (c).   12 January.
Clementine de Vere (s).   20 January.
Yvonne de Tréville (s).   25 January.
Allen Hinckley (bs).   28 January.
Ferdinando Ciniselli (t).   30 January.
Ida Bergamesco (ms).   January.
Lidia Kindermann (ms).   January.
Paul Althouse (t).   6 February.
Doris Woodall (c).   7 February.
Hilda Ohlin (s).   10 February.
Zdenka Fassbaender (s).   14 March.
Fritzi Scheff (s).   8 April.
Torsten Ralf (t).   27 April.
Clemens Krauss (cond).   16 May.
Leon Rains (bs).   12 June.
Luigi Montesanto (b).   14 June.
Emmy Zimmermann (s).   21 June.
Ina Bouraskaya (ms).   25 June.
Miguel Villabella (t).   June.
Adelina Agostinelli (s).   6 July.
Richard Manning (t).   7 July.
Lucien Muratore (t).   16 July.
Lambert Murphy (t).   27 July.
Charles Webber (cond).   29 July.
Kurt Taucher (t).   5 August.
Pauline Joran (s).   13 August.
Arthur Cranmer (b).   20 August.
Lansing Hatfield (bs).   23 August.
Alexis Boyer (c).   August.
Peter Anders (t).   10 September.
Licinio Refice (comp).   11 September.
Alessandro Dolci (t).   17 September.

Year Unknown

Umberto di Lelio (bs).
Eduard Habich (b).
Gino Lulli (b).
Felix Vieulle (bs).
Umberto Macnez (t).
Francesco Zaccarini (bs).
Helmut Shcweebs (bs).